Palgrave Macmillan Studies in Family and Intimate Life

Titles include:

Graham Allan, Graham Crow and Sheila Hawker
STEPFAMILIES

Harriet Becher
FAMILY PRACTICES IN SOUTH ASIAN MUSLIM FAMILIES
Parenting in a Multi-Faith Britain

Elisa Rose Birch, Anh T. Le and Paul W. Miller
HOUSEHOLD DIVISIONS OF LABOUR
Teamwork, Gender and Time

Robbie Duschinsky and Leon Antonio Rocha (*editors*)
FOUCAULT, THE FAMILY AND POLITICS

Jacqui Gabb
RESEARCHING INTIMACY IN FAMILIES

Stephen Hicks
LESBIAN, GAY AND QUEER PARENTING
Families, Intimacies, Genealogies

Peter Jackson (*editor*)
CHANGING FAMILIES, CHANGING FOOD

Riitta Jallinoja and Eric Widmer (*editors*)
FAMILIES AND KINSHIP IN CONTEMPORARY EUROPE
Rules and Practices of Relatedness

Lynn Jamieson, Ruth Lewis and Roona Simpson (*editors*)
RESEARCHING FAMILIES AND RELATIONSHIPS
Reflections on Process

David Morgan
RETHINKING FAMILY PRACTICES

Eriikka Oinonen
FAMILIES IN CONVERGING EUROPE
A Comparison of Forms, Structures and Ideals

Róisín Ryan-Flood
LESBIAN MOTHERHOOD
Gender, Families and Sexual Citizenship

Sally Sales
ADOPTION, FAMILY AND THE PARADOX OF ORIGINS
A Foucauldian History

Tam Sanger
TRANS PEOPLE'S PARTNERSHIPS
Towards an Ethics of Intimacy

Elizabeth B. Silva
TECHNOLOGY, CULTURE, FAMILY
Influences on Home Life

Lisa Smyth
THE DEMANDS OF MOTHERHOOD
Agents, Roles and Recognitions

Palgrave Macmillan Studies in Family and Intimate Life
Series Standing Order ISBN 978–0–230–51748–6 hardback
978–0–230–24924–0 paperback
(*outside North America only*)

You can receive future titles in this series as they are published by placing a standing order. Please contact your bookseller or, in case of difficulty, write to us at the address below with your name and address, the title of the series and the ISBN quoted above.

Customer Services Department, Macmillan Distribution Ltd, Houndmills, Basingstoke, Hampshire RG21 6XS, England

Foucault, the Family and Politics

Edited by

Robbie Duschinsky
Northumbria University, UK

and

Leon Antonio Rocha
University of Cambridge, UK

First published 2012 by
PALGRAVE MACMILLAN

Palgrave Macmillan in the UK is an imprint of Macmillan Publishers Limited, registered in England, company number 785998, of Houndmills, Basingstoke, Hampshire RG21 6XS.

Palgrave Macmillan in the US is a division of St. Martin's Press LLC, 175 Fifth Avenue, New York, NY 10010.

Palgrave Macmillan is the global academic imprint of the above companies and has companies and representatives throughout the world.

Palgrave® and Macmillan® are registered trademarks in the United States, the United Kingdom, Europe and other countries.

ISBN 978–0–230–34847–9

This book is printed on paper suitable for recycling and made from fully managed and sustained forest sources. Logging, pulping and manufacturing processes are expected to conform to the environmental regulations of the country of origin.

A catalogue record for this book is available from the British Library.

Library of Congress Cataloging-in-Publication Data
Foucault, the family and politics / edited by Robbie Duschinsky and Leon Antonio Rocha.
p. cm.
Includes bibliographical references and index.
ISBN 978–0–230–34847–9
1. Foucault, Michel, 1926–1984. 2. Families. I. Duschinsky, Robbie, 1986– II. Rocha, Leon Antonio, 1982–
B2430.F724F6887 2012
306.85092—dc23   2012034170

10 9 8 7 6 5 4 3 2 1
21 20 19 18 17 16 15 14 13 12

Printed and bound in Great Britain by
CPI Antony Rowe, Chippenham and Eastbourne

Contents

Acknowledgements

This volume emerged from a conference, 'Foucault, the Family and Politics', held in November 2010 at King's College, Cambridge, convened by Robbie Duschinsky, Jude Browne and Deborah Thom. The conference was supported by the Centre for Research in the Arts, Social Sciences and Humanities (CRASSH) and the Centre for Gender Studies at the University of Cambridge. We gratefully acknowledge the funding for the conference generously provided by the Cambridge Centre for Gender Studies with a grant from Cambridge University Press, the Trevelyan Fund at the Faculty of History at the University of Cambridge, the Department of French at the University of Cambridge, the French Embassy, and the British Sociological Association Theory Study Group.

Many people contributed to the success of the conference and the ensuing volume. We wish to thank, in alphabetical order: Jude Browne, Netta Chachamu, Arlette Farge, John Forrester, Mary Jacobus, Jean Khalfa, Simon Schaffer, Anna Kathryn Schoefert, Chloë Taylor, Malcolm Thompson, Susan Walker, Valerie Walkerdine and Andrew Webber. We also thank the members of staff at the Centre for Research in the Arts, Social Sciences and Humanities (CRASSH) at Cambridge – Helga Brandt, Catherine Hurley, Esther Lamb, Michelle Maciejewska and Ruth Rushworth – for the administrative support for the conference. Leon Antonio Rocha would like to thank colleagues at the University of Cambridge, specifically at the Department of History and Philosophy of Science, the Faculty of Asian and Middle Eastern Studies and the Faculty of History, as well as the Needham Research Institute and Emmanuel College, Cambridge. Robbie Duschinsky would like to thank colleagues at the School of Health, Community and Education Studies at the University of Northumbria. Philippa Grand and Andrew James at Palgrave Macmillan imparted valuable guidance along the way. We are also thankful to Florence Giry at Gallimard for her assistance in seeking the translation rights for the 'Présentation' of Arlette Farge and Michel Foucault's *Le Désordre des familles*. We thank the anonymous referees for their helpful suggestions. Finally, we thank our families for their support and patience throughout our labours on the conference and the volume.

One contribution to the conference, by Malcolm Thompson at the University of Toronto, was published as a separate peer-reviewed paper with *History and Theory*. The full citation for this article is: Malcolm Thompson, 'Foucault, Fields of Governability, and the Population–Family–Economy Nexus in China', *History and Theory*, 51 (2012), 42–62.

At the conference on 'Foucault, the Family and Politics', David Macey was due to speak on 'A Race of Monsters', exploring Michel Foucault's account of the family as a fundamental institution for the organisation and naturalisation of 'race'. He pulled out of the conference on the grounds of ill health and, sadly, he died on 7 October 2011. We thank David for his encouragement in our project, for his wonderful scholarship and for his generosity and friendship.

Robbie Duschinsky and Leon Antonio Rocha

Abbreviations

Titles of works by and collections of Michel Foucault

ABN *Abnormal: Lectures at the Collège de France, 1974–1975*, Arnold I. Davidson (ed.) and Graham Burchell (trans.) (London: Verso, 2003)

BOB *The Birth of Biopolitics: Lectures at the Collège de France, 1978–1979*, Arnold I. Davidson (ed.) and Graham Burchell (trans.) (Basingstoke: Palgrave Macmillan, 2008)

DE1 *Dits et écrits, I, 1954–1975*, Daniel Defert and François Ewald (eds), with the collaboration of Jacques Lagrange (Paris: Quarto Gallimard, 2001)

DE2 *Dits et écrits, II, 1976–1988*, Daniel Defert and François Ewald (eds), with the collaboration of Jacques Lagrange (Paris: Quarto Gallimard, 2001)

DEF Arlette Farge and Michel Foucault, *Le Désordre des familles: Lettres de cachet des Archives de la Bastille au XVIIIe siècle* (Paris: Gallimard, 1982)

DIE 'Dream, imagination, and existence', in Keith Hoeller (ed.) and Forest Williams (trans.), *Dream and Existence: Michel Foucault and Ludwig Binswanger* (Atlantic Highlands, NJ: Humanities Press, 1993 [1954]), 31–105

DOL 'Appendix: the discourse on language', in *The Archaeology of Knowledge and the Discourse on Language*, Rupert Swyer and Alan Mark Sheridan-Smith (trans.) (New York: Pantheon Books, 1972), 215–37

D&P *Discipline and Punish: The Birth of the Prison*, Alan Sheridan (trans.) (London: Penguin, 1979 [first published in French in 1975])

EW1 *Ethics: Subjectivity and Truth: Essential Works of Foucault, 1954–1984, Volume 1*, Paul Rabinow (ed.) (New York: New Press, 1998)

EW2   *Aesthetics, Method, and Epistemology: Essential Works of Foucault, 1954–1984, Volume 2*, James D. Faubion (ed.) (New York: New Press, 1998)

EW3   *Power: Essential Works of Foucault, 1954–1984, Volume 3*, James D. Faubion (ed.) (New York: New Press, 2001)

GSO   *The Government of Self and Others: Lectures at the Collège de France, 1982–1983*, Arnold I. Davidson (ed.) and Graham Burchell (trans.) (Basingstoke: Palgrave Macmillan, 2010)

HBA   *Herculine Barbin: Being the Recently Discovered Memoirs of a Nineteenth-Century French Hermaphrodite*, Richard McDougall (trans.) (New York: Pantheon, 1980)

HES   *The Hermeneutics of the Subject: Lectures at the Collège de France, 1981–1982*, Arnold I. Davidson (ed.) and Graham Burchell (trans.) (Basingstoke: Palgrave Macmillan, 2005)

HOM   *History of Madness*, Jean Khalfa (ed.) and Jonathan Murphy and Jean Khalfa (trans.) (London: Routledge, 2006)

HS1   *The History of Sexuality, Volume 1: An Introduction*, Robert Hurley (trans.) (New York: Pantheon, 1978 [first published in French, Paris: Gallimard, 1976]), reprinted as *The Will to Knowledge* (London: Penguin, 1998)

HS2   *The History of Sexuality, Volume 2: The Use of Pleasure*, Robert Hurley (trans.) (New York: Pantheon, 1985 [first published in French, Paris: Gallimard, 1984])

HS3   *The History of Sexuality, Volume 3: The Care of the Self*, Robert Hurley (trans.) (New York: Pantheon, 1986 [first published in French, Paris: Gallimard, 1984])

IPR   Michel Foucault (ed.) *'I, Pierre Rivière, Having Slaughtered My Mother, My Sister, and My Brother': A Case of Parricide in the Nineteenth Century*, Frank Jellinek (trans.) (Lincoln, NB: University of Nebraska Press, 1975 [first published in French in 1973)

PAO   'Preface' in Gilles Deleuze and Félix Guattari, *Anti-Oedipus: Capitalism and Schizophrenia*, Robert Hurley, Mark Seem and Helen R. Lane (trans.) (London and New York: Continuum, 2004), pp. xiii–xvi

PPC *Politics, Philosophy, Culture: Interviews and Other Writings, 1977–1984*, Lawrence D. Kritzman (ed.) (London: Routledge, 1988)

PSP *Psychiatric Power: Lectures at the Collège de France, 1973–1974*, Arnold I. Davidson (ed.) and Graham Burchell (trans.) (Basingstoke: Palgrave Macmillan, 2006)

SMD *Society Must Be Defended: Lectures at the Collège de France, 1975–1976*, Arnold I. Davidson (ed.) and Graham Burchell (trans.) (New York: Picador, 2003)

STP *Security, Territory, Population: Lectures at the Collège de France, 1977–1978*, Arnold I. Davidson (ed.) and Graham Burchell (trans.) (Basingstoke: Palgrave Macmillan, 2007)

Notes on Contributors

Vikki Bell is Professor in Sociology at Goldsmiths College, University of London. Her books include *Interrogating Incest: Feminism, Foucault and the Law* (1993), *Feminist Imagination: Genealogies in Feminist Thought* (1999), and *Culture and Performance: The Challenge of Ethics, Politics and Feminist Theory* (2007).

Terrell Carver is Professor of Political Theory at the University of Bristol. Some of his publications include *The Postmodern Marx* (1998), *Men in Political Theory* (2004), and *Judith Butler and Political Theory: Troubling Politics* (2008, with Samuel Allen Chambers).

Robbie Duschinsky is Senior Lecturer in Social Science for Social Work at Northumbria University. He recently completed his thesis, entitled 'The Politics of Purity', at the Faculty of Politics, Psychology, Sociology and International Studies at the University of Cambridge.

Gillian Harkins is Associate Professor of English at the University of Washington, Seattle. She is the author of *Everybody's Family Romance: Reading Incest in Neoliberal America* (2009). She is currently working on her second monograph, entitled, *Screening Paedophilia: Virtuality and Other Crimes Against Nature*.

Thibaud Harrois is Lecturer in French at Trinity College, Cambridge, and a graduate student at the École Normale Supérieure, Lyon. He is currently studying contemporary British and European Politics under the supervision of Pauline Schnapper at the Université de Paris III: Panthéon Sorbonne.

Rémi Lenoir is Professor of Sociology at the Université de Paris I: Panthéon Sorbonne. He has numerous publications on French society, many concerning family policies, and is the author of *La Généalogie de la morale familial* (2003).

Katherine Logan is a doctoral candidate at the Department of Philosophy at the University of Oregon.

José Luis Moreno Pestaña is Professor of Philosophy at the University of Cádiz, and the author of *Pierre Bourdieu y la filosofía* (2009) and *Foucault, la gauche et la politique* (2011).

Véronique Mottier is Fellow and Director of Studies in Politics, Psychology, Sociology and International Studies at Jesus College, Cambridge, and is part-time Professor in Sociology at the University of Lausanne. Her publications include *Politics of Sexuality: Identity, Gender, Citizenship* (2006, edited with Terrell Carver), *Sexuality: A Very Short Introduction* (2008), and *French Social Theory: From Merleau-Ponty to Bourdieu* (forthcoming with Polity Press).

Leon Antonio Rocha is Research Fellow at Emmanuel College, Cambridge, and is affiliated with the Department of History and Philosophy of Science, University of Cambridge, and the Needham Research Institute, Cambridge.

Deborah Thom is Fellow and Director of Studies for the Faculty of History and the Faculty of Politics, Psychology, Sociology and International Studies at Robinson College, Cambridge. She also lectures at the Department of History and Philosophy of Science, University of Cambridge, and is the author of *Nice Girls and Rude Girls: Women Workers in World War I* (1998).

Introduction:

The Problem of the Family in Foucault's Work

Robbie Duschinsky and Leon Antonio Rocha

The family and *History of Sexuality*, *Volume 1*

The index of *Dits et écrits*, which contains all of Michel Foucault's writings and interviews besides his monographs, does not have an entry for 'family'. In part, this is because almost none of the voluminous number of books and articles produced by Foucault directly offer sustained discussion of the family. *Le Désordre des familles* (with Arlette Farge, 1982), for instance, brings together letters between family members and the state regarding the incarceration of abnormal or delinquent individuals in eighteenth-century France, but contains no in-depth theorisation on families. There is some discussion of 'the marital role' in some chapters of *The History of Sexuality*, *Volume 2* and *Volume 3* (first published in French in 1984), but Foucault's account sticks closely to the primary texts. Although contributing an incisive account of ethical subjectivity, these chapters by Foucault have not generally been seen as a theoretical contribution on the topic of the family. The family can seem like a spectre in the works that Foucault published in his lifetime: an amorphous, somewhat shapeless thing that he consistently mentions, flirtatiously alludes to and fleetingly gestures towards. Yet the family is a crucial theme in the Collège de France lecture series given between 1973 and 1978. In these lectures, Foucault explores the transformation of familial dynamics – most notably at the intersection between kinship, sexuality and the state – that occurred with the rise of the bourgeoisie in the nineteenth century.

Until the publication of the Collège de France lectures, the most sustained treatment of the family by Foucault had been 'The Deployment of Sexuality', which stands as Section 4 of *History of Sexuality*, *Volume 1*, first published in French in 1976. Here 'sexuality' is framed by Foucault as less 'a stubborn drive' than 'an especially dense transfer point for relations of power: between men and women, young people and old people, parents and offspring, teachers and students, priests and laity, an administration and a population'.[1] Already the family weaves tantalisingly in and out of Foucault's characterisation. Men and women, young people and old people, parents and offspring all can relate to one another within discourses on sexuality without the family being explicitly invoked; however, 'the family' as an ideal will haunt such discourses, as a constitutive figure in shaping the true and proper form of such 'sexual' or 'asexual' relations. Foucault's list thus begins with the family, but makes a beeline for administration. This does not only indicate the role of sexuality as 'one of those [elements in power relations] endowed with the greatest instrumentality' for biopolitics at the level of public administration. It also identifies the biopolitics of sexuality as an apparatus that organises the family, and the relationship between the family and institutions of public governance. The biopolitics of sexuality is therefore not simply a system for ensuring that 'all of sex' is organised according to its true and proper form within the family, but a 'manifold' apparatus 'employed in the different sexual politics concerned with the two sexes, the different age groups and social classes'.[2]

Foucault then goes on to identify the emergence in the eighteenth century of four discursive 'figures' who, by the nineteenth century, operate as 'the four great strategies' in the organisation of discourses on 'sexuality'.[3] These figures were 'privileged objects of knowledge, which were also targets and anchorage points for the ventures of knowledge: the hysterical woman, the masturbating child, the Malthusian couple, and the perverse adult'.[4] The argument is captivating. Foucault is suggesting here that discourses on sexuality have not happened upon these four topics by chance, but rather that the way in which we perceive our sexuality and broader identity today has been shaped by the *constitutive* role of these four figures. Each of these strategies, he argues, 'went by way of a family which must be viewed, not as a powerful agency of prohibition, but as a major factor in sexualisation':[5]

1. The middle-class 'mother' was constituted and policed in relation to the figure of the 'hysterical woman'. The biological and cultural reproduction of the nation, the class, and the familial dynasty was placed in the hands of the mother of the household, whose behaviour was thus subjected to medical intervention if it veered away from the tacit norm of 'regulated fecundity' and 'biologico-moral

responsibility lasting through the entire period of the children's education'.[6] Foucault argues that:

> in the family, parents and relatives became the chief agents of a deployment of sexuality which drew its outside support from doctors, educators and later psychiatrists [...] then these new personages made their appearance: the nervous woman, the frigid wife, the indifferent mother.[7]

With abnormality in women positioned as the result of a deficiency or deviancy located in the sexual instinct, psychiatry could take charge of middle-class mothers when their behaviour running contrary to social norms could be situated as a consequence of 'hysteria'.

2. The middle-class child was constituted and policed in relation to the figure of the 'masturbating child'. Masturbation was situated by psychiatry as simultaneously a natural thing for children to do and 'contrary to nature', capable of perverting their identity and of corrupting their heredity. This 'double assertion' mandated a continual parental, educational and medical surveillance of the middle-class child, since 'this sexual activity posed physical and moral, individual and collective dangers'. With abnormality in children situated as the result of a 'dangerous and endangered sexual potential', parents, educators and doctors could take charge of policing the subjectivation of children to ensure that they would achieve what could thereby be situated as their true and proper form.[8]

3. Intercourse between sexual partners was constituted and policed in relation to the figure of the 'couple'. Sexual partners would not only put society in danger, but risked causing themselves medical and psychological damage, if they ventured away from imputed norms in organising their acts of intercourse. They therefore required economic, social and political incentives and sanctions to ensure that their acts of intercourse were in line with this ostensive norm, constructed by dominant institutions as in line with the perceived needs for the 'regulation of births' of 'the social body as a whole (which had to be limited or on the contrary reinvigorated)'.[9]

4. Underpinning each of these previous three familial figures was the capacity for personal abnormality and social harm if the sexual instinct, as the inner truth of the individual, became perverse. Thus sexuality 'was assigned a role of normalisation or pathologisation with respect to all behaviour'. A 'psychiatrisation of perverse pleasure' made even the most 'imperceptible' desires of the individual a

legitimate object of institutional concern and the body a legitimate object of institutional regulation.[10] On the one hand, preventative measures of surveillance and discipline could be established to supplement the natural desires of 'normal individuals'; these measures could themselves be deployed to shape an imputed ideal of 'normality' itself. The family is placed as the origin of desire, providing the site of the inner truth of the individual, and is also situated as the ultimate object of 'normal' desires. On the other hand, those observable forms that deviated from the norm could, through the figure of the 'perverse adult', be subjected to legitimate management by governmental discourses mobilising a particular model of existence as the true and proper form of human life. The family here is situated as the eyes, ears and hands of educationalists, the medical profession and ultimately the state.

Foucault thus turns his attention to the way in which a construction of the sexual instinct as the secret of normal or abnormal identity was constituted through discourse on these four figures. An ongoing differentiation between 'normal' and 'abnormal' forms of desire and behaviour by dominant discourses could, in this way, produce the appearance that there exists a natural form of human life from which deviation would always mean danger. These emergent discourses on 'sexuality' were indelibly tied to the family. Such a tie appeared and appears to us today as inevitable and natural, but Foucault is insistent that the position of the family as the origin and ultimate goal of desire is a contingent historical construction. The dividing line between normal and abnormal sexuality is ultimately familial, as it is produced by the moral and medical problematisation of perverse desire as the common thread linking hysterical mothers, masturbating children and the capacity of adults to have inappropriate intercourse with – or without – their heterosexual spouse.

Sexuality was thus tightly woven together with an infrastructure of 'kinship', or 'alliance', which predated and conditioned it.[11] Kinship relations, organised according to 'mechanisms of constraint', had served as an effective substrate for the political economy of an ancien régime, which had also been organised by a model of power as legal constraint. However, Foucault argues, from the eighteenth century, kinship 'lost some of its importance as economic processes and political structures could no longer rely on it as an adequate instrument or sufficient support'.[12] The two forms could be overlain, with kinship undergirding sexuality, because at stake in the latter are the desires that are taken to originate naturally in and lead back to the former: 'for the first what is pertinent is the link between partners and definite statutes; the second is concerned with the sensations of the body, the quality of pleasures, and the nature of impressions'.[13] 'It was around and on the basis of the deployment of alliance that the deployment of sexuality was constructed,' as 'normal' sexuality was delineated precisely by the way in which it mediated familial kinship. This mediation occurs not only through the role of sexuality in the reproduction of the kinship group, but primarily through the role of the family as the 'natural' and 'normal' origin and object of desire.[14] Foucault therefore concludes that: 'the family is the interchange of sexuality and alliance: it conveys the law and the juridical dimension in the deployment of sexuality; and it conveys the economy of pleasure and the intensity of sensations in the regime of alliance'.[15]

Kinship does not contain a sexuality naturally directed towards heterosexual partners and away from incestuous objects, as modern discourses commonly presume. Nor is sexuality a drive naturally directed towards heterosexual partners as a substitute for incestuous objects, as psychoanalysis has argued. Rather, familial relations are situated by key institutions such as psychiatry and education as the formative origin of desire.[16] They must therefore be carefully managed to ensure 'normal', 'healthy' development: 'the family, the keystone of alliance, was the germ of all the misfortunes of sex. And lo and behold, from the mid-nineteenth century onwards the family engaged in searching out the slightest traces of sexuality in its midst.'[17] Moreover, familial kinship relations were situated as the true and proper outcome of such forms of individual growth and development: 'the family has become an obligatory locus of affects, feelings, love; [and] sexuality has its privileged development in the family [...] for this reason sexuality is "incestuous" from the start'.[18] Incest, Foucault argues, serves as an 'indispensable pivot'[19] between alliance and sexuality; it ties together the determination of forbidden and permitted relationships (kinship) with the incitement to desire that can serve as justification for the governance of individuals in relation to an imputed norm (sexuality).

Thus, relations of sex, Foucault suggests, gave rise to two systems: the deployment of alliance: 'a system of marriage, of fixation and development of kinship ties, of transmission of names and possessions', and the deployment of sexuality. On the one hand, the deployment of alliance: (i) is 'built around a system of rules defining the permitted and the forbidden, the licit and illicit'; (ii) has 'as one of its chief objectives to reproduce the interplay of relations and maintain the law that governs them'; (iii) as 'the link between partners and definite statutes' is pertinent; (iv) is 'firmly tied to the economy due to the role it can play in the transmission or circulation of wealth'; (v) 'is attuned to a homeostasis of the social body, which it has the function of maintaining; whence its privileged link with the law; whence too the fact that the important phase for it is "reproduction"'. On the other hand, the deployment of sexuality: (i) 'operates according to mobile, polymorphous, and contingent techniques of power'; (ii) 'engenders a continual extension of areas and forms of control'; (iii) is concerned with 'the sensations of the body, the quality of pleasures, and the nature of impressions'; (iv) is 'linked to the economy through numerous and subtle relays, the main one of which is the body'; (v) 'has its reason for being, not in reproduction itself, but in proliferating, innovating, annexing, creating, and penetrating bodies in an increasingly detailed way, and in controlling populations in an increasingly comprehensive way'.[20]

The family, then, comes into this system as the unit that makes it possible for the deployment of sexuality ('the feminine body, infantile precocity, the regulation of births ... the specification of the perverted') to develop along the 'husband–wife' axis and the 'parents–children' axis.[21] The family anchors sexuality; the family becomes the 'interchange of sexuality and alliance: it conveys the law and the juridical dimension in the deployment of sexuality; and it conveys the economy of pleasure and the intensity of sensations in the regime of alliance'.[22] Parents are recruited as agents of the deployment of sexuality, bolstered by scientific and medical knowledge of normal and abnormal forms of being. The overall effect is that family has come to be the primary location for the regulation of the behaviour of the population.

Beyond the *History of Sexuality, Volume 1*

In recent years, however, our understanding in the English-speaking academia of Foucault's thought has been substantially deepened and widened by the publication of the Collège de France lectures. At the time of the writing of this Introduction, nine of the thirteen lecture series have been published in French and eight in English. These translations have encouraged scholars to pay closer attention to the evolution of Foucault's ideas. Furthermore, they enable us to challenge established orthodoxies in reading Foucault – for instance, the mass of scholarship and commentaries based on the oblique and compressed treatments of the Western nuclear family in *History of Sexuality, Volume 1*. Jacques Donzelot's *Policing of Families*, first published in French in 1977, has generally been used by scholars to fill out the account of the *History of Sexuality, Volume 1*.[23] Yet the more elaborate account of the family by Foucault in the newly translated and published material offers powerful resources with which to reinvigorate our historical, sociological and political analyses, with insights that are not available in Donzelot. Given the strong demand for explorations of the family with reference to a Foucauldean perspective, there is space for new, cutting-edge work on the topic.

It is the conviction of the editors and contributors of the present volume that Michel Foucault's theory continues to be a powerful source of insights into the way in which the internal power-relations of the family interface and interleave with the politics of society more generally. Foucault places the family as an absolutely integral institution to judgements in modern societies regarding the normal and the abnormal, the acceptable and the unacceptable. On the one hand, Foucault discerns the way in which the family became a point of intervention and an object of knowledge – how social politics impact family structure and dynamics through legal judgments, medical interventions, social work, and many other mechanisms and institutions. On the other hand, Foucault analyses the way in which members within the family regularly call on discourses from society at large in order to manage or transform the operation of and the intimate relationships within the family.

Foucault describes the complex emotional, geographical, economic and social relations that comprise 'the family', suggesting that all these play an essential role in linking individuals to one another, to social systems, to the government and the state. The obligation to attend school, to go to work and be productive, to perform military service, to stay healthy, to follow the law – 'being a good son, a good husband, and so on', as Foucault wryly remarks in the 1973–74 Collège de France Lectures *Psychiatric Power* – are frequently policed and disciplined in the first instance through the family.[24] Foucault rather brilliantly adds:

> When an individual is rejected as abnormal from a disciplinary system, where is he sent? To his family. When a number of disciplinary systems successively reject him as inassimilable, incapable of being disciplined, or uneducable, he is sent back to the family, and the family's role at this point is to reject him in turn as incapable of being fixed to any disciplinary system, and to get rid of him either by consigning him to pathology, or abandoning him to delinquency, etcetera.[25]

The Collège de France lectures affirm that if we find ourselves subjects of the family, this is not simply a fact of biology. Through a host of social and physical forms, the family operates as both a social institution and an acute psychological experience. Foucault notes that even as we engage in our daily projects, the family seems to follow closely behind. Within and beyond psychoanalytic discourses, we tell ourselves and one another: 'Look into my life choices, and you will see my family; look into my family and you will see the ground of my longings.' The family promises a space full of warmth and happiness for some, threatens others with chill and bleakness, and always demands in exchange a ceaseless activity in its name. Our desires and our self-management are thus in many ways – although never totally or monolithically – shaped by the family as a social formation and a discursive entity, and by the opportunities for happiness and for hope that are constituted and deferred by this institution. Foucault describes how the family has a singular capability to be retained within our very affect, shaping the way in which we know how to live, to feel peace or anguish, to meet the eyes of a friend or a stranger. Yet this is not due to any intrinsic and necessary property of the family, but rather is the result of the way in which this social institution serves to refract broader discursive, material and affective structures in society.

Both the family and Foucauldean thought often stand as idealised objects in academic discourse, thanks to the operation of something akin to an obsessional neurosis. This discourse is compulsively impelled to touch ritually upon 'the family' and 'Foucault', and each has become a ubiquitous reference in discussions of the other. However, these fleeting engagements frequently do not allow their subjects the narrative space for complexity or fallibility. To enact a thoroughgoing conjunction risks the accounts upon which we have been trained to rest. Could there be power dynamics in the micro-physics of the way in which I care for my infant? Could there be gendered differences within contemporary familial life that make 'sexuality' an untenable analytical construct? The direct conjunction of Foucault and the family risks the heartbreak of showing our ideals and our safety to have been in ruins all along. Foucault reveals the family's emotional majesty and social utility to be strategically tied to a structural and tragic perniciousness. Simultaneously, the family reveals the theoretical scotomata and weaknesses in Foucault's theorising, in troubling proximity to the sites of his most extraordinary insights.

The goal of this volume, *Foucault, the Family and Politics*, is twofold. First, the editors wish to bring together a variety of new, unpublished papers engaging in the exposition and elaboration of Foucault on the family, from some of the best-known international scholars in sociology, politics, history, philosophy, gender theory, literary criticisms and cultural studies. We want to clarify Foucault's theories on the politics of the family and intimate life for advanced undergraduate and graduate students, and aim to push Foucault's analyses further and discuss their relevance for current academic research. Second, we offer a number of critical considerations of Foucault's ideas. Comparisons will be drawn between Michel Foucault and, for instance, Karl Marx, Judith Butler, Pierre Bourdieu and other theorists. *Foucault, the Family and Politics* is the first book in any language that explicitly concentrates on Foucault and the family in light of the incomparably richer account presented in the Collège de France lectures.

Corresponding to our twin goals, this volume is divided into two parts: 'Part I: Expositions' and 'Part II: Evaluations'. In 'Expositions', Rémi Lenoir with Robbie Duschinsky, Vikki Bell, Katherine Logan and Gillian Harkins offer close readings of Foucault's texts, particularly the recently published English translations of the Collège de France lectures, in which the question of the family is more directly confronted. Lenoir with Duschinsky, Bell and Harkins offer expositions to Foucault's theorisation, which will be of interest to general readers as well as specialist scholars in the field.

Rémi Lenoir was a protégé and colleague of Michel Foucault (and then of Pierre Bourdieu). Advancing the remarks of this Introduction, Lenoir with Duschinsky begin by observing that Foucault makes reference to the family in a few dazzling yet brief passages. They argue that Foucault conceives the family as a fundamental and peculiar node in the operation of modern 'mechanisms of power'. In fact, they discern, it is primarily in relation to power that Foucault mentions the family. The family as a theme appears time and again when Foucault theorises power. In the early 1970s, the family is a crucial lens for Foucault as he distinguishes between sovereign and disciplinary forms of power, the distinction that will underpin his text *Discipline and Punish* (first published in French in 1975). The family appears again as a key object in the mid 1970s, as Foucault battles the Marxist conceptualisation of the state. Against a monolithic account of state power, Foucault traces the specific figures and relations that organised the relationship between psychiatry, law and familial dynamics.

Lenoir with Duschinsky then attend to Foucault's work on the family in the *History of Sexuality, Volume 2* and *Volume 3*. Although these texts have not been seen to offer a theory of the family as they do not abstract a great deal from the ancient texts under discussion, Lenoir with Duschinsky incisively read them as a revision of the account of the family from *Volume 1*. In the 1970s, Foucault treats subjectivity mainly as an effect of power relations: the requirements of 'the social body as a whole' could be situated as the main cause of the emergence of the conjugal 'couple' as a discursive figure in nineteenth-century discourses on sexuality. Yet by the 1980s, Foucault wishes to illustrate, using the family, the importance of practices of self as providing a fundamental mediator between power and the formation of subjectivity. Drawing together these different arguments, Lenoir with Duschinsky close their chapter with a consideration of what may be Foucault's contributions to sociological works on the family.

Vikki Bell is among the most authoritative scholars of Foucault and the family. In her chapter, Bell traces the place of the family in Foucault's thought, considering three key discussions of the topic. First, building upon Lenoir, she examines Foucault's discussion of the family in the 1970s. She argues that while the family seems to be the very source of sexuality, Foucault worked to show that actually it *reflects* the activity of the expert agents of the apparatus of sexuality surrounding the family. Illustrating this claim, Bell focuses on incest as a potential sexual activity located between systems of alliance and the apparatus of sexuality. Although the prohibition on incest was longstanding, she argues that in modern societies this prohibition is remobilised as a constitutive outside of 'normal' sexuality. She shows how constructions of normal and abnormal desire were mobilised within professional discourses to justify interventions in order to ensure the successful biopolitical reproduction of the national population.

Second, Bell considers Foucault's examination of self-governance and care for the self in antiquity. She argues that 'the family' was not an object of thought and reflection in antiquity, in the way that it is now. It was not 'the family' that was the focus of critical reflection. Instead, the relations within and outside 'the household' – including relationships between married couples and with boys – are problematised through the relations that the free man conducts with others because each of these implies a relationship with himself. Between ancient Greece and Stoic ethics, Bell shows that Foucault traces a shift, as the marriage bond became constructed as essential to true human existence. The conjugal bond emerges here as a relationship through which appropriate and inappropriate forms of human life can be assessed. Third, Bell considers Foucault's discussion of relations of alliance in the play *Ion* by Euripides. She describes Foucault's attention to the way in which the play relates the emergence of new relationships between politics, truth and kinship with the advent of democracy. The kinship status of an individual was positioned as crucial to establishing their relative capacity to access authorised public discourses within a democratic state. She concludes that the red thread guiding Foucault's concerns in these three discussions is the question of how we came to believe that the family is the site of our deepest truth as ethical beings and as citizens. Yet Foucault's writings make this belief seem peculiar: although the family was used in each case as a site for discussing the deepest truth of the human being, the nature of this deepest truth in each case is far from the same.

Katherine Logan uses the Collège de France lecture material to deepen the account of the family offered in the first volume of *History of Sexuality* by identifying gendered relations of power that Foucault describes but upon which he does not focus his attention. She argues that although Foucault often refers generally to 'the family', this should be taken as lacking necessary specificity, as the mother ought to be regarded as the chief parental target with respect to biopolitical strategies for children's normalisation. In the first volume of the *History of Sexuality*, Foucault indicates the particular role and responsibilities that mothers came to be assigned and the way in which this shift was necessary for the emergence in modernity of the apparatus of sexuality. Thus, many aspects of what we take to be the 'normal' identity and role of a mother are the contingent results of this historical transformation in the way in which we conceptualise sexuality.

Logan further argues that articulating the implications of Foucault's description of the family in his lecture material shows that discourses on sexual normality and abnormality altered the way in which we both understand and enact motherhood, producing both oppressive and anti-oppressive effects. Mothering became an intense site of biopolitics, as the mother's subjectivity became organised as a site at which class, race, nation and the heterosexual family itself must be stabilised and reproduced. In achieving this, the mother became constructed as the primary familial agent in the surveillance and normalisation of her children and 'the physics of family space', as a delegate and privileged ally of medical and pedagogic agents. In addition, she has been enjoined to exercise her authority through embodied and affective means, experiencing feelings of extreme closeness with her children as well as responsibility and social blame when her children are seen as deviant from imputed norms. Logan thus identifies the way in which the figure of the 'mother' has become an important site of contestation in civil society as the masked site of its biological and cultural reproduction, or transformation.

Gillian Harkins moves from the history of modern familial relations to an account of the family and politics as they are changing today.

Her chapter adventurously builds from Foucault's own insights into the genealogy of monsters and into the rise of neoliberalism to interpret his activism in the late 1970s aiming at the decriminalisation of adult–child sexual activity. She brings together Foucault's Collège de France lectures *Abnormal* (1974–75) and *The Birth of Biopolitics* (1978–79) in order to explore neoliberal revisions to the division between normal and abnormal forms of subjectivity. Harkins contests Foucault's appeal to the decriminalisation of adult–child sex as the solution to the new forms of sexual governmentality that have emerged since the 1970s. Instead, she mobilises Foucault's work on the emergence of neoliberalism to make sense of the transformation and increased visibility of the figure of the paedophile since the late 1970s as a core object of public concern.

Harkins links the way in which we have constructed the paedophile as the ultimate monster to the vilification of the state as the enemy of the free market. Each form of discourse is linked to, and helps support the other, through a shared model of human nature and its interests. The state and the paedophile, depicted as stealing the natural potentiality of the child, serve in neoliberal discourse as the two core constitutive outsides of a politically invested and gendered model – heedless of the effects of material inequalities – of what it is to be a sexually and economically consenting and responsible adult. In presenting this analysis she explains why neoliberal discourses call both for a further liberalisation and a re-moralisation of our lives: neoliberalism must ever work to construct, through moralisation, the subject that it takes to be simply set free by liberalisation.

The second part of the book, 'Evaluations', includes contributions from José Luis Moreno Pestaña, Véronique Mottier, Deborah Thom and Leon Antonio Rocha, who critically evaluate the promises and limits of Foucauldean theorisation of the family and intimate life. There is also a chapter of a translation by Leon Antonio Rocha and Thibaud Harrois of Arlette Farge and Michel Foucault's 'Présentation'.

The chapter by José Luis Moreno Pestaña places Jacques Donzelot's *The Policing of Families* (1977) in an academic and social context. With many scholars presuming that Foucault does not offer a theory of the family, Donzelot's work has been taken as the paradigmatic Foucauldean approach. Pestaña situates the text on the critical pole of accounts of the relationship between social work and the family, a position within the academic field opened up by Foucault's research into the relationship between psychiatry and the family. Pestaña's chapter explores the logic of Donzelot's account of social work as exercising a totalising power, and examines the relationship between the academic, professional and political fields in which this account participates. Pestaña's incisive analysis of Donzelot in context not only serves as a genealogy of the influence of Foucault on later theorists, but also functions as a diagnosis of the relationship between fields that has influenced Foucauldean theorising on the family more generally.

Véronique Mottier's chapter reflects upon Michel Foucault's writings on biopolitics and sexuality in the context of a specific area of the politics of the family: eugenic policy-making. Historical examples of eugenic policy-making in various European countries between the 1920s and 1970s serve as a basis for theorising the role of the state in regulating and policing the reproductive sexualities, sexual practices, sexual identities and future families of its citizens. In doing so, Mottier draws on Foucault; however, she also attempts to identify and go beyond some of the blind spots in his work. Mottier highlights in particular the importance of gender for exploring both the power relations linking families to the state and the architecture of state institutions themselves.

Deborah Thom's chapter argues that Foucault's concern with the role of systems of thought and the work of professionals neglected the subjects' experiences of families, their emotions and imaginative life. These concerns enter into the case studies edited by Foucault, such as *'I, Pierre Rivière'*. However, Thom argues, the experience of particular subjects of their families and the psychological and social forces that they navigate do not receive sustained conceptualisation or elaboration by Foucault at a theoretical level. The result of his focus on official, prescriptive texts was a profound political and social theory of the family as a site in which future citizens are subjected to physical surveillance and social normalisation. However, Foucault's account missed out key elements for an adequate account of the family. In particular, Thom argues that Foucault neglects the feelings and emotions of family members, embedded within economic and cultural structures and relations of power. At times he treats experience, emotions and imagination as no more than an epiphenomenon of discourse, although at other times his account is more subtle. He misses issues of great importance to the organisation of family life, such as gender, mutual aid and love – and their complex role in both enacting and contesting relations of power. By contrast, she argues, the later work of Pierre Bourdieu on sexual difference and commercial exchange offers a more effective account of such phenomena.

Le Désordre des familles: Lettres de cachet des Archives de la Bastille au XVIIIe siècle is a volume co-edited by Arlette Farge and Michel Foucault, published in French in 1982. The book collects together 'poison-pen letters' from eighteen-century France, written to state institutions by ordinary men and women who wanted their 'deviant' or disgraced family members – sometimes their own sons and daughters – to be confined in a hospital, an asylum or a prison. Some of the responses given by the authorities and the police dossiers are also included in Farge and Foucault's volume, and throughout the two scholars provide commentary on the primary materials. At the time of writing this Introduction, *Le Désordre des familles* has still not found an English translator and publisher, and has gone out of print in France as well. Leon Antonio Rocha and Thibaud Harrois provide an English translation of Farge and Foucault's introduction, and Rocha supplies an additional chapter on *Le Désordre des familles*, explaining its context of production, its place within the 'Foucauldean canon', Foucault's engagement with other historians and his preoccupation with archival materials. Rocha argues that *Le Désordre des familles*, despite rarely being read, is absolutely crucial in understanding Foucault's thinking in the late 1970s on power and the question of 'experience' – in relation to the family and in general. It is hoped that the translation of the introduction along with this chapter on the background of *Le Désordre des familles* will renew attention to its fascinating content and the insight that it offers into Foucault's thought and scholarly practice.

No one since Marx has made a more profound change to the way in which we think about society, power and politics than Foucault. But the focus of his work – on major public institutions – tracks exactly the issues that feminism forced conventionally masculinised social studies to face. These are the exclusion and marginalisation of women from public space and voice, the relegation of the 'gender issues' with which they are identified to a realm of triviality, and the most formative human experiences of all – 'in the family' – to an anthropological orientalism uncritical of 'Western' practices. However, for feminists the 'family' was never a given and was often an object of attack. After a brief discussion of the feminist appropriation of Foucault, Terrell Carver assesses the extent to which Foucault's work – *malgré lui* – continues to make the family look as different in theory as it does in practice.

Notes

1. Foucault, HS1, 103.
2. Ibid.
3. Ibid., 114.
4. Ibid., 105.
5. Ibid., 114.
6. Ibid., 104.

7. Ibid., 104, 110.
8. Ibid., 104.
9. Ibid., 105, 108.
10. Ibid., 105–6.
11. Ibid., 106.
12. Ibid.
13. Ibid.
14. Ibid., 107.
15. Ibid., 108.
16. Ibid., 111.
17. Ibid.
18. Ibid., 108.
19. Ibid., 109.
20. Ibid., 106–7.
21. Ibid., 108.
22. Ibid.
23. Jacques Donzelot, *The Policing of Families*, Robert Hurley (trans.) (Baltimore, MD: Johns Hopkins University Press, 1979 [first published in French in 1977]). Other important texts filling in for the compressed account of the family in the *History of Sexuality, Volume 1* include Nikolas Rose's *Governing the Soul: The Shaping of the Private Self* (London: Free Associations Books, 1989; new edn 2001), and Vikki Bell's, *Interrogating Incest: Feminism, Foucault and the Law* (London: Routledge, 1993).
24. Foucault, PSP, 116.
25. Ibid., 81.

Part I
Expositions

1

Foucault and the Family:

Deepening the Account of *History of Sexuality, Volume 1*

Rémi Lenoir with Robbie Duschinsky

In the *History of Sexuality, Volume 1*, first published in French in 1976 and translated into English in 1978, Michel Foucault refers to the family in a few brief and dazzling pages (103–14 in the English edition, HS1). The prose is compressed, almost telegraphic, but profoundly evocative in characterising the 'domain' within which sexuality ever operates 'by way of a family'.[1] The family is situated as the formative site within which desire is originally formed, and as 'the family has become an obligatory locus of affects, feelings, love; sexuality has its privileged development in the family'.[2] Building upon these brief suggestions, numerous works on the family claim to speak from a Foucauldean perspective, elaborating on what appears to be Foucault's fleeting – or even non-existent – attention to the issue.[3] Indicative of the widespread scholarly consensus that the family is not a major concern for Foucault, there is no entry for 'family' in the index of the *Dits et écrits*, a collection not only of Foucault's works but of his interviews and lectures.

In fact, however, Foucault can be said to be quite preoccupied with the history of the family. The brief pages on the family in the *History of Sexuality, Volume 1* summarise elements of a sustained genealogical investigation of the family during the early 1970s. Attention to the family coincided notably with Foucault's focus on forms of the exercise of power. In fact, it is primarily in relation to the question of power that Foucault discusses the family. The family is given a unique place in the history of the shift from the ancien régime to modernity: the family has played a significant role in the construction of middle-class life; it has been implicated in the identification of each human subject as in possession of a 'personal identity'; it has entered into an intricate and constitutive relationship with the modern psy-disciplines. Moreover, the family did not cease to be an object of thought for Foucault after 1976.

It retained its position as a privileged object of reflection in Foucault's thinking about power into the 1980s. The family was the subject of further discussion in the Collège de France lectures of this period as Foucault moved to a consideration of technologies of the self as key in the formation of subjectivity within particular regimes of truth and power. In particular, he attends to the emergence of conjugality as a technology of the self, which Foucault situated as having formed 'the basic framework of modern European sexual morality'.[4]

Drawing on the rich material from the Collège de France lectures, this chapter will address three questions left unanswered in the *History of Sexuality, Volume 1*. First, what are the relationships between forms of power and structures of the family? Second, what are the relationships between class structures and family structures? Third, how does Foucault analyse the social conditions of the emergence of the 'conjugalisation of the family' in Greece during the Hellenistic period, and its connection with 'practices of the self'? In the conclusion, the answers to these questions will be used to draw out the contribution of Foucault's more detailed reflections in the Collège de France lectures to contemporary sociological work on the family.

Forms of power and familial structures

In his work during the 1970s, Foucault draws a distinction between two forms of power, 'sovereign' and 'disciplinary'. The former characterises the ancien régime, whereas the latter characterises modernity. Sovereign power operates primarily through a legal register in determining the permitted and the forbidden, rights and responsibilities and punishing misdemeanours as attacks on the sovereign's rulership. By contrast, 'ascetic exercises taken from a whole tradition of religious exercises, defined disciplinary methods for daily life and pedagogy':[5]

> One type of power, that of sovereignty, is replaced by what could be called disciplinary power, and the effect of which is not at all to consecrate someone's power, to concentrate power in a visible and named individual, but only to produce effects on its target [...] who must be rendered 'docile and submissive'.[6]

This is achieved through permanent supervision within a delimited territory or institution, an optimal and rationalised use of time, the application and exploitation of the body's forces, and the strict identification of the subject with all of his good or bad actions through written records.[7] Disciplinary power positions each subject as what Foucault terms a 'somatic singularity'. By this Foucault means that each subject is pinned to all of their 'body, actions, time and behaviour', and these are subject to normalisation and optimisation with reference to a scale of subtle incentives and punishments.[8] Whereas sovereignty is legitimated by a founding act in the past, whether conquest or contract, the disciplines are legitimated by their orientation towards the betterment of subjects in the future according to a given norm. The disciplinarisation of society, Foucault argues, is associated with the demand of capitalism to achieve 'the maximum possible use of individuals'.[9] The disciplines allow the physical, social, semiotic and economic forces of human beings to be disaggregated and reordered in such a way as to ensure that they can work optimally as part of a wider system. Such a strategy also serves to:

> make all of them usable, not so that they can all be used in fact, but, precisely, so that they do not all have to be used; extending the labour market to the maximum in order to make certain of an unemployed reserve enabling wages to be lowered.[10]

Under the ancien régime, 'a post-feudal, pre-industrial government',[11] Foucault argues that the family served as a 'kind of complete model' for the operation of the state.[12] The government of the state is conceived of as similar to the governance of a family: it must manage individuals, goods and wealth, in the manner of a beneficent head of a family. In *Psychiatric Power*, Foucault identifies three ways in which the family operates according to a logic parallel to that of 'sovereignty'. First, 'in the family you have individualisation at the top, which recalls and is of the very same type as the power of sovereignty, the complete opposite of disciplinary power'.[13] Second, 'in the family there is constant reference to a type of bond, of commitment, and of dependence established once and for all in the form of marriage or birth'. This is the 'blood tie', as both the sovereign and the family found their legitimacy on the social meaning of descent:

> And it is this reference to the earlier act, to the status conferred once and for all, which gives the family its solidity; mechanisms of supervision are only grafted on to it, and membership of the family continues to hold even when these mechanisms do not function.[14]

Third:

> in the family there is all the entanglement of what could be called
> heterotopic relationships: an entanglement of local, contractual
> bonds, bonds of property, and of personal and collective com-
> mitments, which recalls the power of sovereignty rather than the
> monotony and isotopy of disciplinary systems.[15]

A further parallel between the family and the ancien régime is identified in *Le Désordre des familles*. Arlette Farge and Michel Foucault demonstrate the structural and functional correspondences between the
family and the absolutist state up to the eighteenth century. Farge and
Foucault establish the affinity between family honour and an administration's public order, since they both share the same goal – to establish
a permanent regulation of the behaviour of the individuals.[16] Honour
is to the family what public order is to the state.

Whereas under the ancien régime the family served as a model for the
operation of state power, in the eighteenth century the family became
no more than a 'segment' of the 'population'. And with the formation
of the modern state, the population became the primary unit for the
management of public affairs. The population had its own aggregate
reality, and these effects are irreducible to those of the family. Foucault
points to the political concern for 'the great epidemics, the endemic
expansion, the spiral of work and wealth'. In such a context, 'the family as model of government is going to disappear'. For Foucault, there
would remain only 'a certain number of residual themes that may well
be religious or more themes'.[17] Yet among the different segments of
the population, the family was nevertheless a privileged 'instrument'
for modern government. The reason is that 'when one wants to obtain
something from the population concerning sexual behaviour, demography, the birth rate, or consumption, then one has to utilise the family'.[18] Moreover, for Foucault the family has become the bridge, 'the
hinge, the interlocking point, which is absolutely indispensable to the
very functioning of all the disciplinary systems'.[19] Why is this?

The family is not a disciplinary institution in the manner of the
school, barracks, workshop or prison. Foucault speaks of the family as
an 'alveolus of sovereignty', a form of power that intensifies relationships between parents and children, and between the husband and the
wife, by binding together economic, political, geographical and affective ties.[20] This is an extraordinary analysis. Whereas readers of *History
of Sexuality, Volume 1* have commonly taken the family to be no more

than another disciplinary institution, Foucault argues explicitly that this is not the case. Disciplinary power may be engaged within the family to ensure the regulation of sexuality, the effective conduct of homework and so forth. The family does not solely look backwards to the blood tie for its authority, but into the promised future of normalising, disciplining and helping the child become a citizen of value and esteem. It is in this regard that Foucault speaks of the 'disciplinarisation of the family'.[21] Yet primarily the family is, according to Foucault, 'a sort of cell within which the power exercised is not, as one usually says, disciplinary, but rather of the same type as the power of sovereignty'.[22] Foucault argues that this underlying logic of sovereignty demarcates the family as a unique institution, although, strangely enough, one that is for this precise reason integral to the very operation of disciplinary apparatuses. He is adamant that there is not only one type of power in modern societies; the disciplinary organisation of the school, for example, cannot be understood without taking into account the 'multiple subjugations' such as 'family to administration, and so on'.[23] 'Between familial sovereignty and disciplinary panopticism, the form of which is, I think, completely different from that of the family cell, there is a permanent game of cross-reference and transfer.'[24]

'It is because', states Foucault, 'you have this system of sovereignty operating in society in the form of the family, that the obligation to attend school works and children, individuals, these somatic singularities, are fixed and finally individualised within the school system.'[25] The same applies for the other disciplinary apparatuses:

> Look at how, historically, the obligation of military service was imposed on people who clearly had no reason to want to do their military service: it is solely because the State put pressure on the family as a small community of father, mother, brothers and sisters, etcetera, that the obligation of military service had real constraining force.[26]

The constraining force of the family's potent amalgam of economic, political, geographical and affective ties for the operation of the disciplines can be seen again in the case of the insertion of subjects into the labour pool as docile workers:

> What meaning would the obligation to work have if individuals were not first of all held within the family's system of sovereignty, within this system of commitments and obligations, which means that

things like help to other members of the family and the obligation to provide them with food are taken for granted? Fixation on the disciplinary system of work is only achieved insofar as the sovereignty of the family plays a full role.[27]

As well as serving to 'inject them, so to speak, into the disciplinary apparatuses', the family plays another key role. The family acts as:

the switch point, the junction ensuring passage from one disciplinary system to another, from one apparatus (*dispositif*) to another. The best proof of this is that when an individual is rejected as abnormal from a disciplinary system, where is he sent? To his family. When a number of disciplinary systems successively reject him as inassimilable, incapable of being disciplined, or uneducable, he is sent back to the family, and the family's role at this point is to reject him in turn as incapable of being fixed to any disciplinary system, and to get rid of him either by consigning him to pathology, or by abandoning him to delinquency, etcetera.[28]

If the sovereign form of power is not effective within the family, it is precisely its sovereign form of power that mandates the operation of the disciplinary apparatuses as a compensatory system. It is the amalgam of economic, political, geographical and affective relations conjoined in discourses on the family that mandate and organise 'the appearance of supplementary disciplinary systems in order to retrieve these individuals' who do not become docile bodies within disciplinary systems.[29]

New experts and specialists thus appear – criminologists, psychotherapists, sociologists, social workers and so forth – who deal with problems of the family without being from the family themselves. Foucault draws a distinction between 'social assistance' on the one hand, and 'the psy-function' on the other, as forms taken by the disciplines with respect to the family. Social assistance is 'all the social work which appears at the start of the nineteenth century'. Social work forms 'a kind of disciplinary tissue which will be able to stand in for the family, to both reconstitute the family and enable one to do without it'. It works to discipline the family itself, and to ensure that those without the minimal adequate familial experience are given a form of this experience outside their birth family.[30] Foucault finds it highly significant that 'within this disciplinary system which rushes in where there is no longer a family, there is a constant reference to the family', even to the extent that in early forms of extra-familial care for 'young delinquents', 'the supervisors, the chiefs, etcetera, are called father, or grandfather, and [...] supposed to constitute a family'.[31]

In contrast to social assistance, the 'psy-function' is less a 'substitute for the family' than disciplinary apparatuses 'with a familial reference'. 'The psychiatric, psychopathological, psycho-sociological, psycho-criminal' professions are 'agents of the organisation of a disciplinary apparatus that will plug in, rush in, where an opening gapes in familial sovereignty' – as defined precisely by the fabrication within and beyond the home of future adequate citizens, and the physical, emotional and sexual sustenance of its adult worker members.[32] When detached from the institution of the family home in the form of social assistance or the psy-function where it is naturalised by the appearance of self-evident referents, the discourse of 'family' reveals more clearly its normalising operation and function. 'The family' is the hinge and switch-point for the disciplines because of the way in which it can operationalise its assemblage of potent affects with economic, political and geographical ties in the service of determinate forms of biopolitics. The position of the family at the intersection of kinship and sexuality allows it to mask the concerted organisation or reorganisation of cultural and biological processes associated with the disciplines as merely the 'cultivation' of natural forms or the 'rectification' of deviant individuals.

Foucault provocatively suggests that 'as for the mentally ill, they are no doubt the residue of all residues, the residue of all the disciplines, those who are inassimilable to all of a society's educational, military and police disciplines' that are hinged by the family. The family are responsible, in conjunction with the state, for conveying their member into psychiatric power by 'consigning him to pathology'.[33] This conclusion is aligned with Foucault's previous analysis in the *History of Madness*. There, Foucault had suggested that 'confinement and the whole police structure that surrounded it served to control a certain order in family structures', since the family had an importance to dominant institutions as 'a social regulator'. Thus 'family and its requirements became one of the essential criteria of reason', and 'it was above all in its name that confinement was demanded and obtained'.[34] Foucault argued that, with madness constructed in the eighteenth century as the alienation of the 'system of the passions', any behaviour that disrupted 'the organisation of the bourgeois family' and that could be positioned as such an alienation risked being placed as mental illness.[35] The authority that 'the doctor' would henceforth hold as an ostensive property of his or her profession, was initially 'borrowed from order, morality and the family' as the three key 'great massive structures of bourgeois society and its values'.[36]

However, Foucault's analysis of the relationship between the family and psychiatric power in the Collège de France lectures diverges in another respect from that of his previous work. In the *History of Madness*, Foucault had claimed that the asylum had been 'closely modelled on the family unit'.[37] Tuke's early asylum, The Retreat, was 'a great fraternal community of patients and helpers, under the authority of the directors and the administration. It was a rigorous family', since 'the belief was that the 'family' placed the patient in a milieu that was both normal and natural', conducive to their return to reason and mental health.[38] The asylum was 'a structure forming a microcosm' of societal values regarding 'the relationship between Family and Children structured around the theme of paternal authority',[39] and discourses on madness more generally became 'inextricably linked to the half-real, half-imaginary dialectic of the Family'.[40] In *Psychiatric Power*, Foucault attempts to correct this thesis. He argues that the asylum was not constituted on the model of the family because, whereas the asylum was organised according to disciplinary power, the family is fundamentally oriented by a sovereign-style form of power. 'The joining of the family model to the disciplinary system takes place relatively late in the nineteenth century – I think we can put it around the years 1860 to 1880,' Foucault contends.[41] The child became the target of a psychiatric intervention differentiated by social class: penal settlement or incarceration in asylums for the masses, and individual psychiatric treatment for the upper classes. The disciplinary apparatuses were joined to the family: psychiatry would make a profit from the adjudication and correction of familial irregularities; and in turn, the family would be recompensed for deferring its sovereign power to disciplinary expertise by being situated by psychiatry as the origin and secret truth of personal identity.[42] In this way, Foucault's research on the development of the psychiatric field in relation to the forms of power that intersect in the family, allows us to understand why this field invested heavily in the field of sexuality, to the point of almost becoming synonymous with it.

Social classes and familial structures

In the *History of Sexuality, Volume 1*, Foucault argues that in the first third of the nineteenth century, the 'organisation of the "conventional" family' as an ideal served as 'an indispensable instrument of political control and economic regulation for the subjugation of the urban proletariat: there was a great campaign for the "moralisation of the poorer classes"'.[43] These brief remarks are not given substantial elaboration in the text, and subsequent commentators on the *History of Sexuality*, *Volume 1* have not only described a text in which social class is under-theorised but have also occasionally accused Foucault of ignoring the issue of class. The Collège de France lectures indicate a thoroughgoing account of class in Foucault's analysis of the family in the period of the early to mid 1970s.

Foucault situates aristocratic and bourgeois families under the sovereign power of the ancien régime as comprising a system of relationships – relations with ancestors, descendants, collaterals, as well as marriages. These relationships, he argues, were organised by social and economic apparatuses for the division and distribution of goods and status from one generation to another:

> However, to the extent that the family was thus homogenous with all the other apparatuses of sovereignty, you can see that basically it had no specificity, no precise limits. This is why the family's roots spread far and wide [...] it merged into a whole series of other relationships with which it was very close because they were of the same time: relationships of suzerain to vassal, of membership of corporations, etcetera.[44]

Within the context of the 'imprecise and fuzzy' interaction between different forms of power that characterised sovereignty, the body of the king played a crucial role. Sovereign power holds together 'multiple, different and irreconcilable relationships' in society in the individu-alised body of the sovereign; the figure of 'the crown' as a corporate personage 'was necessary of the mutual adjustment of heterotopic sovereignties within the game of societies of sovereignty'.[45] Yet discipli-nary power did not need the king for this purpose, as the family could serve as the hinge and switch-point between different social, political and economic apparatuses. Foucault therefore argues that 'what the king's body was in societies of mechanisms of sovereignty, the family is in societies of disciplinary systems'.[46] The family thus superseded the king; it preserved some feudal relations, such as the law of status in the encounters between parents and children, but also facilitated their obsolescence. Yet in turn there was also a substantial shift in the form of the normative family across society over the course of the eight-eenth and nineteenth centuries. This shift was played out in republican rhetoric. On the one hand, representing the perfection attained by the Revolution over monarchy, Jean-Sylvain Bailly is described by Foucault as having conceived of the union of nobility, clergy and Third Estate against the King as 'Now the family is reunited.'[47] On the other hand, republican characterisations of the monarchy depicted them as engaged in monstrous familial relations. With republican rhetoric in relation to 'Marie-Antoinette, the dominant theme seems to be sexual debauchery, and incest in particular'.[48] Yet this characterisation of royalty as 'the incestuous (the princely monster) later served as the grid of intelligibility for and means of access to a number of disciplines', including psychoanalysis.[49]

Foucault describes the emergence of the bourgeois home as a 'family cell' towards the end of the eighteenth century. In contrast to the family within sovereign societies, the family within a society of disciplinary apparatuses constituted a narrower, more affective, space and was structured around the direct relations between parents and children. According to Foucault, the control and regulation of the children's sexuality was positioned as a key constituent of the family cell; this control was the parents' role and duty. The potential for deviation within the desires of the child justified a totalising surveillance. Foucault's description of the family cell evokes a topology in which the child's bed is situated at the centre of the home. The bodies of the parents form protective walls against outside threats, the parental gaze focuses inwards upon the child's body, and their voices call outward to summon doctors, educationalists and other professionals to aid their cultivation of the natural propensity of their child towards an ideal norm. All the economic, political, geographical and affective ties that comprised the family were mobilised in the cause of the effective normalisation of the family's offspring.

Fundamental to this normalisation was the problematisation of familial 'sexuality', which varied by class. The bourgeois and aristocratic families were the first to become the object of discourses that urged a surveillance of sexuality, and the necessity of a rational technology of punishment. Animating these new discourses, Foucault argues in *Society Must Be Defended*, were not 'the bourgeoisie in general' but 'the real agents that exist in the immediate entourage: the family, parents, doctors, the lowest level of the police, and so on'.[50] In these new discourses on sexuality, subjects were impelled to propagate their family and class through the production of healthy descendants. Fundamental to this injunction were discourses on heredity and degeneracy: 'the theory of heredity allows psychiatry of the abnormal to be [...] a technology of the health or unhealthy, useful or dangerous, profitable or harmful marriage'.[51] At stake in the 'constant apparatus of the parental surveillance of children was the discovery of a political and economic interest'.[52] Foucault describes this medico-moral concept of heredity as 'racism against the abnormal', the function of which 'is not so much the prejudice or defence of one group against another as the detection of all those within a group who may be the carriers of a danger to it. It is an internal racism that permits the screening of every individual within a given society.'[53] Oscillating between an account of these eugenic discourses as a consequence of class identity and a constitutive element in class identity, Foucault describes that 'the surveillance apparatus, the medicalisation of sexuality [...] came at a certain moment to represent, to constitute the interest of the bourgeoisie'.[54]

Foucault argues against the hypothesis that 'the child's sexuality that is tracked down and prohibited is in some way the consequence of the formation of the nuclear family'. Instead, he wishes to suggest of the 'parental family' of the nineteenth century that 'this sexuality is one of [its] constitutive elements'.[55] To illustrate this claim that the primary goal of discourses on sexuality was not repression but surveillance and subjectivation, Foucault pays particular attention to concerns regarding 'the masturbation of bourgeois children and adolescents'.[56] The invention of masturbation is part of what Foucault calls the 'family drama of the nineteenth and twentieth centuries', the key component of which was the relationship between the bodies of parents and the bodies of the children. Prior to the mid-eighteenth century, sexual prohibitions were concerned with relations between family members. The focus then shifted to the child's sexuality and the problem of masturbation. Foucault associates this with the process of transformation within the bourgeois family, which became a sort of 'restricted, close-knit, substantial, compact, corporeal, and affective family core'. He describes this new apparatus as a 'cell family', distinguished from prior forms of the family by 'its corporeal, affective, and sexual space entirely saturated by direct parent–child relationships'. The potential for deviance within the desires of the child, which may draw them away from their 'natural' innocence and towards sickness and immorality, demanded two great projects.[57] First, the potential of the masturbating child to become 'abnormal' (in the form of an 'individual to be corrected') necessitated the continual protection of children by parents from 'seduction by an adult', 'the ideal solution being the infant alone in a sexually aseptic family space'. Thus 'the family space must be a space of continual surveillance. Children must be watched over when they are washing, going to bed, getting up, and while they sleep. Parents must keep a lookout all around their children, over their clothes and bodies.'[58]

Second, the potential for 'abnormality' in the child necessitated the intervention of medical professionals and medical discourses. Foucault suggests that 'at the very moment that the cellular family is enclosed in a dense, affective space, it is endowed with a rationality that, in the name of illness, plugs it into a technology, into an external medical power and knowledge'.[59] This new 'family space' is so invested with medical rationality that Foucault speaks of the family as being 'medicalised'. He coins the term 'medico-familial mesh' to describe the way in which the interaction between the family and psychiatric power 'organises a field that is both ethical and pathological in which sexual conduct becomes an object of control, coercion, examination, judgement, and intervention'. Foucault expands this analysis and argues that 'in short, the medicalised family functions as a source of normalisation'.[60] It is this 'medico-familial mesh' that will henceforth allow the distinction between the 'normal' and the 'abnormal' in the sexual domain to appear, beginning in the first decades of the nineteenth century.

In *History of Sexuality, Volume 1*, Foucault had implied that 'the "conventional" family' was an ideal that was then imposed as a norm on the urban proletariat. The Collège de France lectures deepen this account by documenting how this norm operated differently between the middle and working classes. Foucault draws a distinction between 'two processes of formation, two ways of organising the cellular family around the dangers of sexuality', one in the bourgeois family, the other appearing in the working-class family.[61] Medical control is first aimed particularly at the bourgeoisie, 'for the sake of a general protection of society and race', while judicial control is aimed more particularly at the working classes.[62] Whereas in the bourgeois family Foucault identifies that the central concern is the desire of the child, which must be monitored in order to avoid perversion, in the working-class family it is adult sexuality that is constructed as dangerous. The curious implication is that two types of incest must be acknowledged as operating within nineteenth-century discourses on sexuality, depending on whether we are considering the bourgeois or working-class family. These two types of incest have two corresponding types of treatment: in the case of the bourgeois family, 'the child's sexuality is dangerous and calls for the coagulation of the family; in the other case, adult sexuality is thought to be dangerous and calls instead for the optimal distribution of the family'.[63]

For the bourgeois family, danger was perceived to lie in the abnormal personality that may result from problems or precociousness in the emergence of a child's sexuality, requiring the intervention from the medical field, and more precisely, the intervention of psychoanalysis 'which appears as the technique of dealing with infantile incest and all its disturbing effects in the family space'.[64] For the working-class family, however, what was considered dangerous was the 'incestuous appetite of parents or older children, sexualisation around a possible incest coming from above, from the older members of the family', resulting in social, judicial and police intervention.[65] The peasant who enters the city as a new member of the proletariat finds himself without institutional supports or systems of stabilising obligations. Foucault claims that in the nineteenth century, as 'the European proletariat was being formed, conditions of work and housing, movements of the labour force, and the use of child labour, all made family relationships increasingly fragile and disabled the family structure', leading to 'bands of children' unsupervised by adults and an increase in 'foundlings, and infanticides, etcetera'. Foucault argues that:

> faced with this immediate consequence of the constitution of the proletariat, very early on, around 1820–1825, there was major effort to reconstitute the family; employers, philanthropists, and public authorities used every possible means to reconstitute the family, to force workers to live in couples, to marry, have children and to recognise their children. The employers even made financial sacrifices in order to achieve this refamilialisation of working class life.[66]

The ideal of the family would serve as a means of stabilising workers, through 'mechanisms like the saving banks, housing policy, and so on'.[67] Within this family, a strict rule would be the segregation of the sexes and the generations, apart from the married couple in the conjugal bed. On the basis of this class analysis of the family, Foucault makes one further point, arguing against the universality of the psychoanalytic theory of incest: 'there have been two modes of [...] the familialisation of sexuality, two family spaces of sexuality and sexual prohibition. No theory can validly pass over this duality'.[68]

The invention of conjugality

In the final part of Foucault's work, dedicated to what he calls the 'stylistics of existence' and more precisely, the stylistics of love, Foucault studies the invention of the 'conjugal bond', which he also calls 'conjugal duality'.[69] In *History of Sexuality, Volume 1*, subjectivity was conceptualised mainly as an effect of power relations. The requirements of 'the social body as a whole' were situated as the main cause of the emergence of the conjugal 'couple' as a discursive figure in nineteenth-century discourses on sexuality.[70] This has often been treated as the 'Foucauldean' approach to the family by subsequent researchers. Yet in revising his account of power and subjectivity in the later works, Foucault revises his history of the conjugal 'couple' to the degree that Foucault would become no 'Foucauldean' in this sense. In *History of Sexuality, Volume 1*, Foucault was interested exclusively in the family as a crucial biopolitical node; he is happy to use the term 'the regulation of populations' as a simple synonym for 'the socialisation of procreative behaviour'.[71] In the later volumes of the *History of Sexuality*, Foucault wishes to illustrate, using the family, the importance of practices of the self as mediating between power and subjectivity. Marriage appears as one of the 'great domains of relations' that have long defined the Western sexual subject.

'At first glance', Foucault notes, classical forms of sexual subjectivity in discourses on 'household management' 'bear a close resemblance to the forms of austerity that will be found later, in the Western, Christian societies'.[72] Yet the ethical relation within which marital sexuality was positioned changed dramatically within this period. For 'a free man in classical societies', sexual intercourse within marriage was a way 'to develop and display his activity without encountering any major prohibition'.[73] By contrast, subsequently there was a 'codification of married life to which Christianity was to give a universal form, an imperative value, and the support of a whole institutional system'.[74] This codification was oriented by 'a way of thinking that sought to rarefy sexual behaviour, to moderate and condition it, and to define an austere style in the practice of pleasures'.[75] Foucault is thus able to show that between power and subjectivity lie practices of the self, which may form very different ethical projects even while appearing to 'bear a close resemblance'.

In *History of Sexuality, Volume 2*, Foucault begins his attention to the family with the question, 'How, in what form, and why were sexual relations between husband and wife "problematical" in Greek thought?'[76] He notes that a defining difference of Hellenistic practices was that 'the married man was prohibited only from contracting another marriage; no sexual relation was forbidden him as a consequence of the marriage'.[77] Sex outside marriage for a man was not, then, prohibited. However,

> the principle that obligated a man to have no partner outside the couple he formed [...] was because he exercised authority and because he was expected to exhibit self-mastery in his use of this authority, that he needed to limit his sexual options [...] For the

husband, having sexual relations only with his wife was the most elegant way of exercising his control.[78]

The husband does not remain sexually faithful to his wife because of a moral prohibition, but because of an ethical desire for self-mastery and self-perfection. By contrast to her husband, the wife is indeed subject to a moral prohibition. However, Foucault contends that the way in which the wife recognises this moral prohibition, the 'mode of subjectivation', is quite different in Christian and modern ethics. Rather than offending nature or divine law, 'for the wife' in the Hellenistic era, 'having sexual relations only with her husband was a consequence of the fact that she was under his control'.[79] An equivalent, though subordinate, ideal of self-perfection as moderation in women, Foucault argues, was not felt in the sexual domain but in 'the way in which she conducts the household and conducts herself in the household' in the 'regulation of expenditure'.[80] Foucault concludes that 'in the cases of two spouses, marital status, management of the *oikos* [domestic sphere], and maintenance of the lineage could create standards of behaviour, define the rules of that behaviour, and determine the forms of the requisite moderation'.[81]

Yet in considering the Stoic revision of these Hellenistic ethics, Foucault identifies the beginnings of a tendency towards the moral prohibition of sexuality that will be fully developed in Christianity: 'Marrying, for Musonius, Epictetus, or Hierocles, is something one does, not because it is "better", but because it is a duty. The marital tie derives from a universal rule,' proper to all human beings according to the dictates of Nature.[82] The Stoic ideal of self-control restricted appropriate sexual pleasure to the production of legitimate progeny. This ethics, 'which tends to exclude, even for men, sexual intercourse outside marriage [...] will be one of the anchor points for a subsequent "juridication" of marital relations and sexual practices'.[83] Foucault, tying this shift in practices of the self to broader relations of power in Roman society, argues that 'a set of legislative measures marks little by little the hold of public authority on the marriage institution'.[84]

Foucault finds this 'phenomenon [...] all the more interesting' because the evolution of law regarding marriage and sexuality 'offers nothing new in the way of legal definition of acts. It reproduces precisely the traditional schemas of ethical valuation, merely transferring to public power a sanction previously under familial authority.'[85] Moreover, he considers the way in which this juridification was 'the effect, the relay, and the instrument' of socio-political and economic changes, impacting differently upon the various groups in society. Politically, marriage for the 'upper classes' shifted as 'status and fortune came to depend on proximity to the prince, on a civil or military "career", on success in "business" more than simply on the alliance between family groups'. A study of tomb inscriptions evidenced to Foucault that the 'lower classes' found marriage economically 'more accessible'.[86] Marriage thus becomes a common, politically regulated union of subjects, and increasingly problematised as 'a form of living, a shared existence, a personal bond [...] having its own force, its own difficulties, obligations, benefits, and pleasures'.[87] The case of marriage, then, illustrates his broader theoretical claims that mediating power and subjectivity are practices of the self, since the same injunctions on the subject can be organised from within a variety of ethical systems.

Within Stoic ethics, 'it is in order to satisfy the specific requirements of the relation to oneself, not to violate one's natural and essential being, and to honour oneself as a reasonable being that one must keep one's practice of sexual pleasure within marriage'.[88] By contrast, with the increasing juridification of ethics that occurred in Christianity, 'even within marriage, a precise code will say what one is permitted or forbidden to do, to want, or even to think'[89] and 'the principle of a perfect conjugal fidelity will be, in the pastoral ministry, an unconditional duty for anyone concerned about his salvation'.[90] Whereas for the Stoics, pleasure and desire had to be mastered and moderated, for the Christian they had to be deciphered and purified.[91] Sexual relations outside of marriage will retain their place as morally objectionable, but from within a different ethical frame. Foucault concludes the *History of Sexuality, Volume 3* with the claim that 'the code elements that concern [...] conjugal fidelity [...] may well remain analogous, but they will derive from a profoundly altered ethics and from a different way of constituting oneself as the ethical subject of one's sexual behaviour'.[92]

Conclusion

The most valuable of Foucault's contributions regarding the sociology of the family is his conception of the family as an object of thought and experience, shaped by a variety of historically situated dynamics.[93] Deepening the account of *History of Sexuality, Volume 1*, we have seen this historicity in Foucault's description of the family as: (i) a relay between different, changing apparatuses of power; (ii) problematised differently according to class; and (iii) organised according to practices of the self that may vary independently of moral norms regarding family life. A further analysis that could have been conducted is of the changing organisation of the family under the form of power known as 'security' in *Security, Territory, Population*; we have not pursued this task, as Gillian Harkins' chapter presents such an analysis and more.

Yet a path can be travelled with and beyond Foucault, as the subsequent chapters of this volume will show. What may be emphasised briefly in the conclusion to this chapter is the need for further attention to the complex relationships between the various fields of expertise, power and the family. Discourses on eugenics in the twentieth century have been shown by Véronique Mottier and Ladelle McWhorter to be crucial in constituting the hidden horizon of contemporary political discourses on the family.[94] Dietetics is another important example, and is currently the subject of genealogical investigation by Chloë Taylor. And curiously, Foucault, who was so interested in the emergence of structures of knowledge with respect to the family and psychiatry, never seriously considered the emergence of demography. In fact demography perhaps constituted the knowledge that was most immediately apposite to both the problematisation and regulation of families, and the shifts in psychiatric knowledge. A statistical science – numerical and statist – demography applies both to the population and to the family;[95] demography not only reflected but contributed to the changes in constructions of normal and abnormal behaviour with which Foucault was concerned.[96] The celibate individual, for example, is not the same form of subjectivity after the science of demography situates him or her as a deviation menacing the family.

A final remark on different types of power. Within sovereign forms of power, family was taken for granted. Family participated to the '*doxa*' of that time – Pierre Bourdieu's term for the taken-for-granted assumptions that frame a particular reality as obvious and necessary. Nobody could question the family, if only because it would also be to question the absolute power of the monarch. With the arrival of disciplinary power, the family was questioned: defending the family no longer belonged to the taken-for-granted *doxa*, but to 'orthodoxy' – a dominant view that had to justify continually the *raison d'être* of some type of family or another. And a power that has to justify itself is already that little bit more vulnerable, more potentially malleable.

Notes

1. Foucault, HS1, 114.
2. Ibid., 103.

3. For instance, Ellen K. Feder, *Family Bonds: Genealogies of Race and Gender* (Oxford: Oxford University Press, 2007), 17.
4. Foucault, HES, 2.
5. Ibid., 41.
6. Foucault, PSP, 22.
7. Ibid., 71.
8. Ibid., 45–6, 55. Foucault criticises previous social scientists and political philosophers, who collude with dominant discourses in society by taking the outcomes of the disciplines as the true form of the human being, rather than examine the political technology of his or her fabrication.
9. Ibid., 71.
10. Ibid., 71–2.
11. Ibid., 27.
12. Foucault, STP, 140.
13. Foucault, PSP, 80.
14. Ibid.
15. Ibid.
16. Farge and Foucault, DEF.
17. Ibid., 107–8.
18. Foucault, STP, 141.
19. Foucault, PSP, 81.
20. Ibid., 83.
21. Ibid., 114.
22. Ibid., 79.
23. Foucault, SMD, 45.
24. Foucault, PSP, 84.
25. Ibid., 81.
26. Ibid.
27. Ibid.
28. Ibid., 81–2.
29. Ibid., 54.
30. Ibid., PSP, 82–3.
31. Ibid., 85.
32. Ibid.
33. Ibid., 54, 82.
34. Foucault, HOM, 489.
35. Ibid., 82.
36. Ibid., 507.
37. Ibid., 490.
38. Ibid., 474, 489.
39. Ibid., 507.
40. Ibid., 490.
41. Foucault, PSP, 123.
42. Foucault, ABN, 250.
43. Foucault, HS1, 122.
44. Foucault, PSP, 82.
45. Ibid., 45, 82.
46. Ibid.
47. Foucault, SMD, 233.

48. Foucault, ABN, 98.
49. Ibid., 102.
50. Foucault, SMD, 32.
51. Foucault, ABN, 315.
52. Ibid., 255.
53. Ibid., 317.
54. Foucault, SMD, 32.
55. Foucault, ABN, 248.
56. Ibid., 237.
57. Ibid., 255.
58. Ibid., 243.
59. Ibid., 250.
60. Ibid., 254.
61. Ibid., 271.
62. Foucault, HS1, 122; ibid., ABN, 272.
63. Foucault, ABN, 271.
64. Ibid., 272.
65. Ibid.
66. Foucault, PSP, 83.
67. Foucault, ABN, 270.
68. Ibid., 273.
69. Foucault, HS3, 154.
70. Foucault, HS1, 105.
71. Ibid., 114, 104.
72. Foucault, HS2, 249.
73. Ibid., 24.
74. Ibid., 181.
75. Ibid., 24.
76. Ibid., 143.
77. Ibid., 146.
78. Ibid., 151.
79. Ibid.
80. Ibid., 157, 165.
81. Ibid., 202.
82. Foucault, HS3, 154–5.
83. Ibid., 184.
84. Ibid., 73.
85. Ibid.
86. Ibid., 74.
87. Ibid., 78–9.
88. Ibid., 184 after 'marriage'.
89. Ibid., 184.
90. Ibid.
91. Ibid., 239.
92. Ibid., 240.
93. See also Robert Nye, *Masculinity and Male Codes of Honour in Modern France* (Oxford: Oxford University Press, 1993); Jon Simons, 'Foucault's mother', in Susan J. Hekman (ed.), *Feminist Interpretations of Michel Foucault* (University Park, PA: Penn State University Press, 1996), 179–209.

94. See Véronique Mottier, 'From welfare to social exclusion: eugenic social policies and the Swiss national order', in David Howarth and Jacob Torfing (eds), *Discourse Theory in European Politics: Identity, Policy, Governance* (London: Palgrave MacMillan, 2005), 255–74; and Ladelle McWhorter, *Racism and Sexual Oppression in Anglo-America: A Genealogy* (Bloomington, IN: Indiana University Press, 2009).

95. See Rémi Lenoir, *Généalogie de la morale familial* (Paris: Seuil, 2003), 268–403.

96. Arnold I. Davidson, *The Emergence of Sexuality: Historical Epistemology and the Formation of Concepts* (Cambridge, MA: Harvard University Press, 2001).

2
Foucault's Familial Scenes:
Kangaroos, Crystals, Continence and Oracles

Vikki Bell

Foucault did not write about the family *as such*, and certainly not as the sociology of the family has come to write about it, *viz.* as a discrete domain of predominantly functionalist sociological thought and empirical endeavour. To read his work through the lens of the family is therefore to set oneself upon a task that must be approached with some caution. Indeed, as this chapter aims to show through selected moments in Foucault's books and lectures, his interest was always in the modes by which 'the family' has served as a site for the exercise of the power/knowledge relations that have surrounded it. Indeed, if 'the family' is an arrangement of figures and concerns, it is co-emergent, in a very real sense, with our understandings of it.

As with so much of Foucault's writing, his concern is thus to problematise how terms such as 'the family' have been endowed with quasi-natural status. He reconsiders the term's fragmented, dispersed histories and maps the often paradoxical power relations involved in its production. So, while the concerns of his genealogies meant that he wrote about 'the family', it is clear that he meant to wrest the analysis of the family's import from its customary coding in psychoanalytic, sociological or Marcusian discourse. In gathering his analyses under this rubric, therefore, one must not present Foucault's analysis of 'the family' in such a way that it attempts to rehabilitate his critical stance within debates that he was attempting to critique and to explode. For these reasons, this chapter will explain arguments from different moments in Foucault's later writings and lectures without seeking to make the substance of these arguments consistent. Each might be construed to address 'the family', but they are bound less by that theme and more by their mode of critique. In each of these scenes, Foucault's intention was to attend to the past in order to disaggregate and disturb our present modes of understanding.

The kangaroo and the crystal: the 'family' as a key site of activity and production

In the lecture on governmentality in *Security, Territory, Population*, Foucault argued that the middle of the eighteenth century saw a shift from the family as an aspirational model of government to the family as a privileged target, key to the concept of 'population' and a principal focus of biopolitical governmentality. In tracing shifts in how political treatises understood government, Foucault argues that – in contrast to Machiavelli, where the Prince's essential discontinuity with the other forms of power was presumed – the arts of government that emerged in sixteenth- and seventeenth-century Europe proposed that the state power should be continuous with other forms, including and especially that of the father towards his family. The art of government that emerged in this period began to understand the task of government as concerned not with sovereignty and territory but more akin to running a household, which is to say, with attention to relations between the people and things within it and their possible relations in the future. As Rémi Lenoir and Robbie Duschinsky have established in their chapter, Foucault argued that this invocation of the family as the model for government came to be replaced during the next centuries, when the family was no longer a model for government but became subservient to the notion of population.[1] The family thus becomes a 'privileged instrument' of biopolitics. As a field of intervention the notion of population relied upon the development of the disciplines, and these worked through the family, inscribing it with concerns that operated at both poles of what Foucault came to term biopolitical government. That is, biopolitics employs the micro, anatomical disciplinary techniques of power described throughout *Discipline and Punish*. But through these disciplinary techniques, truths emerge that come to be articulated in the macro or aggregate terms of governmentality, allowing forms of rationality that predict, control and create situations to which they seem merely to respond to.

Foucault argued in *History of Sexuality, Volume 1* that sex occupies a particular place within this history because sex is not simply an example of the operations of biopolitical power, but is a crucial target due to its pivotal place between the two 'ends' of the biopolitical spectrum: the micro politics of the disciplines, and the macro politics of the governmentality of populations.[2] In other words, the success of biopolitical strategies is articulated and monitored governmentally, at the level of the aggregate, but depends upon encouraging people to behave in a disciplined manner in relation to their bodies and not least, their sexual behaviour. 'The family' is the principle site and vehicle through which biopolitics works. In part, the reason for this is that it is the privileged site of the 'apparatus of sexuality': the veritable explosion of discourses on and about sexuality that operated through incitement (even and maybe especially when they appear to mimic a juridical form of condemnation and repression).

I have explored this activity of power around the family and its paradoxes at length elsewhere.[3] Let it suffice to recall the following key points. The family is paradoxical. On the one hand, Foucault places it at the heart of the apparatus of sexuality. He describes it as a 'crystal'.[4] The family seems to be the very source of sexuality, while actually it *reflects* the activity of the expert agents of the apparatus of sexuality surrounding the family. It was their attention to sexual matters within the family – between children and their bodies, between parents and their children, in relation to fertility and contraception, and so on – that problematised and 'sexualised' the familial domain.[5]

Thus, as a key example, late eighteenth- and nineteenth-century concerns about the dangers of masturbation and the instructions to parents to watch over their children's sexual behaviour did not aim to repress sexuality. On the contrary, as Foucault had explained in the *Psychiatric Power* lectures from 1973–74, the silencing or *discretio maxima* that had seemingly fallen over sexual matters was broken not least by this 'immense jabbering' around the dangers of masturbation that started up in the eighteenth century and continued for over a century. The exhortations to watch over children 'from the cradle' in order to prevent the dangers of ill-health into which masturbation might lead them, as well as the suspicion that adult servants might be to blame with their 'careless and ticklish hands', had the effect of folding the family into a tighter unit.[6] If parents were to watch over their children 'when they are washed, going to bed, getting up, and while they sleep [...] [if] the child's body must be the object of their permanent attention', then what was required was essentially a 'new physics of family space'.[7] The family became a space of 'continual surveillance'.[8] Between parents and children, then, a new drama of family life 'brings the adult's curiosity ever closer to the child's body',[9] as the parent is urgently advised to watch over the child's body in a 'sort of physical clinch'.[10]

Foucault draws upon the comment by Rozier, who advised parents through the example of the possum mother who 'when danger threatens [...] does not confine herself to fearing for them [her young], she puts them in her flesh'.[11] Foucault was a little unsure as to what a possum is, it seems – 'a kind of kangaroo I think' – but he uses this idea of a mother enveloping her children within her pouch to express this 'central objective of the crusade' against masturbation, which was 'the constitution of a new family body'.[12] There was a 'folding' of the parents' bodies over the child's bodies, in a 'sort of restricted, close-knit, substantial, compact, corporeal and affective family core: [...] the cell family' or what he calls the 'kangaroo family'.[13] These terms do not survive in the *History of Sexuality, Volume 1*, where Foucault talks rather of the 'affective intensification of familial space'.[14] However, the argument that the concerns of experts about masturbation brought about the reorganisation of familial relations survives as one of the key strategies of the 'apparatus of sexuality'. That is, it is understood as one important strand in a range of concerns and activities that surrounded the family and that brought the very notion of sexuality into existence through its attendant figures – not only the masturbating child but the Malthusian couple, the hysterical, frigid wife, the indifferent mother, the perverse adult.

In the *History of Sexuality, Volume 1*, Foucault clarifies and extends his argument that this intensification and 'folding' of familial space also meant familial relations were subordinated, penetrated by expertise, not least medical expertise. This development formed the 'apparatus of sexuality', making sexuality 'a dense transfer point for relations of power'. At the same time as the family was becoming sexualised in this manner, it became understood, within other discourses, as the site at which the rule of all rules operated. The incest taboo, in the form that the 'apparatus of sexuality' was supposed to replace, the juridico-discursive formulation par excellence – 'thou shalt not' – was discovered and analysed as the founding rule of civilised society. 'Incest [...] occupies a central place', wrote Foucault, 'it is constantly being solicited and refused; it is an object of obsession and attraction, a dreadful secret and an indispensable pivot'.[15]

Foucault suggested that the attention given to the incest prohibition by anthropological and sociological theories in the twentieth century – as well as, of course, Freud – was a reaction to the effects that the apparatus of sexuality was starting to have. This attention was a reassertion of the importance of systems of alliance. 'Alliance' here refers to relations understood in terms of blood and legal-marriage ties, by rules rather than desire:

> By asserting that all societies without exception, and consequently our own, were subject to this rule of rules, one guaranteed that this deployment of sexuality, whose strange effects were beginning to be felt – among them, the intensification of family space – would not be able to escape from the grand and ancient system of alliance.[16]

In their different but concerted efforts to elevate the incest taboo into its 'gateway' position signalling the threshold between nature and culture, sociologists, anthropologists and Freud's psychoanalytic theories clung to the system of power relations that the apparatus of sexuality was encroaching upon. Thus could Lévi-Strauss assert that '[the incest prohibition is] the fundamental step *because of* which and *by* which, but, above all, *in* which, the transition from nature to culture is accomplished'.[17]

But it is not the case that one can see this as an archaic discursive formulation that lingers into the twentieth century. Rather, one has to understand this discourse around incest prohibition as part of that present, an articulation that mimics older, predominantly religious modes of speaking, while being fully part of its moment of government. The two diagrams of power (the system of alliance and the apparatus of sexuality) are not historical stages. Indeed, Foucault states in the final section of *History of Sexuality, Volume 1* that 'it is not the soul of two civilisations or the organising principle of two cultural forms that I am attempting to express'.[18] The system of alliance, with its lines of descent and inheritance, and its symbols of blood and the sword, is operative within the present, maintaining the legalistic form of the family with its simple licit/illicit divisions. Yet the family becomes increasingly governed through attention to the quality of its pleasures, judged through measurements tracing its degree of variation from sexual norms.

So, not only was the symbol of blood called up within the apparatus of sexuality in the sense that it was enfolded in Sade's peculiar intervention, or in Nazi philosophy, but it was also less spectacularly sustained because the family was *required*; it was 'one of the most valuable tactical components of the deployment of sexuality'.[19] The state governs not against but through the family (see José Luis Moreno Pestaña's chapter on Jacques Donzelot in this volume), and as such has an interest in maintaining the desire for familial life, for its self-sufficiency and privacy. While the state retains its right to intervene there – since it is also constantly exposed as the most dangerous and damaging of places – the family is encouraged to self-discipline, to govern its own resources, both economic and sexual.

One analytic direction, among many, that may open up fruitfully here is to ponder the sense in which moral codes continue to be sought and fought over in relation to the family and the government of its conduct, and relatedly, how that thoroughly modern enterprise is obliged to articulate itself via truths articulated within biopolitical knowledges. In other words, relations are governed, subjects' self-conceptions arise and ethical modes of life are posited according to the truths found within the very power/knowledge complexes that entangle us in the biopolitical assemblage. As James Bernauer argued some time ago, it is for this reason that Foucault became interested in texts of Antiquity in which he argued one could find a prior alternative approach to ethics: 'Foucault's effort to liberate ethical reflection from its modern dependence upon knowledge makes his work a counter-ethic to that "ethic of knowledge" [*connaissance*] which promised "truth only to the desire for truth itself and the power to think it".'[20]

The family as a site for the stylisation of freedom

In the second and third volumes of *History of Sexuality*, Foucault's interest was in exploring an ethics of existence that did not engage in a search for truths on which to base one's conduct, but was instead about the practice of one's own liberty. In Antiquity – long before the rise of the 'psy' experts with their empirically generated or statistically significant truths, long before psychoanalytic formulations of the unconscious machinations of sexual truths, and before even the Christian articulation of sexual austerity – sexual practices and pleasures were debated by the philosophers as part of a suite of ways of living an exemplary life, one to be admired, emulated and remembered. Foucault wrote:

> The will to be a moral subject and the search for an ethics of existence were, in Antiquity, mainly an attempt to affirm one's liberty and to give one's own life a certain form in which one would recognise oneself, be recognised by others, and which even posterity might take as an example.[21]

As a key example of his arguments here, Foucault discusses, in the *History of Sexuality, Volume 2*, the classical notion of *enkrateia* that interests him precisely because it is a mode of problematisation and self-governance that is posited as concerning the practice of the relation of self to self. In his reading of Aristotle, principally, Foucault suggests that *enkrateia* is located:

> on the axis of struggle, resistance and combat; it is self-control, tension, 'continence'; *enkrateia* rules over pleasures and desires but has to struggle to maintain control. Unlike the moderate man, the 'continent' one experiences pleasures that are not in accord with reason, but he no longer allows himself to be carried away by them, and his merit will be greater in proportion as his desires are strong [...] the incontinent individual lets himself be overcome in spite of himself, and despite the reasonable principles he embraces, either because he does not have sufficient strength or because he has not given them sufficient thought: this explains why the incontinent person can come to his senses and achieve self-mastery. Thus, *enkrateia* can be regarded as (the prerequisite of *sophrosyne*, as) the form of effort and control that the individual must apply to himself in order to become moderate (*sophron*).[22]

It is this 'combative attitude toward the pleasures'[23] that constituted the practice of ethics, an attitude that was, Foucault points out, a relationship of the free man with himself. At the beginning of Plato's *Laws*, it is stated that 'to be defeated by oneself is the most shameful and at the same time the worst of all defeats'.[24] The ideal here, therefore, was to construct oneself as virtuous and moderate in the use of one's pleasures by constituting a relation to the self that took the form of 'domination–submission', 'command–obedience' 'master–docility' and not, Foucault points out, the form of 'elucidation–renunciation' or 'decipherment–purification' as it would take in Christian spirituality. Desire, including of course the desire for boys, was not by its presence understood as problematic. Instead, it was the management of one's desire that was problematised. It was there that men required guidance and reflection.

The relation of self to self was likened to several models. Plato's driver of his team was one such. But mostly this relation was likened to the government of a household. The 'family' in this scenario is not the *site* of the production of sexuality (as we saw Foucault argue in relation to later developments, discussed above) but instead, the 'household' was a *model* of governing one's sexual desire. '[A] man would be moderate only insofar as he was able to rule his desires as if they were his servants. Conversely immoderation could be likened to a household that was mismanaged.'[25]

The practice of *enkrateia* required time of course, and it was through training that the ability to control one's self and therefore *the right to govern others* was earned. Several different types of exercises were discussed by philosophical traditions – training, meditation, tests of thinking, examination of conscience, control of representations[26] – as in Plato's *Republic*, where he mentions these practices in relation to desires that are dangers to the soul. This training is posited as an ongoing practice, not something that can be neglected after it has been tested and one has succeeded. Practical training, *askesis*, was not 'distinct from the practice of virtue itself; it was the rehearsal that anticipated the practice'. These would later separate, argued Foucault:

> but in classical Greek thought, the 'ascetics' that enabled one to make oneself into an ethical subject was an integral part – down to its very form – of the practice of a virtuous life, which was the life of a 'free' man in the full, positive and political sense of the word.[27]

Rémi Lenoir and Robbie Duschinsky have explored the other places in the *History of Sexuality, Volume 2*, where Foucault discusses the wisdom of marriage, and depictions of the management of the household, that are relevant to this discussion. The point that I wish to emphasise here is that it is not 'the family' that is the focus of the problematisations in these texts. Instead, the relations within and outside the household – including relationships between married couples and with boys – are problematised through the relations that the free man conducts with others because each of these implies a relationship with himself. In other words, these are sites at which to trace the 'stylisation of freedom',[28] where the definition and forms of moderation were debated. This was not a time simply of toleration therefore, but was one in which sexual activity was thought to require a 'meticulous economy that would discourage unnecessary indulgence'.[29] The ethical strategies for self-mastery that this economy implied were not articulated in the law-like form that would emerge later in history. Instead, they were 'principles of stylisation of conduct' for those who aimed to give their existence 'the most graceful and accomplished form possible',[30] a form that illustrated one's right to deem oneself fit to govern the conduct of others.

The history of sexuality, and the family's place within it, have therefore to be regarded as entwined with the history of ethics, of the relations between self and self in the context of other relations, and the transformation of their problematisation. Foucault suggests that in these early texts there was not one set of rules or techniques that applied to sex as a domain of behaviour. Rather, the different domains of dietetics, economics, erotics, all had their implications for the sexual conduct and activity of the free adult male. This was an 'aesthetics of existence', then, a purposeful art of freedom 'perceived as a power game'. Sexual ethics, wrote Foucault, 'was problematised in thought as the relationship, for a free man, between the exercise of his freedom, the forms of his power, and his access to truth'.[31]

History of Sexuality, Volume 3 considers developments in the debates on sexual pleasures and practices in texts from the first centuries AD. Here, Foucault sought to explore changes from the earlier period, in particular in terms of whether the outline of a coming Christian morality was foreshadowed. This morality would be the one that came to confine sexual practices to the heterosexual married couple, considering its excesses sources of moral and physical danger both for the self and the community. Did these texts mark a break with the earlier period? Was a more austere, restrictive and prohibitive sexual morality taking shape in the texts that survive? Foucault's answer is that as well as important lines of continuity, there were some changes in the ways that sexual pleasures and conduct were debated; but he cautioned that these constitute a specific period in the history of sexuality, and one should not be too quick to read them as proto-Christian moral discourse.

Foucault characterises this period as one in which rumination on sexual practice came to be dominated by the question of the self. Whereas previously control of sexual practices and their excesses were understood in terms of how best to master oneself in order to dominate others, in this period the debate became how best to achieve and maintain a self-control and constitute complete dominance and supremacy over the self. The issue was how to develop an 'art of existence' within a context that debated obligations to community and to reason, and that also began to problematise sexual practices in terms of the dangers that they posed.[32]

Thus in relation to conjugal relations, as one of the key aspects of debate among philosophers, Foucault argues that one can see a relatively new mode of philosophical reflection that posited the relationship in terms of what he called a 'stylistics of living as a couple'.[33] The art of being together, the art of dialogue and an identity in moral attitude were extolled in an image of fusion that elevated the dual heterosexual relationship above other familial or friendship relations. While there were still those who argued against the marriage bond – especially for those who chose the philosophical life who needed to guide the community and had little time for marriage – the texts came in general to speak about the conjugal relationship as essential to one's existence, both because humans are 'conjugal by nature' (as Hierocles argued), and since it is integral to the cultivation of self.[34] Indeed, and most strongly for the Stoics, there was a duty and an obligation to marry. 'Such is the paradox,' writes Foucault: if we are to believe these texts, the marriage bond became privileged to the extent that the woman was understood as forming a unity with the man but only as it were insofar as the relation had import 'within' his cultivation and care of the self.[35]

This period saw philosophers suggesting a more active attention to the specificities of sexual practice than had been the case earlier: to its effects on the body, its function within marriage and its difficulties in relation to boys. With this attention to its function and difficulties there also came a caution. These were cautions about how sexual practice might endanger relations, and which came to distrust it, and to advise increasingly that it be confined to marital relations. Seeking sexual pleasure outside marriage was to risk a hurt that wounded deeper than its 'trivial' pleasure justified (argued Plutarch), although wives were also advised to practise tolerance and even to consider a husband's seeking pleasure elsewhere as a sign of his respect for guarding her against his debauchery and excess.[36] But the advice did not yet speak in terms of *illicit* sexual practice or make law-like regulations between permitted and forbidden.

Indeed, with regard to sexual monopoly, Foucault argued that the relation most endangered according to the ethics inspired by Stoicism was that to the self. It was in order 'not to violate one's natural and essential being, and to honour oneself as a reasonable being' that one must practice sexual pleasure only within marriage, and even for men to authorise it only under certain specific circumstances.[37] Instead of condemnation or the talk of evil or sin that was still to come, what was at stake here was one's 'mode of being, a style of relations' that would enable one to give oneself an existence that was 'honourable and noble'.[38] A principle of symmetry and of monopoly in relation to sexual pleasure was articulated in the texts that Foucault studied, most strictly in those of Musonius, but also in other authors, such that Foucault identifies the emergence of different 'modes of acting and conduct and ways of acting'.[39] He identifies the emergence of a fidelity 'defined less by a law than by a style of relating to the wife, by a way of being and behaving with respect to her'.[40] The texts posit the 'pursuit of refinement in marital relations', not least in maintaining, as far as possible, a reciprocal fidelity.[41] Moreover, there was at this time a distrust of pleasure, specifically of too much hedonistic pleasure in sexual intercourse between the spouses, and a general recommendation of reserve and of mutual affection and communication was articulated. The purpose of marriage and sexual intercourse – the birth of progeny – was to be kept in mind.

These texts do not imply a simple continuity of this 'monopolistic' code from Platonic utopia to Christianity, therefore, but had their own particular inflections that Foucault regards as related to the ethics of 'cultivation of the self'. In this ethics inspired by Stoicism, there is no longer the concern with self-mastery as it was articulated in the earlier texts (that Foucault studied in *Volume 2*), nor was there a concern that was to come later, with Christian duty, in relation to one's own salvation. Rather, in this ethics of the first centuries,

> it is in order to satisfy the specific requirements of the relationship to oneself, not to violate one's natural and essential being, and to honour oneself as a reasonable being that one must keep one's practice of sexual pleasure within marriage and in conformity with its objectives.[42]

Emphasising this point throughout the third volume, Foucault insists that this ethics is no longer about the need for self-mastery in order to allow for the domination of others, nor is it about the accentuation of forms of prohibition. This sexual ethics is an 'arts of existence' that understands sexual pleasures and activities to expose one to 'manifold ills'[43] such that they need to be given a universal form, one 'grounded in both nature and reason'.[44] It was without later legislative formulations, self-renunciation or hermeneutic self-interrogation, that this sexual ethics sought to develop an arts of living and a care of the self.

Ion: the 'tragedy of truth-telling'

In this section, I want to consider Foucault's explorations of kinship in his discussion of the concept of *parrhesia*, or truth-speaking, in his lectures of 1982–83. I will focus on Foucault's reading of Euripides' play *Ion* (from 418 BC), which Foucault argued was 'entirely devoted to the problem of *parrhesia* since it pursues the question: who has the right, the duty, and the courage to speak the truth'.[45] Again, one must be cautious insofar as Foucault's interest in the play was not to provide an analysis of the changing notion of 'the family'; yet it is of interest here because Foucault uses the play to consider how lines of descent were tied up with questions of authority, not least the authority between gods and

mortals, and the highly contested political rights in the city. The genealogy of the central character, Ion, is the secret that the play will reveal,
its central plot. This genealogy is politically charged because the play
itself is a mode of participation in the question of the division of rights
between citizens and foreigners. It is a play in which, unusually, the
gods remain silent, speaking only through the oracle, a form of truth-
telling that is 'reticent, enigmatic and difficult to understand',[46] leaving
human beings to speak truth to one another through the Athenian
practice of *parrhesia*. The attempt to clarify lines of alliance between
the main characters obliges them to stage scenes of questioning and of
truth-telling in which prior authorities and modes of seeking the truth
are challenged.

Foucault situates the play in relation to changing political relations of
the time, understanding it as scholars before him had done as part of an
attempt to articulate reasons for Athens to be understood as leader of the
Hellenic world, and to give weight to a pan-Hellenic coalition against
Sparta. *Ion* the play is an attempt to intervene in the mythical legend
that created an ancestor to those people from the Peloponnese who were
known as Ionians. According to myth, Ion had been an immigrant who
nonetheless had made a significant reform to Athens' constitution. In
Aristotle's version, Ion makes the first of many revolutions in the constitution, that of dividing Athens into four founding tribes.[47] But at the
time that the play was written, Athens wanted to claim its purity and
its superiority over other parts of Greece; to have a foreigner play such
a foundational role was awkward for these claims to Athenian autoch-
thony. The play presents a mythical genealogy, therefore, that through
the retelling of Ion's story unites Greek cities, finding genealogical reasons to build alliances. Ion's legend is retold, such that he was misrec-
ognised as a foreigner and is in actual fact Athenian, of both divine and
Athenian blood. The play partakes therefore in an assertion of Athenian
supremacy, and through the transformation of the immigrant into a
native,[48] its alliance with the Ionians. Furthermore, Foucault reads the
play as shifting the site of truth's disclosure from Delphi to Athens, again
reflecting the political moment in which Delphi was rather hostile to
Athens. That Athens should be understood as central is clear in the play's
implication of a shift from the oracular form of truth (where humans
were told the truth by the gods through utterances of the Pythia) to that
where human beings speak the truth to each other without the intervention of gods, 'politically' as it were, in Athens and through *parrhesia*.

But this shift is not straightforward, and Foucault was interested in
the play's movement through different scenes of truth-speaking and

attempts at truth-speaking. His lectures attended closely to the processes by which the truth emerges, and the connections that are thereby established, as well as making an argument about the shadows or illusions that accompany the truths by which connections are settled. In the play, Creusa, who is the sole survivor of the Athenian dynasty – her father being Erechtheus, said to be born not from a woman but from the very earth of the land – and her husband Xuthus, a foreigner (whom she had been obliged to marry as a token of gratitude for aid in war), come to Apollo's temple at Delphi to ask the oracle whether they will ever have children as they have remained childless. Unbeknownst to Xuthus, however, eighteen years earlier, when a young girl, Creusa had been 'ravished' – it is debatable whether this should be understood to mean as the result of a rape or a seduction – by Apollo himself. As a result of this encounter, she had borne a son. Out of shame, she abandoned the boy in the same cave where the rape/seduction had taken place. She believed the baby to have died. But in fact Apollo had ordered the child to be brought to the temple at Delphi and he had been raised there as the god's servant, the keeper of the temple's gold. In the play, Xuthus emerges from his consultation with the oracle with his wish granted, having been told that the first person that he meets outside the temple is his son. That person is the young man Ion, who is henceforth given that name. So it appears, on the most literal, straightforward reading of the play, that Apollo tries to send Ion back to his mother without need for speaking the truth to her or to her husband, while reuniting them nonetheless.

It is therefore a depiction of a god who is seemingly ashamed of his own actions, who will not in fact tell the truth but who instead attempts to rearrange relations while 'hiding' (indeed, even at the end of the play he still fails to appear, as would be usual, but instead sends Athene to speak the truth). The ability of the characters to speak the truth to one another is affected, gods and mortals alike, out of shame at their previous behaviour. Apollo cannot tell the truth because he would have to confess his misdeed; the enigma of the oracle is not only stylistic but based on guilt. Foucault suggests that 'the oracle's reticence is also the hesitation to confess'.[49] So the play stages a shift away from any notion that the gods were the source of unimpeded authority on all questions. It is left to Ion, the one born of a god and a mortal, to attempt to make truth emerge through human speech. At their meeting, when Xuthus leaves the temple and meets Ion, the two of them are obliged to establish how it could be true that they were father and son. In the course of this attempt, the two explicitly abandon the oracular form of truth-telling, which does not convince Ion. 'How could I be yours?' he asks; 'Apollo, not I, has the answer,' replies Xuthus, to which Ion says, 'Let us try another tack,' a phrase which Foucault privileges as making this scene significant. For here human beings propose to speak the truth to each other, abandoning as it were, the idea that truth comes from gods to men. Instead, truth emerges from modes of speech adopted between mortals.

Xuthus suggests that he must have had sex with a girl from Delphi as a young man, as he did, now that he is prompted by Ion, recall a drunken encounter there while celebrating the Dionysian torch feast! Ion is convinced by this rational explanation, but he is also most unhappy with this explanation of events, because while he might live as 'the son of a rich and powerful king',[50] if he is not born of an Athenian then he would not have the rights of an Athenian citizen. Athens claimed itself to be autochthonous, unlike other Greek peoples, as Foucault explains in his lectures, insisting that 'the Athenians have always inhabited Athens, they are born from its very soil, and Erechtheus, born from the soil of Athens, is the guarantee of this'.[51] But Xuthus was a foreigner, so although he has power and authority over the city, his sovereignty is not of the type that Ion craves. He does not want the monarchical or tyrannical sovereignty that Xuthus can give him: he wants *parrhesia*. Of course Ion does not know at this stage that Creusa is his true mother. He says:

> And if I might choose I would like her to be an Athenian; then I should have free speech in my blood! A foreigner, coming to a city of unmixed race must curb his speech: the law can enfranchise his name but not his tongue.[52]

For Foucault, Ion displays the characteristics of a good *parrhesiastes*. Certainly, he is sceptical of stories that humans tell about the gods. To Creusa's story of a young girl raped by Apollo, his first reaction is disbelief: 'Impossible! Some man wronged her and she is ashamed to own it.'[53] And in the conversation with Xuthus, Ion's response to Xuthus' inability to name his mother is to scornfully cite the myth that Creusa wholehearted accepted about her own father's birth, that he was born of earth and that his mother remained a virgin. His scorn quickly draws the agreement of Xuthus contradicting his wife's belief about her own genealogy:

Ion: How could such a thing happen?
Xuthus: I know; it puzzles me too.

Ion [with a sudden cry of joy]:	Ah! Then you know my mother! Who is she?
Xuthus:	I have no idea.
Ion:	Apollo said nothing?
Xuthus:	I didn't ask him; I was too delighted –
Ion [bitterly]:	Ha! Another child of the earth!
Xuthus:	The earth doesn't bear children.[54]

Ion distances himself from reliance on the gods, therefore, and both Xuthus and he suggest that Creusa's acceptance of her father's birth from the earth is 'merely' myth. 'The earth doesn't bear children,' Xuthus states baldly. Yet Ion suggests that mortal attempts to organise their speech and modes of living together are also flawed. He points out for Xuthus, and thence for the audience, that Athenian democracy is stratified and flawed, and that if he were to accompany Xuthus back to Athens he would neither legally nor institutionally be allowed to exercise his *parrhesia* by rules of Athenian political life, and is likely to be resented and even reviled. Foucault suggests that Euripides is presenting a critique of this state of affairs through Ion and through the play as itself an instance of what Foucault terms *political parrhesia*. But the twist of course is that since Creusa *is* his mother, Ion should have that right. He only does not at this stage because the god Apollo failed to speak the truth to Xuthus, so that, despite Xuthus' attempt to be truthful with Ion, he cannot tell the truth because he is simply ignorant of it.

Nor is Ion's mother Creusa told the truth by Apollo; from her point of view, she has instead to face a situation in which a young man will return with her and her husband to Athens, the child it seems of her husband's youthful dalliance with an unknown woman. She had come to Delphi to seek a child of her own, a child whom in fact she knew existed – this is the secret that she had withheld from her husband – but would leave having been asked to accept that she would instead be a step-mother to a grown son.

For her elderly slave and the Chorus who surround her as she struggles to comprehend the turn of events of which they had informed her about, it is Xuthus' mendacity that is revealed:

it's clear enough now: after coming and planting himself on Athens – a foreigner – and marrying you, and taking over your palace and everything you inherited, he goes and secretly breeds children with another woman – yes, secretly. Listen: when he saw you were childless, he was not content to be childless too and share your misfortune [...] It was not Apollo who told lies, but your husband.[55]

The slave appeals to a xenophobia that painful as it might be also protects Creusa's beliefs. In direct contrast with Ion's mode of reasoning, which implied a withdrawal from the gods as the route to truth, rejecting the god's 'half-truths' as Foucault calls them,[56] Creusa's slave, and the Chorus likewise, believe Apollo that Ion is Xuthus' son. They turn their fury on the foreigner Xuthus, and then on Ion himself, culminating in their incitement to Creusa to murder the 'slave's brat, brought along to lord it in your house!'[57]

Creusa herself is furious with both Apollo and Xuthus. Her passion prompts her *parrhesiastic* scene, a 'tirade' against Apollo in which, throwing off her shame, she publicly accuses him, still not knowing that Ion is the very boy infant that she had left in the cave. She does not accuse him of lying, but of not speaking the truth:

> My soul, how can I keep silence?
> Yet, how strip off shame, and show
> That lustful act in open light?
> What is left now to hinder me?
> What prim glance now could make me blush?
> My husband has turned traitor!
> I have no home now, no child; no hope left now.
> I thought, if I hid my ravishing,
> If I hid my baby's birth, and all my tears,
> I could bring these hopes to fulfilment;
> But I could not.
> [...]
> I will ease the load from my heart,
> Hold my secret no longer.
> With tears falling from my eyes, my soul tormented
> By the scheming cruelty of man and god alike,
> Who demand love and give treachery in return –
> I will expose them!
> [...]
> Listen Apollo, you who wake to song
> The seven strings of your lifeless lyre
> Till they chant immortal music to lonely shepherds –

Here in the white light of heaven I denounce you!
You came to me, with the gleam of gold in your hair,
As I was picking an armful of yellow flowers
Whose petals, pinned on my dress, mirrored the same golden gleam;
You gripped my bloodless wrists,
Dragged me, shrieking for help, into the cave,
Bore me to the ground – a god without shame or remorse! –
And had your will – for the honour of Aphrodite!
[...]
I shout it in your ear: vile betrayer!
My husband never did you service,
Yet you give him a son to inherit his house,
While my child – yes, and yours – like a beast you leave to die.[58]

Her accusation is, Foucault argued, a 'discourse of humiliation, a discourse of weeping, a discourse in tears'.[59] It is a second sort of truth-speaking, a further example of *parrhesia*, although in contrast to Ion's, it is not termed as such by Euripides and will not be recognised as such until later in history. Its form is one in which the weak reproach the powerful; an agonistic and dangerous form of truth-speaking, then, since the speaker's inferiority means that they take a risk in making such an accusation publicly. Inter alia, Foucault emphasises how Creusa's explosive speech contrasts the music and song of Apollo to the shrieking and shouting of Creusa herself, both at her ordeal in the cave and again now, as she resorts to shout the truth in Apollo's ear, a truth that he knows well but refuses to speak. Immediately after this imprecation, however, Creusa's old servant and she enter into a dialogue that, by contrast with her emotional outburst directed at Apollo, adopts a question-and-answer form that allows the truth of the events of her son's birth and abandonment to emerge. Here then, a third form of truth-speaking takes the form of a dialogue or an interrogation,[60] one in which the elderly servant prompts and guides her answers, and in which Creusa accuses herself as much as Apollo, recalling her own weaknesses and misdeed in exposing the child. This form of truth-speaking Foucault sees as further dialogic form of confession that he clearly regards as foreshadowing later forms of confessions that he had previously analysed.

In the lecture of 26 January 1983 in which Foucault considers the forms of truth-telling exemplified by Creusa's two rather different modes of telling her story, he was clearly rushed for time and summarises the end of the play, pointing out as he did so a key conclusion regarding the transfer of truth-speaking from the gods to humans:

> it is humans and human passion which will be the source, the mainspring, the force which will push aside this difficulty of telling the truth, which will push aside the shame of humans to tell the truth and the god's reluctance to utter a clear oracle.[61]

Creusa is persuaded by her servant that her only course of action is to murder Ion, and this she attempts to do by asking the servant to add the poison from her phial of the Gorgon's blood to Ion's drink as he celebrates having found his father, Xuthus. Apollo, still not speaking or revealing the truth directly, intervenes at this point – if somewhat minimally and still without speaking, notes Foucault – arranging an event that will ensure that the wine is discarded, and sending his doves to the scene, one of which drinks the poisoned wine from Ion's spilt cup, thereby sending Ion on an enraged path to discover who had wished him dead. This path leads him in due course to Creusa, who has taken refuge in the temple. It is here, finally, where she is protected from Ion's wrath, that the Pythia brings a sign of the truth of their relationship. Still the Pythia does not speak, but offers an object, a basket, the one in which the infant Ion was carried to Delphi, and which Creusa recognises as the basket in which she had left her child. Within it still is the cloth woven by Creusa as a girl, with its pattern of the Gorgon and fringe of snakes, and the sign that the child was of the Erechthean line – Athene's gift of a necklace of golden serpents to be given to every child. Ion is once more suspicious and does not accept that this object can reveal the truth until he has quizzed Creusa about the contents of the basket. Still more surprised is he by her next revelation: that it is Apollo and not Xuthus who is his father.

At first Ion questions whether this is a human half-truth to cover up another love-child before her marriage – which is of course the same suspicion that he had had of Xuthus – and his suspicion is only somewhat calmed when Creusa suggests, in stark contrast with her emotional outburst, that they might understand Apollo's actions as an attempt to be kind by giving Ion to Xuthus. Moreover, she suggests, the outcome will be a favourable one for Ion, not least materially because he will inherit Xuthus and Creusa's house in Athens. But Ion is still not entirely convinced, and declares that he will ask Apollo himself whose son he is: 'That is mere trifling. I am looking for a better answer. I will go into the temple and ask Apollo himself whose son I am.'[62]

It is at this point, at the very end of the play, when usually the god himself would appear, that Athene appears in his stead to convince Ion. In doing so, argues Foucault, she 'superimposes her authority on that of the god who did not want to speak'.[63] She gives the instruction to Creusa: 'take your son home with you to Athens, and give him the place and power of royalty; he is descended from Erechtheus, and it is his right to rule my land'.[64] Athena predicts then the events that will see Ion's descendents founding cities throughout Greece, lending 'their strength to my city', and the birth of Creusa and Xuthus' own sons, Dorus and Achaeus.[65] In this way, then, the play asserts the unity of different parts of Greece, while portraying Athens as its true centre.

As we have seen, Euripides' *Ion* provides a 'tragedy of truth-telling' within which Foucault could explore the several different modes of truth-speaking presented. The foreshadowing of modes of speech and confrontation associated with theories of democracy is his primary interest in the play. For our purposes, one can see how to interrogate what constitutes the 'family' is to understand how it was constituted and valued through lines of descent and inheritance, mainly of rights within the city and its rule-bound political machinery, but also of property. This is not to say that the family implied a cool and calculated set of relations (to be contrasted with later notions of conjugal love); on the contrary, the characters – and especially Creusa in relation to the baby that she had abandoned out of shame – display intense emotion and longing for familial ties. But ultimately the play is a political intervention that asserts a political vision in which the familial relations were given a new narrative that offered a unity to fragmented peoples. It drew upon myths while re-narrating them to fit contemporary purposes.

Foucault argues that this is the way in which to understand the play's intention, and gives his attentions to the implications that this new organisation of kinship genealogies also involved a new organisation of relations between speech and truth turning, not least, on the question of whether it is through the gods or between mortals that truths should be sought. Moreover, Foucault was also clearly intrigued by how the play undermines the subject's faith not only in his or her kinship genealogy but also in the structure of his or her belief more generally, while these mistaken beliefs or half-truths continue to structure relations, familial and political. Thus Creusa is seen to hold beliefs about her genealogy that are contrary to simple logic – 'the earth doesn't bear children' – while that same genealogical myth is to facilitate Ion's right to rule the city. Apollo speaks only 'half-truths' through the invariably enigmatic form of the oracle and the appearance of the Pythia herself brings only objects,

leaving humans to fathom their meaning. And while Xuthus is sceptical of Erechtheus' birth from the soil, he is content to take the power
that Creusa's position has given him in Athens and to pass it on to his
own son. The announcement by Athene, the reasonable rather than the
oracular god, furthermore, advises that no one tell Xuthus that Ion is
not his son, so that he may 'enjoy his delusion'.[66] Moreover, Athene's
suggestion protects Creusa and Ion, sparing them the need to confess
and to face Xuthus' disappointment (and possibly his withdrawal of
Ion's power). Such a confrontation would pit the human-father against
the god-father. Instead, the 'problem of two fathers' as Foucault calls
it, is solved by allowing the human father to live 'under the reign of a
share of illusion', the price of which 'establishes the order in which
speech which commands can become a speech of truth and justice,
free speech, *parrhesia*'.[67] For the sake of a democracy to come and the
modes of government, critique and debate that it will enable to be fos-
tered due to Ion's *parrhesiastic* qualities, this illusion will accompany the
newly constituted family as they return to Athens.

Conclusion

While Foucault's research and teaching took him further and further back
in history, he remained concerned with the forms of truth and the figures
of authority that espouse them. Through them our institutions have
been shaped. His work has become so influential in how we approach
these social histories that stated in this generalised form his arguments
start to sound platitudinous. But it is in the detail of each of these three
moments from Foucault's later writings that we can better see why for
him 'the family' has always to be disaggregated, approached not as a unit
but as a resultant of the historically specific apparatus (dispositif) that has
produced not only its modes of organisation but also the various modes
of self-understanding adopted by its constituent members.

   To reiterate some key arguments. From his work of the mid to late
1970s, we can argue that for Foucault, the rise of experts around 'the
family' have produced normalising knowledges that collectively, if
not uniformly, came to organise and (re)produce familial relations.
To understand this expertise historically is also to understand the
pronouncements of experts as forms of power/knowledge. How these
discourses have been supported and reproduced sustains normalised
modes of government of the family. Indeed, this work approached the
family as a target of biopolitical activity, the key site for the apparatus
of sexuality that intensified affect 'within' the nuclear family through

nineteenth- and into twentieth-century Europe. Paradoxically, however, because the family was so central to this new form of governing sexual bodies, it also maintained the 'old' emphasis on the importance of lines of alliance through its reiterations of the incest taboo as pivotal. In the second section of this chapter, we saw how in the work from Foucault's next period of research, his focus was on modes of ethical self-stylisation in texts from the fourth century BC. The family as such was not the primary focus there but Foucault shows how 'the household' is used as a model for controlling one's desires; indeed, one could make the case that seen through the lens of the history of ethics, the relation of self to self was privileged to the extent that the family featured only as a site for the exercise of a man's relation to himself. In the third volume, where Foucault considers texts from the first centuries AD, the conjugal relationship began to be understood as symmetrical and natural; yet this focus is not to be taken as a proto-Christian monogamy. Rather, Foucault suggests that the duality of the couple is one aspect of several in which the free man was advised in the practice of his aesthetics of existence.

The final section of this chapter considered how, in his last explorations of *parrhesia*, Foucault underscored how understandings of lines of descent and inheritance – what he had called the 'system of alliance' – were entwined in that era not only with questions of how mortals should understand their relation to the gods but also with how the rights to Greek citizenship were understood in relation to the geopolitics of that time. With his attention to Euripides' *Ion*, Foucault argues that the importance that *parrhesia* will assume within Greek democracy is foreshadowed in the character Ion, whose genealogy is also re-narrated in order to address and resolve the contemporary questions of political rivalry. The relations between the characters display the fundamental importance of lines of alliance to rights in the city, with Ion seeking to establish his parentage in order to establish his right to practice *parrhesia* once he arrives in Athens. At that point in history, Foucault suggests in his reading of *Ion*, these rights were also entangled with dominant myths that established purity of lineage with reference to the gods. In *Ion* we can see that a new political myth was being formulated to bring new understandings of how present peoples might understand themselves as in fact, *relations*, bound together by lineage. In particular, Foucault's interest is held by the fact that, as these lines are revealed in the play, several different modes of truth-telling are adopted that not only establish lineage but establish modes of speech that will become part and parcel of what constitutes the future practice of democracy. (Indeed, as we have seen, the new conceptualisation of relations is accompanied by modes of critique that are in tension with the dramatic or mythical resolution of political discord.) The lines of alliance, therefore, are crucial not only for how people were being asked to imagine their past but also for how they were asked to imagine their political present and its possible futures.

For the contemporary sociology of 'the family', Foucault's work advises, the task is that of Foucault's approach *tout court*. That is, one should try to decentre, to 'make strange' those conceptions of the family that have become taken-for-granted, by tracing the changing relations between forms of expertise, government action and subjective experience. Moreover, sociological endeavour is part of the complex that it studies, adding to and potentially altering the course of 'expertise' and the government of relations, such that the task also entails a profound reflexivity and a certain responsibility for one's interventions. Inter alia, this means that wherever the agenda of sociological endeavour is set by the interests and infused with the rhetoric of government interests, it is likely to be compromised from the outset. Beyond these general points, Foucault's own investigations and lectures offer rich examples of how through the interrogation of texts and scenes we might consider the political, social and ethical relations that are reflected in the crystal of 'the contemporary family'. These include but are not restricted to the most radical of changes that have occurred in the governmentality of 'the family' in contemporary times. Alongside the most striking changes in how 'the family' is understood, research must consider the continuities across time within re-narrations of conservative genealogies. This suggests a wide and complex research agenda that remains highly relevant. It proposes that through our interrogations we consider how discourses of sexuality, of desire and of loathing entwine themselves around notions of alliance, changing but not necessarily replacing the latter. It proposes that we consider how changing notions of subjectivity, of ethics and 'ethical behaviour' are articulated through matters of sex or desire more generally. And it proposes that political relations, including the constitution of a nation or *demos* from multiple ethnicities, be interrogated not only for the deployment of re-narrated lines of alliance that they produce, but also for new modes of subjectification and relationality in both the 'political' and the 'familial' spheres.

Notes

1. Foucault, STP, 105.
2. Foucault, HS1, 104, 114.

3. Vikki Bell, *Interrogating Incest: Feminism, Foucault and the Law* (London: Routledge, 1993); ibid., 'Biopolitics and the spectre of incest: sexuality and/ in the family', in Mike Featherstone and Scott Lash (eds), *Global Modernities* (London: Sage, 1995), 227–43.
4. Foucault, HS1, 111.
5. Ibid., 120.
6. Foucault, PSP, 244.
7. Ibid., 245.
8. Ibid.
9. Ibid., 247.
10. Ibid., 248.
11. Ibid.
12. Ibid.
13. Ibid., 248–9.
14. Foucault, HS1, 109.
15. Ibid.
16. Ibid.
17. Claude Lévi-Strauss, *The Elementary Structures of Kinship*, Rodney Needham (ed. and trans.) (London: Eyre and Spottiswoode, 1969 [1949]), 24.
18. Foucault, HS1, 148.
19. Ibid., 111.
20. James Bernauer, 'Beyond life and death', in Timothy Armstrong (ed.), *Michel Foucault, Philosopher: Essays* (Brighton: Harvester Wheatsheaf, 1992), 260–79 at 268.
21. Foucault, 'An aesthetics of existence', in PPC, 47–53 at 49.
22. Foucault, HS2, 64–5.
23. Ibid., 66.
24. Quoted in ibid., 69.
25. Ibid., 70–1. Besides the driver and the family, the other model was, of course, the city; in Plato's *Republic*, desires are likened to low-born populace who must be kept in check lest they grow agitated and disrupt civic life.
26. Foucault, HS2, 74.
27. Ibid., 77.
28. Ibid., 97.
29. Ibid., 250.
30. Ibid., 250–1.
31. Ibid., 253.
32. Foucault, HS3, 238–9.
33. Ibid.
34. Ibid., 163.
35. Ibid., 164.
36. Ibid., 175.
37. Ibid., 184.
38. Ibid., 185.
39. Ibid., 173.
40. Ibid.
41. Ibid., 173–4.
42. Ibid., 184.
43. Ibid., 238.

62   *Foucault, the Family and Politics*

44. Ibid.
45. Foucault, GSO, 27.
46. Ibid., 81.
47. Ibid., 77.
48. Ibid., 79.
49. Ibid., 89.
50. Euripides, *The Bacchae and Other Plays*, Philip Vellacott (trans.) (London: Penguin, 1973), 59.
51. Foucault, GSO, 89–90.
52. Euripides, *The Bacchae and Other Plays*, 62; Foucault's quotation has been translated slightly differently: 'If I may do so I pray that my mother is Athenian, so that through her I may have rights of speech. For when a stranger comes into the city of pure blood, though in name a citizen, his mouth remains a slave: he has no right of speech,' in Michel Foucault, 'Discourse and truth: the problematisation of *Parrhesia*: six lectures given by Michel Foucault at the University of California, Berkeley, October–November 1983 – Lecture 2, *Parrhesia* in the Tragedies of Euripides', available at: http://foucault.info/documents/parrhesia/foucault.DT2.parrhesiaEuripides.en.html (last accessed 1 March 2012).
53. Euripides, *The Bacchae and Other Plays*, 52.
54. Ibid., 58.
55. Ibid., 66.
56. Foucault, GSO, 90.
57. Euripides, *The Bacchae and Other Plays*, 66.
58. Ibid., 67–8.
59. Foucault, GSO, 120.
60. Ibid., 138–9.
61. Ibid., 140.
62. Euripides, *The Bacchae and Other Plays*, 86.
63. Foucault, GSO, 144.
64. Ibid., 144–5.
65. Ibid., 144.
66. Euripides, *The Bacchae and Other Plays*, 87.
67. Foucault, GSO, 145.

3
Foucault, the Modern Mother and Maternal Power:

Notes Towards a Genealogy of the Mother

Katherine Logan

> I would say that the small, affective, close-knit and substantial family that is characteristic of our society and that arose at the end of the eighteenth century was constituted on the basis of the caressing incest of looks and gestures around the child's body. It is this incest, this epistemophilic incest of touch, gaze, and surveillance that was the basis of the modern family.
>
> Michel Foucault[1]

In his work of the mid to late 1970s, Michel Foucault analysed various social phenomena: abnormality, sexuality, neoliberalism. He rendered these objects of inquiry problematic by, in part, giving detailed descriptions of various figures[2] – the masturbator, the hysteric, the physiocrat – whose emergence was made possible within what Foucault called *dispositifs*[3] or *problematisations*, that is to say, complex intersections of various practices.

With respect to Foucauldean research concerning sexuality, the implications of Foucault's recently published lectures at the Collège de France have as of yet been only minimally explored. It is the aim of this chapter to contribute to this growing body of scholarship, particularly through articulating latent content in the material from this period. When this lecture material – especially *Abnormal* – is read alongside Foucault's first volume of *The History of Sexuality*, a particular figure may be described as a key figure in the deployment of sexuality without being explicitly described as such. While she herself was only passively figured as relevant to the deployment of sexuality, she was essential to the emergence of sexuality as a form of *assujettissement*. This figure was the *mother* or, more specifically, the *modern* mother.

This chapter re-describes Foucault's genealogical analyses of this period for the purposes of taking the mother as a key figure in the deployment of sexuality, so as to begin to tell the Foucauldean story of the development[4] of the modern mother. Foucault argues that the deployment of sexuality was intimately bound up with (and within) the family. However, when Foucault refers more generally to 'the family', we ought to take this as lacking its necessary specificity in terms of the way in which the members of the family are individuated with respect to the deployment of sexuality. In an attempt to make Foucault's own analysis more specific, I argue that, within the family, the mother can be described as a central figure and maternal power as a central mechanism in the deployment of sexuality. While the mother is necessarily linked to the father within the sovereign realm of the family,[5] the mother ought to be regarded as having been quite distinctly individuated with respect to familial participation in the deployment of sexuality. In short, maternal practice underwent a significant transformation within this deployment, such that some of those practices that we now take to be part of being a 'normal' mother can be traced back to this deployment.

Unfortunately, it is beyond the scope of this chapter to address the vast body of literature, both feminist and otherwise, on the mother and the family. Furthermore, I will not attempt to develop the genealogy of the mother beyond the primary indications that I develop out of Foucault's more general observations on the family. Instead, I have the far humbler aim of making visible the 'fragmentary genealogy' of the mother that is implicit in Foucault's accounts of normalisation and the deployment of sexuality. As such, I do precisely what Foucault advised against – scholarship on Foucault – for the sake of beginning the project that Foucault himself might approve of instead: a genealogy of the mother.[6]

Before becoming absorbed in the details of this latent and fragmentary genealogy, however, it will be helpful to provide an overview regarding what I take the purpose and promise of a genealogical analysis to be. Here, I follow Colin Koopman in his description of genealogy as problematisation, rather than subversion. Rather than understanding genealogy as a way of subverting norms, genealogy as problematisation uses 'history to show the way in which certain practices have structured the core problematics which a given period of thought, most notably our own modernity, must face'.[7] Put differently, a genealogical analysis employs historical material for the purposes of clarifying the problems that we face in our own time.

The historicisation of the problem via genealogical analysis does two things for us. First, in detailing the emergence of some object of inquiry – sexuality, for example – we will develop an account of the ways in which certain practices simultaneously emerged or developed as part of a complex solution (or a complex of solutions) to the problem posed. For example, with respect to sexuality, we find that there is a tendency to think that conventional social norms are repressive. In other words, we take our sexuality to be a problem for which the solution is liberation. Yet Thomas W. Laqueur, in trying to point to exactly what is at issue in the modern obsession with sexuality, and especially masturbation, suggests that:

> masturbation became [...] the particular form of sexuality in which the success or failure of moral self-government was most apparent – not through the work that the state did, or even what professionals with strong links to the state did, but through the work of civil society on its members.[8]

In other words, sexuality is problematic, masturbation in particular, because it was through the disciplinary control of these practices that the individual's relationship to civil society, that is, his or her liberty, was negotiated. Rather than civil society merely acting to repress one's already pre-existing sexuality, it was in fact the rise of liberal civil society – and its demand upon its members that they be sufficient to govern themselves, that is, to maintain liberty – that was productive of some of the disciplinary practices that were then taken to be repressive and in need of liberation. With respect to the genealogical analysis as 'problematisation', then, when sexuality and its 'corollary conceptions of what might count as a solution' are problematised, we find that precisely what is at issue in sexuality is our own freedom.[9]

Through genealogical inquiry into the problems that we face – for example, the need for the liberation of our sexuality – we are 'able to open these problems up to more rigorous forms of critical scrutiny'.[10] As in the example above, thoughtful consideration of the issue of sexual repression leads us into a far more complex problem space. Furthermore, in opening up this expanded, historicised, critical field for inquiry, we begin to recognise the contingency as opposed to the necessity of the 'hybrid networks of problems and solutions' with which we are faced.[11] Sexuality, it turns out, is not something that merely pre-existed our demand for liberty in civil society. In fact, sexuality is one of those aspects of modern subjectivity in which the very means by which we are to define our freedom is produced alongside of restraints on our freedom. The result of the problematisation of sexuality then is not the 'subversion' of the repressive hypothesis and thus the notion of freedom as liberation, but instead is the further specification of that initial problem such that we become capable of reflecting upon the very conditions for the possibility of our demand for liberation. As such, that which we take to be repressive, for example the prohibition of masturbation, is shown to be a disciplinary practice that was *also* constitutive of our freedom in civil society.

However, this is not an account of genealogy that is incompatible with the destabilisation of problematic practices. On the contrary, this form of genealogical inquiry 'brings into critical focus the problems which further critical work must attempt to develop solutions for'. In other words, genealogy as problematisation is a process of inquiry in which a critical field is opened up for the sake of more adequately specifying the problems with which we are faced, as well as those places within the 'hybrid networks of problems and solutions' that might hold out promise for targeted intervention.[12]

It is in relation to this notion of genealogical inquiry that I hope to situate a fragmentary, Foucauldean narrative regarding the modern mother so as to draw out some pointers, some indications as to how we might problematise the mother in our own time. In other words, a genealogical analysis that adequately problematises the mother will indicate, as a matter of course, some of the specific points at which we might resist the domination or restraint that befalls mothers, while in turn recognising the ways in which the modern mother developed as a figure whose activity was integral to the development of freedom in civil society.

The mother and the abnormal individual

Foucault goes so far as to say that it is the deployment of sexuality that gave rise to the close-knit, nuclear, middle-class family:

> What is now being constituted is a sort of restricted, close-knit, substantial, compact, corporeal, and affective family core: the cell family in place of the relational family; the cell family with its corporeal, affective, and sexual space entirely saturated by direct parent–child relationships. In other words, I am not inclined to say that the child's sexuality that is tracked down and prohibited is in some way the consequence of the formation of the nuclear family, let us say of the conjugal or parental family of the nineteenth century. Rather, I would say that this sexuality is one of the constitutive elements of this family.[13]

Here, we ought to hear echoes of Foucault's critique of 'the repressive hypothesis' in the first volume of *History of Sexuality*. Foucault is arguing that, rather than pointing to the nuclear family as repressive of sexuality, we ought to see the increasing normalisation of sexuality, that is to say the deployment of sexuality, as that which was (at least in part) constitutive of the transformation of the 'relational' family into the nuclear family. In other words, we ought to take the normalisation of sexuality as a process of the normalisation of the family, as well. Yet, despite Foucault's detailed attention to the family in the work of this era,[14] he fails to draw any explicit distinction between paternal practice and maternal practice with respect to the deployment of sexuality. Given this failure, it falls to his successors to draw out the implications that are to be found in his accounts of familial responsibility in the normalisation of childhood sexuality for a description of maternal practice and thus the development of the modern mother. It is to this project that I now turn, by exploring and elaborating on Foucault's account of sexuality in *Abnormal* and the first volume of *History of Sexuality*.

In his course lectures of 1974 to 1975, Foucault analyses the emergence of the 'technology of human abnormality' that began in the seventeenth and eighteenth centuries and crystallised in the nineteenth century as a result of a 'regular network of knowledge and power' being established that united three figures who came to be known as 'abnormal'.[15] The third of these figures was the 'masturbator', that is to say 'the child masturbator', a figure who emerged as a central impetus to a reorganisation of the family in which the intimate concerns of the family 'become the domain of investigation, the point of decision and site of intervention for psychiatry'.[16]

There are three chief features of the masturbator that mark him or her out as a specific target for the discipline of abnormality. First, the masturbator was that abnormal figure whose abnormality issued within the frame of reference of the body, and whose constant surveillance was necessary in order to prevent this abnormality.[17] Second, the masturbator and thus masturbation are figured, of all the forms of abnormality, as 'the possible root, even as the real root, of almost every possible evil'.[18] Finally, the prohibition of masturbation, given that it was an abnormality that occurred within the narrow frame of the body and its immediate environs, demanded a form of intimacy between parents and children that was heretofore unexpected within the strict confines of the bourgeois family: 'The parent's body envelops the child's and at this point the central objective of the maneuver or crusade is revealed: the constitution of a new family body.'[19] Whereas the family was once a diffuse network of extended relations and household help, the parents are now invested with 'absolute power over the child', except to the extent that 'the internal parental control that fathers and mothers are required to exercise is necessarily plugged in to an external medical control', and due to which the family 'must become an agency for transmitting medical knowledge'.[20]

These features of the child masturbator have substantial implications for the development of modern maternal practice. First, the masturbator, in contrast to the 'monster' and 'the individual to be corrected', possessed a frame of reference that immediately brings to mind the apparatus of disciplinary power: 'His frame of reference is [...] a much narrower space. It is the bedroom, the bed, the body; it is the parents [...] it is a kind of microcell around the individual and his body.'[21] In other words, the family became the site for the constant surveillance of the young child, in which the 'child's body must be the object of their permanent attention', and through which the child will learn to maintain control over his or her own autoeroticism.[22] Foucault indeed draws a connection to disciplinary power as an integral method employed for the purposes of achieving oversight of abnormality. This relationship is established when criminal individuals come to be regarded as possessed of a kind of illness:

> The question of the illegal and the question of the abnormal, or of the criminal and the pathological, are now bound up with each other, not on the basis of a new ideology that may or may not arise from a State apparatus, but according to a technology defining the new rules of the economy of punitive power.[23]

In other words, with the pathologisation of criminal behaviour, methods for the punishment and oversight of criminals now become tools for managing other pathologies.

For the masturbator then, the parents are the agents of oversight in the campaign against the evils of masturbation. In contrast to a form of family in which responsibility for a child's care might have been dispersed among various family members and household help, the form of family that emerges as a result of the interdiction of masturbation is one in which surveillance is a parental imperative. For the mother then, to the extent that her productive role within the family demanded her presence in and oversight of the private rather than the public sphere, it is reasonable to assume that the burden of the responsibility for the oversight of the child's abnormal sexuality would have fallen to her.[24]

In other words, maternal practice is transformed to include the responsibility for disciplinary surveillance of children: the mother is invested with a familial form of disciplinary power.[25]

This responsibility takes on great importance because masturbation was considered, while still a form of illness, an illness that might betoken the development of all manner of evil: 'It is the secret all possess that never emerges into self-consciousness or universal discourse [...] This secret [...] is posited in its quasi universality as the possible root, even as the real root, of almost every possible evil.'[26] The prevention of masturbation – that amoral and infantile source of evil – thus demands from parents, and especially mothers, the utmost kind of vigilance. The child, who innocently engages in this abnormal and ill-fated behaviour, cannot be held responsible: 'it is the average and unhealthy household that is blamed more than the child [...] The parents are ultimately guilty since these problems occur because they do not want to take direct responsibility for their children.'[27] To the extent that the mother, whose oversight of the household is her primary vocation, is primarily responsible for caring for, attending to and exercising the utmost vigilance in the prevention of the child's masturbation, she is thus also guilty of allowing evil to flourish at its source if she avoids this responsibility. Because of this tendency of the mother to be the primary caregiver,[28] I now begin to substitute 'mother' for 'parent', in order to see how far we can go in re-describing Foucault's genealogical analyses for the sake of making the development of the modern mother visible.

The caring, attentive, concerned and vigilant mother, who is routinely valorised as the source of our earliest comfort and security, is here implicitly figured as having developed those characteristics for the sake of policing and staving off the earliest signs of malevolence in the development of each individual human being. Furthermore, the mother is now the subject of surveillance herself; she either effectively polices herself and provides adequate oversight of her child's tendency to a wayward sexuality, or fails to do so effectively and thus becomes subject to blame by those agents of public health who must then intervene to ensure that the child's masturbation is effectively curtailed.

The mother's responsibility to discipline herself and her child for the sake of curtailing an abnormal sexuality thus demands a deeply embodied, affective form of maternal control:

> There is the instruction for the direct, immediate, and constant application of the [mothers'] bodies to the bodies of their children. [...] There is extreme closeness, contact, almost mixing; the urgent

folding of the [mothers'] bodies over their children's bodies; the insistent obligation of the gaze, of presence, contiguity, and touch. [...] The [mother's] body envelops the child's.[29]

This form of maternal control necessitates a narrowing of the sphere of influence over the individual child. The mother's responsibility for and intimate enforcement of the prohibition of masturbation demands a 'new organisation, a new physics of the family space', which entails 'the elimination of all intermediaries and the suppression, if possible, of domestics, or at least a very close supervision of domestics, the ideal situation being the infant alone in a sexually aseptic family space'.[30] In her vigilant struggle against the potential evil of childhood masturbation, the mother must divest herself of a substantial support network in her broader household responsibilities. She does so for the sake of ensuring that her children are not daily exposed to anyone who is not equally committed to this project or, even worse, would encourage the child's precocious sexuality.

Furthermore, this new family space, in its 'little cultural involution of the family around the [mother]–child relationship', leads to the investment of this space with an affective and physical potency that demands a shift in familial intimacy away from its extended members (including household help) and towards a primacy of the affective bond between mother and child. Proper nurturance and the bodily intimacy that this requires now becomes the sole responsibility of the 'parents'. However, once again, to the extent that the management of the household is the mother's primary vocation, it is implied that the mother will become the chief bearer of the responsibility for this intensive, bodily and exclusive relation to the child.

Following this line of reasoning, Foucault is led to conclude that 'the child's non-relational, autoerotic sexuality [...] was one of the factors in the constitution of the close-knit and interdependent family, of a physical and affective family'.[31] On this analysis, much of what is taken to be natural to expect from the mother – sensitivity to her child's physical and psychological well-being, physical affection, vigilance with regard to the child's moral development, and so on – at least in part[32] owes its emergence as a novel necessity to a time when prohibition of the child's masturbation became a matter of significant public concern. Furthermore, the mother's isolation in the home, with minimal reliance on household help and limited influence by extended family, ought to be at least partially attributed to this emergent importance of control over the child's sexuality, a control that was to be directly exercised by and thus became the primary responsibility of his or her most immediate family members, that is, the parents and more specifically the mother.

The mother and the deployment of sexuality

We may further extend this description of the development of the modern mother via Foucault's account of the family's deep imbrication with the deployment of sexuality in his first volume of *The History of Sexuality*. The family is described as the privileged site of the 'interchange of sexuality and alliance: it conveys the law and the juridical dimensions in the deployment of sexuality; and it conveys the economy of pleasure and the intensity of sensations in the regime of alliance'.[33] The family's historical importance as the source of sexual alliance (through birth and by blood)[34] comes to be entangled with the deployment of sexuality. The historic sense of sex (reproduction) becomes newly invested as the site of the origin of sexuality. Here, the family's apparent centrality to the emergence of sexuality renders the family as:

> the crystal in the deployment of sexuality: it seemed to be the source of a sexuality which it only reflected and diffracted. By virtue of its permeability, and through that process of reflections to the outside, it became one of the most valuable tactical components of that deployment.[35]

In other words, the family becomes an ideal locus for the deployment of disciplinary power with respect to sexuality. As such, we might expect Foucault to remark on the ways in which individual members of the family are disciplined or serve as the disciplinary agents in the deployment of sexuality.

In fact, it is here that Foucault explicitly speaks with respect to the subject formation of the mother. It is in the newly constituted and thoroughly sexualised nuclear family where the mother becomes fully invested by her own form of sexuality as a result of the medicalisation and subsequent 'hysterisation of women's bodies', bodies that were analysed 'as being thoroughly saturated with sexuality'.[36] While Foucault states that all women are affected by this process, he also claims that it is the mother, 'with her negative image as "nervous woman", [who] constituted the most visible form of this hysterisation',[37] and this sexualisation of the mother came with at least two normative constraints on her behaviour. The first was within family space, in which '[her body] has to be a substantial and functional element'. The second was in the life of children, who '[her body] produced and had to guarantee, by virtue of a biologico-moral responsibility lasting through the entire period of the children's education'. Maternal sexuality demanded that the mother's body is a primary target of sexuality within the family, taking on particular functions relevant to sexuality. One of the most important aspects of this was that, due to the biological and moral imperatives of motherhood,[38] the mother must work to ensure that her children grow to become healthy, responsible adult members of society.

Furthermore, based on other aspects of Foucault's genealogy of sexuality, there are two more significant features of the modern mother, both of which indicate that the modern mother serves as a norm that only serves to represent a portion of the social reality pertaining to the ways in which mothers have enacted their relationships to their children. In other words, the modern mother is a norm to measure other mothers against. First, she is middle class. Foucault makes the point that it was, in particular, the 'idle woman' of the middle-class family who was 'assigned a new destiny charged with conjugal and parental obligations'.[39] This implies that motherhood was differentially developed across class lines, and that the particular norm that was developed for the ideal mother was also essentially 'racist' along class lines:

> The works, published in great numbers at the end of the eighteenth century, on body hygiene, the art of longevity, ways of having healthy children and of keeping them alive as long as possible, and methods for improving the human lineage, bear witness to the fact: they thus attest to the correlation of this concern with the body and sex to a type of 'racism' [...] a dynamic racism, a racism of expansion.[40]

Here, Foucault refers to the 'racism' of the middle class, and this form of middle-class dominance thus extends to the mother as well. Mothering, as it developed into its contemporary form, has always been deeply implicated with class differentiation, racial differentiation and so on.[41]

Second, this mother cannot be easily replaced. By virtue of the bonds that inhere in familial relations resulting from the deployment of alliance, which are only strengthened by the class dominance that is established through the middle-class family, the modern mother is one whose children belong to her by birth. It is for them that she will perform all those 'backward-looking rituals, such as birthdays', that solidify those family bonds.[42] It is through this bond that the mother's irreplaceability is established at birth, and it is through her subsequent enactment of the duties of motherhood that her irrepleaceability is reiterated in the daily life of the family. While in a certain sense the importance of the family as a whole can be described as being put into question through disciplinarisation of the family, as is argued by Rémi Lenoir and Robbie Duchinsky in this volume, it could be said that the bond between mother and child is only strengthened. As the mother enacts the requirements placed on her through the disciplinarisation of her blood relation to her children – her more substantial and functional place within the family, her biologico-moral responsibility to her children[43] – the necessity of her care for her own children becomes more deeply entrenched.

While it is only once that Foucault takes the emergence of sexuality as his analytical target that he specifically addresses the conditions of the subject formation of the mother, it is only by simultaneously taking into view his analysis of both abnormality and sexuality that we can fully draw out the implicit description of the development of the modern mother. We have, finally, made visible the characteristics of this figure who is transformed from her position within the 'network family' into her modern form as the locus of responsibility with respect to all matters pertaining to child development: she is the primary agent of disciplinary power within the familial milieu; she is responsible for the direct oversight of children; she is primarily to blame when children go awry; she exercises her authority over her children by deeply embodied and affective means; she must defer her authority and expose her own behaviour to evaluation by experts; she must entrust her children to these same experts if her children do not respond to familial discipline; she is primarily responsible for the successful education and moral development of her children, such that they become productive members of society; she is the agent of the perpetuation of her own 'race'; and she cannot be easily replaced. As such, as the central figure in the familial milieu with respect to the deployment of sexuality, the mother is individuated in unprecedented ways in modernity: she develops a relation to civil society that renders her publicly visible as never before, and she is invested with a power over her children[44] that is not equally wielded by the father.

Conclusion: some notes towards a genealogy of the mother

Having articulated a Foucauldean account of the modern mother, I now turn towards the consideration of some of the many implications that can be drawn from this account for the sake of generating a genealogy of the mother. Rather than begin with some aspect of the description of the modern mother as given above, I will consider only one example in which the mother is taken to be problematic today, drawn from the very small body of literature on Foucault and the mother.

Jon Simons' essay, 'Foucault's mother', is notable for both providing a maternally oriented feminist critique of the androcentrism of Foucault's thought *and* at the same time utilising a Foucauldean orientation to suggest the means by which the domination of mothers might be addressed in our own time. Simons was right to claim that it is 'regrettable' that Foucault's project did not more explicitly address the conditions of the mother in the deployment of sexuality because, as he points out, 'some feminist theories have developed a notion of power that could supplement or refine the notion of empowering subjectification that is needed for Foucault's affirmative project'.[45] Indeed, Foucault's affirmative project relies deeply on the notion of self-creation for the sake of an ethical transformation of those aspects of our subjectivity that are effects of dominance. Simons points out that this move is unnecessary if we take a feminist notion of empowerment, which has been most significantly developed within the care ethics tradition, as a non-dominating power relation: 'Women as caretakers, like teachers, occupy subject positions in which they exercise the power available to them over others for the benefit of those others, empowering them and enhancing their subjective capacities.'[46]

Once again, Simons is right to remark that it is regrettable that Foucault did not pay more explicit attention to the power relations that mothers occupy with respect to their children. This is all the more regrettable given that, as noted in the introduction to this chapter, our freedom is at stake in the development of our ability to moderate our own sexuality. To the extent that the mother is involved in empowering her children to moderate their own sexuality (among other things), she ought also to be considered responsible for empowering her individual children to enjoy their rights as free citizens within a civil society.

However, given the analysis of the modern mother that becomes available to us once processes of the normalisation and sexualisation of the subject are taken into consideration, the empowering role that mothers play in the lives of their children is not without need for criticism. To abstract the mother's context away from the power relation that she holds with respect to her children is to allow for the possibility that the mother will simply empower her children to take up their own subjugation in society. Indeed, this is what is implied in Foucault's analyses: the mother, in her affective and largely total responsibility for the child's development, is the primary agent in the daily installation of norms in the formation of her child's early subjective development. To the extent that these norms are dominating or inegalitarian – racist, for example – the mother's exercise of her authority over her children results in the reproduction of injustice.

The mother's caring and empowering relation to her child only becomes laudable within a social context in which non-dominance and equality are already normatively embedded or, alternatively, when the mother herself takes her position of authority over her children as an opportunity to resist unjust societal norms. The first possibility indicates that the achievement of social justice will require the critical analysis of parenting practices that reinforce unjust norms. The second possibility is one that has already received much attention from theorists and activists, as well as ordinary people, who privilege the mothering relation as one in which social transformation must begin. This is, given the enormous influence that mothers have over their children's development, a necessary strategy. However, too much emphasis on the transformative potential of the mother–child relation has the unfortunate side effect of privatising social transformation, leaving the mother's vulnerable position within the family and social milieu unanalysed. It is in this way that an overwhelmingly unqualified affirmation of the mother, as is characteristic of Simons' essay, does not lend itself to a sufficiently nuanced account of the potential for societal transformation that lies in an analysis of the mother.

Indeed, it is this valorisation of the empowering nature of the mother–child relation that must explain the overwhelmingly conservative nature of Simons' later attempt to suggest the ways in which we might begin to address the inequality that mothers continue to face in a society where their primary role in the child's development is left unreconstructed. Simons seems to get off to a good start, when considering the feminist ameliorative strategies that avail themselves to mothers: 'In general, the [Foucauldean] option for those who struggle against their subjection is to use the capacities and resources available in their particular subject position.'[47] Rather than outright rejection of norms governing the subject position of the mother in society, which would '[disempower] many women', Simons suggests that there is a Foucauldean/Butlerian alternative that will lead to lesser inequality for mothers.[48] This does indeed sound promising.

Yet, once Simons gets into his description of 'subversive mothering as a feminist strategy', he goes so far to say that '(s)ubversive motherhood should aim, as far as possible, to focus on actions in which children are not directly involved'.[49] This is because 'the notion that each child should be reared in a stable domestic environment in which his or her development is optimized, is deeply embedded and would thus be difficult to displace by head-on assault'. Simons is right to point out that the 'scope of playfulness' is not particularly broad.[50] Nevertheless, given the above analysis of the mother that can be developed alongside Foucault's analyses of the deployment of normalisation and sexuality, it strikes me that it is precisely the mother–child relation that must be met head-on, if not 'debunked' or 'subverted', if we are to address effectively the barriers to equality that mothers face as a result of their enactment of modern maternal practice.

The benefit to a genealogical analysis is that it denaturalises and problematises the mother–child relation, indicating that the characteristics of the mother that have come to be the norm are contingent and embedded in a complex network of practices that produce *both* egalitarian *and* inegalitarian effects. Thus, Simons unnecessarily forecloses the possibility of the transformative potential that exists in questioning the mother–child relation and thereby pointing out the ways in which mothering is both empowering and disempowering, for both the mother and the child. In so doing, Simons is led to offer the rather conservative suggestion that social equals might undertake a subversive practice of mothering their peers, which he notes is analogous to Foucault's emphasis on an ethic of friendship, as a primary means to unseating the intransigence of maternal subjugation.[51] It is possible, of course, that the maternalisation of friendship may be one of the many ways by which we may lessen the inegalitarian effects of maternal practice. However, given that the vast majority of women do become mothers at some point in their lives, and that the mother–child relation is precisely the point at which maternal subjectivity, and subjugation, is constituted, then the suggestion that those who are *not* mothers are those best suited to transform the position of the modern mother seems off target.

Certainly, the adoption of maternal practice into the everyday lives of peer relations would undoubtedly mean that peer relations would benefit by it, as Simons suggests: 'Friends who perform mothering subversively can constantly individualize each other without a totality of power developing.'[52] Wonderful. We should do this, too. However, we live at a time when middle-class mothers, for example, feel themselves compelled to adopt 'natural' mothering practices as a means of resisting the barrenness of a life lived in the 'rat race', where the rejection of feminism, the imperative to breastfeed, the benefits of homeschooling, the maintenance of an extraordinarily demanding schedule of enrichment activities for one's children and the 'choice' to leave one's comfortably middle-class profession after giving birth have become common topics of concern for the most socially advantaged mothers.[53] A comparison of these facts against the fragmentary genealogy of the modern mother elaborated out of Foucault's works would suggest that today's middle-class mothers (especially those with careers) continue to find themselves compelled to maintain the norms expected of good mothers, even after 'women's liberation' movements. And rightly so: it is through good mothering in their earliest years that the next generation will achieve their fullest potential, that is, their full freedom as members of civil society. In other words, 'women's liberation' did not account for the ways in which middle-class mothers experience themselves as *achieving* freedom in their work as conventional, middle-class mothers. In other words, middle-class mothers take themselves to be doing meaningful work when they nurture their children, and they are. In fact, they could rightly take themselves to be performing a service for civil society in their work as mothers.

Nevertheless, middle-class mothering stands in need of criticism. For instance, the rate of poverty of divorced mothers suggests that middle-class mothers put themselves at risk when they decide to take up a position of financial dependency in order to mother their young children. Contemporary middle-class mothering needs to be scrutinised for the ways in which it perpetuates other inegalitarian norms, such as racism. Middle-class mothering needs to be analysed regarding the extent to which biopolitical power is exercised through disciplinary means in maternal practice: it may be the case that some discipline is constitutive of freedom in civil society, but how much? What, for example, is the best way to negotiate medical oversight of one's own child? There are numerous questions that arise when considering the experience of middle-class mothers against even a partial genealogy of the modern mother.

And this represents only a small portion of the experience of mothers in our contemporary situation. As such, the suggestion that the disruption of the inegalitarian aspects of modern maternity should neither question nor disrupt norms surrounding the mother–child relationship seems unjustifiable. This is not to say, of course, that mothering and mother–child relationships are deeply suspect and thoroughly unjust. Rather, this indicates that a Foucauldean genealogy of the mother promises to deliver nuanced ethical and political implications.

It is in fact a thorough genealogy of the mother that is most necessary, as a fragmentary genealogy indicates that there are many more aspects of the development of the mother that have yet to be articulated. For example, how might we incorporate work like Elisabeth Badinter's into a genealogical account of the mother? How might we describe the ways in which norms surrounding the middle-class mother are at work in contemporary work–life policies? How are these policies differentially articulated across class lines? How do norms for the mother govern our policies regarding impoverished mothers? What is the role of racism in contemporary mothering practice? How are our children disempowered by contemporary mothering practice? How important is biological sex to the performance of mothering? How intractable is the familial bond with respect to mothering practices? How is caregiving linked to the mother (or not) across class lines, and race lines, and so on?

A thorough genealogical account of the mother will be one that denaturalises the mother–child relationship and suggests alternatives for 'optimising' the child's development while diminishing the inegalitarian effects that mothering has on the development of individual *mothers*. We must utilise all of the resources available to us – research on early child development and childcare best practices, descriptions of maternal practice at a wide diversity of social positions, sociological studies on the unjust workload of mothers, research that offers ameliorative strategies for work–family conflict and so on – in order to fill out the analysis of the mother that is made visible by unearthing latent content in Foucault's work on the deployment of normalisation and sexuality. The genealogy of the modern mother has yet to become a coherent and effective means for reconstructing the unjust conditions under which mothers must live out their lives today.

Notes

This project was funded in part through a 2010–11 Graduate Student Research Award from the Center for the Study of Women in Society at the University of Oregon. I wish to thank Robbie Duschinsky, Leon Antonio Rocha, Naomi Zack, Colin Koopman and the members of the Critical Genealogies Collaboratory at the University of Oregon (http://uocgc.blogspot.com/) for valuable feedback on earlier versions of this chapter. I would also like to thank Chloë Taylor for introducing me to Robbie Duschinsky and Leon Antonio Rocha, the editors of this volume.

1. Foucault, ABN, 248.
2. The term 'figure' is used following Andrew Dilts, 'Michel Foucault meets Gary Becker: criminality beyond *Discipline and Punish*', in *The Carceral*

Notebooks, 4 (2008), available at: http://www.thecarceral.org/journal-vol4. html (last accessed 1 March 2012). I take a 'figure' to be an individual who is targeted as an object of disciplinary or biopolitical power.

3. *Dispositif* is often translated as 'deployment', but also as 'apparatus'. I will use 'deployment' in this chapter.

4. It is inappropriate to speak of the genealogical 'emergence' of the mother, given that 'the mother' preexisted the deployment of sexuality, and thus only developed new characteristics with the deployment of sexuality; it might be most appropriate to speak instead of the 'transformation' or 'evolution' of the mother.

5. See Chloë Taylor, 'Foucault and familial power', *Hypatia*, 27 (2012), 201–18.

6. Jana Sawicki, *Disciplining Foucault: Feminism, Power and the Body* (London: Routledge, 1991), 15.

7. Colin Koopman, 'Two uses of genealogy: Michel Foucault and Bernard Williams', in C. G. Prado (ed.), *Foucault's Legacy* (New York: Continuum 2009), 90–108 at 100.

8. Thomas W. Laqueur, *Solitary Sex: A Cultural History of Masturbation* (New York: Zone Books, 2003), 276–7.

9. Koopman, 'Two uses of genealogy', 101.

10. Ibid.

11. Ibid.

12. Ibid., 103.

13. Foucault, ABN, 248.

14. For an account of the 'fragmentary genealogy of the family' in the work of this period, see Lenoir and Duschinsky in this volume. For a similar account that is concerned with already extant feminist Foucauldean work on the family, see Taylor, 'Foucault and familial power', 201–18.

15. Foucault, ABN, 61.

16. Ibid., 59, 146.

17. Ibid., 61.

18. Ibid., 59.

19. Ibid., 248.

20. Ibid., 249–51.

21. Ibid., 59.

22. Ibid., 245.

23. Ibid., 92.

24. While Foucault does not explicitly state that he takes the mother to be primarily invested with this responsibility for familial exercise of the 'technology of human abnormality', he does state in the first volume of *History of Sexuality* that it was the mother, rather than the father, who was required 'to be a substantial and functional element' within 'the family space' (Foucault, HS1, 104). He describes this process as the 'hysterisation of women's bodies' (ibid.). I will say more about this later on.

25. There is more to be said about the differentiation between the mother and the father, although it is outside the scope of this chapter.

26. Foucault, ABN, 59.

27. Ibid., 244.

28. Foucault is not arguing that the control of masturbation is the cause of the woman's increasing importance as the primary caregiver in the nuclear

family, although he does appear to blame the 'hysterisation of women's bodies' for this increase in responsibility (see below). However, it bears remembering that, given that Foucault's object of analysis was not the family or the mother, the genealogy of the mother that is to be articulated out of Foucault's work on abnormality and sexuality ought only to be considered fragmentary. For more on the development of the mother during this period, see for example Elisabeth Badinter, *Mother Love: Myth and Reality* (New York: Macmillan, 1981), who argues that 'mother love' became important because of an increasing appeal to 'maternal instinct'. This implies a need for a critical engagement between Foucault and Badinter, which is outside the scope of this article.

29. Foucault, ABN, 248.
30. Ibid., 244–5.
31. Ibid., 249.
32. Again, for more on the development of the modern mother, see Badinter, *Mother Love*.
33. Foucault, HS1, 108.
34. See Taylor, 'Foucault and familial power', 212: 'the kinds of bonds in which the family is entangled, involving property as well as personal and collective commitments, are in many ways closer to the conflictual and heterogeneous bonds of sovereignty than to discipline. Family bonds are in fact familial: they are intimate, they involve blood and birth and shared histories, which means that they are not reducible to the anonymous and interchangeable mechanisms of a disciplinary apparatus, however infiltrated by these they may be.'
35. Foucault, HS1, 111.
36. Ibid., 104.
37. Ibid.
38. One might assume that 'maternal instinct', which figures largely in Badinter's study, is the 'biologico-moral responsibility' to which Foucault refers.
39. Foucault, HS1, 121.
40. Ibid., 125.
41. For more on the deeply racialised nature of the development of the family in recent history, see Ellen K. Feder, 'The dangerous individual('s) mother: biopower, family, and the production of race', *Hypatia*, 22 (2007), 60–78; ibid., *Family Bonds: Genealogies of Race and Gender* (Oxford: Oxford University Press, 2007); and Ladelle McWhorter, *Racism and Sexual Oppression in Anglo-America: A Genealogy* (Bloomington, IN: Indiana University Press, 2009).
42. Taylor, 'Foucault and familial power'.
43. Foucault, HS1, 104.
44. See the conclusion for consideration of the 'empowering' role of the mother in her relationship with her children.
45. Jon Simons, 'Foucault's mother', in Susan J. Hekman (ed.), *Feminist Interpretations of Michel Foucault* (University Park, PA: Penn State University Press, 1996), 187.
46. Ibid.
47. Ibid., 196.
48. Ibid., 201.

49. Ibid.
50. Ibid.
51. Ibid., 204.
52. Ibid., 205.
53. See, for example, Lisa Belkin, 'The Opt-Out Revolution', *New York Times Magazine* (26 October 2003). There is a substantial literature that critically engages this article. Nevertheless, the women interviewed for the article report that they left their middle-class professional careers for the sake of full-time mothering.

4
Foucault, the Family and the Cold Monster of Neoliberalism

Gillian Harkins

> Do not think that one has to be sad in order to be militant, even though the thing one is fighting is abominable. It is the connection of desire to reality (and not its retreat into the forms of misrepresentation) that possesses revolutionary force.
>
> Michel Foucault[1]

This chapter takes as its point of departure Michel Foucault's late 1970s intervention in French legal reform, specifically his work to change age of consent laws during the Penal Code reform of 1977–78.[2] Foucault's biographers note the range of his post-1968 activism, including the occupation of a university building at Paris VIII Vincennes (1969), work with the Groupe d'Information sur les Prisons (GIP) (1971–73), participation in efforts to change the age of sexual majority (1977–78), and travel to observe the unfolding Iranian Revolution (1979).[3] This activity has been linked to Foucault's turn towards genealogies of power rather than archaeologies of knowledge.[4] But this activity might also contradict his genealogical work, manifesting belief in radical transformation – even revolution – seemingly undermined by the more diffuse modalities of power described in *Discipline and Punish* (1975) and *History of Sexuality, Volume 1* (1976). This chapter considers Foucault's efforts to change French age of consent law, including decriminalisation of consensual sex with persons under the age of fifteen, in relation to his Collège de France lectures from 1974 to 1979, focusing on the intersections between Foucault's academic writings on monstrosity and his activism in the public arena. This chapter asks how we might more productively understand Foucault's activism regarding the sexual autonomy of children, linked to the decriminalisation of adult–child sexual activity as a key mechanism of governance, by reading it alongside his genealogy of the monster and the rise of neoliberalism.

Across his Collège de France lectures of this period, Foucault explores how the monster emerges where institutions intersect. The monster combines 'the impossible and the forbidden', that which cannot exist according to nature and is not permitted to exist according to law.[5] This chapter reads the monster as a paradox haunting Foucault's approach to the problem of adult–child sex. In particular, I read the monster as a paradox that emerges as a new switch-point between residual and emergent forms of power. Foucault's efforts to problematise adult–child sex, to describe and analyse its emergence as a switch-point in systems of power, founders on this paradox that he cannot entirely grasp within his own analysis. At a 1977 roundtable on 'Confinement, Psychiatry, Prison', Foucault reflects on his choice to target adult–child sex laws: 'People may ask why I have allowed myself to get involved in this – why I have agreed to ask these questions.'[6] While here Foucault answers that he is simply tired of separating academic and political work, in his 1983 interview on 'Social Security' he suggests that academic work cannot understand current politics: 'For the moment, we completely lack the intellectual tools necessary to envision in new terms the form in which we might attain what we are looking for.'[7] In his efforts to engage the 1970s politics of adult–child sex, Foucault suggests that 'the work of the present day historian' is to release alternative potentialities that may not yet be fully understood.[8] But he too quickly labelled the target of such work the erotic potentiality of the child, and he too easily took up the law as a tactic.

This chapter reads Foucault's Collège de France lectures *Abnormal* (1974–75) and *The Birth of Biopolitics* (1978–79) to derive 'intellectual tools' through which to continue the work of the present-day historian. In these lectures Foucault splits his treatment of the abnormal individual (traced from at least 1820 to 1975) from his treatment of neoliberal modes of governance (traced from the 1930s to 1979). This chapter translates the split between abnormality and neoliberalism into a switch-point whose political implications Foucault was only beginning to understand. This helps us to understand the relation between Foucault's activism on age of consent law, his academic analysis of neoliberalism, and the neoliberal transformation of relations between abnormality and monstrosity in which his activism and analysis are situated. In 1978, the figure of the predatory paedophile was just emerging as a necessary supplement to neoliberal governance and a key object for the moralisation of political economic life itself.[9] This figure introduces a monstrous paradox into older systems of abnormality and operates as a switch-point between liberal and neoliberal modes of governance. While the full meaning of this figure eludes Foucault in 1978, we can begin to trace its genealogy by reading Foucault's 1970s works for the monstrous paradox he locates in the emergence of neoliberalism. This chapter therefore focuses on two specific figures: (i) the paedophile, an abnormal individual or 'pale monster' whom Foucault situates in the disciplines of normalisation more than the political economic accounts of neoliberalism; and (ii) the state, that 'cold monster' in Friedrich Nietzsche's terms that Foucault analyses in *Security, Territory, Population* and *The Birth of Biopolitics* as the crossroads of biopower and neoliberalism.[10] In the reading that follows we will find these figures appearing as a switch-point between the family's relation to the liberal state and its emerging relation to the market rationalities of neoliberalism.

Erotic childhood

At a roundtable with Guy Hocquenghem and Jean Danet, broadcast by France Culture on 4 April 1978, Foucault begins by situating their efforts to change sex law in its immediate historical context:

> Things had evolved on such a wide front, in such an overwhelming and at first sight apparently irreversible way, that many of us began to hope that the legal regime imposed on the sexual practices of our contemporaries would at last be relaxed and broken up.[11]

At this roundtable, Foucault periodises the emergence of sex morality in law and its counter-conduct in civil society from the 1960s onward. Here Foucault suggests that morality entered sex law as recently (in France) as 1960, and it has become an object of political struggle only in the last ten years (1968–78).[12] Even more narrowly, he suggests that 1978 efforts to pass 'what may be called liberal' reforms by the Commission for the Reform of Penal Law has been met with civil counter-movements emphasising the moral danger of liberalisation.[13] In the late 1970s, Foucault suggests that the liberalisation of sex law is being countered by moralisation implemented through 'a system of information carried out in the press'.[14] Post-1968 struggles, and 1978 in particular, were marked by different attitudes towards state intervention. Liberalisation, on the one hand, implies the reduction of state intervention into arenas of private conduct, from market to sexual activity. Moralisation, on the other hand, demands intervention in arenas of private conduct to protect against dangerous excesses of liberty.

The claims of this roundtable seem surprising when contrasted with Foucault's other academic work from this period. In his 1976 *History of Sexuality, Volume 1*, for example, Foucault argues that sexuality is not repressed by law but rather produced by diverse mechanisms expanding power beyond the law's immediate reach. Here Foucault famously argues that in the late eighteenth and nineteenth centuries the 'deployment of alliance', a legal system of marriage ties and inheritance rules, is supplemented by a 'deployment of sexuality', which creates 'perpetual spirals of power and pleasure' that operate through disciplinary mechanisms rather than state law.[15] This deployment of sexuality was routed through the family as a key relay for disciplines focused on the management of desire, the cultivation of proper erotic conduct and the subordination of 'perversities' to sexual normalisation. It relied upon an anatamo-politics of the human body governed by a series of prohibitions – the incest taboo symbolically originary but actually only one among many – that inaugurate new and ever-expanding domains of power. Foucault's 1970s Collège de France lectures elaborate this account of power, arguing that state law is only one element of a larger apparatus of regulation and discipline called 'biopower'. Each lecture explores the role of specific institutions and practices in this system: (i) the conjunction of psychiatry and law in *Abnormal* (1974–75); (ii) the relation between social security and racial struggle in *Society Must Be Defended* (1975–76); (iii) the turn towards governmentality as the political rationality of population in *Security, Territory, Population* (1977–78); and (iv) the rise of neoliberalism as a market rationality of governance in *The Birth of Biopolitics* (1978–79).

The first three courses examine how biopower subtends 'liberalism' as a political economic philosophy, practice of governance and discipline of subjectivity. In *Security, Territory, Population* (1977–78), for example, Foucault explains in greater detail how the family emerges as a key relay of liberal governance. Prior to the eighteenth century, Foucault argues, the family was the 'model' for governance.[16] This blocked the development of the 'art of government', which until the eighteenth century was trapped between 'a model of the family that was too narrow, weak, and insubstantial' and an 'excessively large, abstract, and rigid framework of sovereignty'.[17] The art of governance was subsequently 'unblocked' by the establishment of biopower, with its elaborate disciplinary measurements of population, delineation of a distinct 'level of reality' called economy and separation of the 'judicial framework of sovereignty' from government itself.[18] The family was thus transformed from a governmental 'model' to 'an element within the population' and 'a fundamental relay in its government'.[19] This transformed the relationship between the family and sovereignty, creating a host of new problematics resolved through new disciplines and domains of power/knowledge: the problem of the erotic child, the perverse adult, the Malthusian couple and the hysterical woman.

In 1978, however, Foucault noted that this mode of biopower – emergent in the late eighteenth, codified in the nineteenth and dominant by the early twentieth centuries – was undergoing another epistemic transformation whose effects were unclear. In his 1978–79 Collège de France lectures *The Birth of Biopolitics*, delivered while Foucault was engaged in efforts to decriminalise adult–child sex, Foucault stated that: 'we are at the crossroads where a number of old themes are revived concerning family life, co-ownership, and a whole range of recurrent themes criticising market society and standardisation through consumption'.[20] Here Foucault points to a shift in the art of governance emerging in the early twentieth century (the Ordoliberalism of the 1930s) and undergoing a struggle for dominance in the century's final decades (labelled 'neoliberalism' by this later period). Across the mid- to later twentieth century the economy, established as a distinct 'level of reality' in the late eighteenth and nineteenth centuries, becomes a fully developed 'programme of rationalisation' that makes economic rationality the aim and object of governance.[21] The market is not a separate level of reality, but the condition of reality. This is a shift from earlier modes of normalisation (associated with disciplinary liberal societies) to the economic rationalisation of all life, the capitalisation of all forms of existence. But it is a shift that is still in progress, one of which its techniques disrupt earlier relations among the family, the market and the state without yet clarifying what new domains and objects of power/knowledge will emerge.

In these 1978–79 lectures, Foucault expresses concern that we have not yet developed the critical tools needed to understand fully these changing conditions. Too many people who think that they are 'criticising the current objective of governmental policy' are in fact 'criticising something else'.[22] Critical tools designed to understand earlier moments in the art of government are inadequate to the task facing the historian of the present. We cannot critique the 'standardising, mass society of consumption or the spectacle' or other earlier twentieth-century formations because, Foucault says in a rare moment of bald historicism, 'we have gone beyond that stage. We are no longer there.'[23] But where are we precisely in 1978? How does the emergence of neoliberalism discussed in 1978–79 change Foucault's own understanding of relations among the family, the market and the state described in his earlier work?

One way to answer these questions is to turn to Foucault's 1978 activism on adult–child sex. At the roundtable with Guy Hocquenghem and Jean Danet and other interviews of the time, Foucault outlines a post-1960s shift away from the relations between family and sexuality described in *History of Sexuality, Volume 1*. Of this more recent phase, Foucault explains that: 'sexuality will no longer be a kind of sexual behaviour hedged in by precise prohibitions, but a kind of roaming danger, a sort of omnipresent phantom'.[24] This implies a transformation from an older mode of governance – at least partially reliant on the family to organise sexuality through a subjective logic of prohibitions – to one that dismantles the family prohibition and relies instead on a social logic of universal danger. In this new mode of governance, 'sexuality will become a threat in all social relations'.[25] Older modes of social security, associated with the switch-point between family and discipline in the liberal welfare state, will be replaced by demands for a new type of 'security' in the face of universal danger. This security operates through the proliferation of risks and controls rather than the enclosure of disciplinary space. Adult–child sex creates a particularly useful object for power/knowledge that helps dismantle earlier regimes of governmentality – with their emphasis on enclosure and discipline – and put into circulation the wild power of security that Foucault will ultimately associate with neoliberalism. The dangerous sexual predator and the permanently endangered child meet in the demand for increased security that reaches beyond the domain of family or law. Thus we find in the 1970s an efflorescence of sexual moralisation in the law and the press, which seems like a paradoxical tactic in the economic rationalisation of governance and society, until we understand how adult–child sex links neoliberal discourses of marketisation to sexual discourses of moralisation. Only the security risks posed by moral danger limit the market expansion of human capital. The two are joined in the figure of the dangerous sexual predator who threatens all of society by threatening its potential future – embodied in the vulnerable child.

This account does not yet explain Foucault's strange use of the word 'liberal' to describe how sex laws are 'relaxed and broken up', since it is in *The Birth of Biopolitics* that he critiques liberalisation as a key element of neoliberal rationality (part of its effort to shrink state governance). Foucault's own 1978 analysis suggests that 'liberalisation' does not counter 'moralisation' but rather participates in a shared neoliberal discourse of minimal state intervention. Over the course of the roundtable, however, it becomes increasingly clear that Foucault does not believe that liberal legal reform will actually 'liberate' sexual practice. Instead, he justifies his activism by focusing on the potentiality of the erotic child. While discipline operated through the child's universal sexual desire, and security through its constitutive sexual vulnerability, a more revolutionary force might be released by the child's erotic potentiality. In a *Le Nouvel Observateur* interview dated 12 March 1977, Foucault states that the child 'has an assortment of pleasure for which the "sex" grid is a veritable prison'.[26] The '"sex" grid' imposed through the family (as disciplinary nexus of seeming 'sovereignty') and the law (as part of new moral security) imprisons the child. What lies beyond this sex grid is of course not yet available to us, but the child seems positioned to articulate potentiality askew to the normative and normalising injunctions of biopower. As Foucault suggests at the 1978 roundtable, the child might in fact produce a new discourse of desire and pleasure if we allowed it to appear beyond the 'contractual' notion of consent.

In response to Foucault's description of the child's erotic potentiality in the 1977 *Le Nouvel Observateur* interview, Bernard-Henri Lévy asks: 'Is this a paradox?'[27] Lévy implicitly raises the question posed by Foucault's reverse discourse: how can the child's disciplined or securitised sexuality be so easily transformed into revolutionary potentiality? Foucault does not answer this question directly, instead asserting that this description is consistent with his understanding of sexuality as a means for the expansion of power, not its object of fear or repression. For Foucault, the aim is not to liberate the child's sexuality, but to remove legal prohibitions so that the child's erotic potentiality might participate in the expansion of power in 'revolutionary' ways: 'what should follow is the moment of new mobility and new displacement'.[28] As Foucault summarises his position, the aim is not 'to be on the "good side", on the side of madness, children, delinquency, sex',[29] but instead to release revolutionary force as an act of permanent criticism: 'this is where the real work begins, that of the present day historian'.[30] The work of the present-day historian is not to liberate the child's sexuality in a positive sense, but to remove the legal ban on erotic relations with adults in order to actualise a release from both the disciplinary prison of sex and the emergent roaming danger of sexuality.

A number of critics have countered Foucault's historical approach as outlined here, arguing that Foucault misdiagnosed the relation between the family, the market and the state in the power relations of the late 1970s. Vikki Bell and Linda Alcoff have pointed out that Foucault's efforts to lower or eradicate the legal age of consent might replicate, rather than interrupt, the regimes of power produced through adult–child sex.[31] Bell and Alcoff argue that Foucault ignores how power relations are already inscribed onto the diverse sexual practices of childhood, rather than merely in its alleged universal sexuality or constitutive vulnerability. In some conditions, the '"sex" grid' imposed on the child already includes sexual contact with adults, often linked to their vulnerability to disciplinary agents within the family and its related institutions such as school and medicine. Gender is one key variable in how children are rendered vulnerable to sexual contact (and not merely erotic discipline), but race, class and infrastructure certainly condition which children are available to extra-familial sexual contact with adults, whether wanted or unwanted. The erotic potentiality of the child would need to be situated in relation to existing sexual practices of childhood as well as their discursive formations. Foucault's analytic misprision, if installed as legal reform, might in fact reproduce unwelcome force relations rather than open up new and potentially transformative horizons of power and pleasure.

This chapter adds to these critiques by resituating Foucault's legal reform efforts in relation to his 1970s writings on the paradox of the monster. Here I answer Bernard-Henri Lévy's question about Foucault's concept of the child's erotic potentiality – 'Is this a paradox?' – in the affirmative. Foucault's turn to the child's erotic potentiality reveals a paradox in the changing power relations connecting the family, the market and the state: it marks a condition in which existing regimes of representation (discipline and law associated with welfare liberalism) are inadequate to explain emerging relations of power (security and marketisation associated with neoliberalism).[32] Rather than resolve this paradox by arguing for or against decriminalisation in the early 2010s, I turn to Foucault's 1970s writings on the monster to help us better understand the role of the erotic child in creating and resolving paradoxes among domains associated with the family, the state and the market. I agree with Roger Lancaster that age of consent law has been used to mobilise sex panics, and that those sex panics lent themselves to the rise of 'the punitive state' or the intersection of neoliberal economic and carceral rationalities.[33] But here I wish to situate the relation between age of consent and sex panic within Foucault's longer genealogy of monstrous paradox, through which we might discern the unique role of the erotic child in the emergence of neoliberalism and its moralisation of adult–child sex.

Monstrous paradox

Foucault tends to use 'paradox' to mark the conjuncture of multiple domains where seemingly incommensurate relations of force meet.

'Paradox' leaves open the possible effects of such conjunctures while simultaneously drawing attention to their discursive forms. The term itself refers to language: a paradox is a statement that seems to contradict a common belief that may nevertheless be proven true, or a figure of speech 'consisting of a conclusion or apodosis contrary to what the audience has been led to expect'.[34] The paradox appears to be a language game dependent upon an existing regime of truth, one that draws attention to and exploits logic's dependence on grammar and grammar's suspension of social disbelief via a deferral between premise and conclusion. Foucault exploits this sense of paradox and yet redirects it to indicate where a specific episteme of language is itself problematised because changing relations of force can no longer be represented in its discursive forms.[35] This concept of paradox can help us better understand the genealogical figures that Foucault uses to demarcate the crisis of representation that occurs where forces exceed the forms allowed by a particular discursive domain.

There are two domains where Foucault's 1970s genealogies of sexuality are drawn into paradox through the form of the erotic child. The first is the family, where paradox appears as incest; the second is the strange domain of the monstrous, where paradox appears as paedophilia (and, as I will argue later, the state). I have treated the first paradox in my book on father–daughter incest, which I summarise briefly here to move us towards an analysis of the paradox of paedophilia.[36] Across *History of Sexuality, Volume I* and *Society Must Be Defended*, Foucault's account of the family meets its limit in the paradox of incest. Incest appears as both the pivot and secret of biopower, instituting the regularities and dispersions of discursive formations. The 'event' of incest is produced in the changing relations of the deployments of alliance and sexuality; it serves as both the pivot and secret within the modern family, that which appears to regulate sexual desire exogamously (pivot) while also producing sexual discourse (secret). Yet it is also discursively figured as a taboo, which leaves the 'event' of incestuous acts incorporeal even in its materiality (this is called 'fantasy'). Foucault departs from the Freudian reading of incest by situating this taboo/pivot/secret as a bar running through the discourse of sexuality. This bar in fact hides its epistemic function for biopower more generally: to mask the government's interest in regulating reproduction on the grounds of protection from racial degeneracy. Foucault says that incest appears as paradox where biopower meets its limit, creating the illusion of 'law' precisely as power no longer relies on legality or sovereignty to function. In *Society Must Be Defended*, however, Foucault points to another place where biopower meets its paradoxical limit: in the sovereign right to kill. While biopower generally operates through the right to make live and let die, here the right to cause mortality appears as a new form of state 'racism', what he calls a 'caesura' through the biological population. Across these two texts, I have argued that the paradox of incest allows Foucault to create an account of biopower that desexualises racism (or keeps birth and death at a distance from each other). In so doing, it also mistakenly enfolds 'reproduction' fully into the operations of biopower rather than allowing us to see how biopower reaches its limit in birth as much as it does in death.

The rest of this chapter explores the second domain, that of the monster, where paradox appears as the paedophile (and ultimately the state). This second is much harder to discern: it is the domain where paradox seems to appear in the form of the predatory paedophile (but whose figures of roaming danger, prisons and phantoms equally reveal the 'cold monster' of the state). As a preliminary summary, one might describe the monstrous as a peculiar domain where alliance and sexuality do not meet. Foucault describes the monster as 'essentially a legal notion', that which within the '"juridico-biological" domain' figures 'the limit, both the point at which the law is overturned and the exception that is found in extreme cases'.[37] Within the conception of biopower described above, the paedophile emerges as a kind of 'pale monster' across the later nineteenth century and is in a state of transition during the late 1970s, where Foucault encounters and attempts to diagnose its paradoxical image. If incest appears as taboo and fantasy where alliance and sexuality meet (pivot), inaugurating a discourse of the sexual secret, paedophilia appears by contrast as roaming danger and phantom where sexuality operates without the limits and protections of alliance. It produces a discourse of securitisation against increasingly intangible dangers, figured as monstrous exceptions to the law that demand new modes of control. While incest creates the illusion that biopower operates successfully, paedophilia creates the paradoxical occasion for its failure and the demand for its expansion into new domains. The paedophile figures a perpetual roaming danger expanding carceral efforts into increasingly intangible domains (represented most easily by the informational systems of moralisation discussed earlier).

It seems easy enough at first to situate the paedophile as a monster. In *Child-Loving: The Erotic Child and Victorian Culture*, James Kincaid strikes a common note when he says that all talk of child-loving is 'monster-talk'.[38] Yet Foucault uses the concept of the monster somewhat differently in his discussion of adult–child sex in *Abnormal*. According to

Foucault, the modern paedophile emerges precisely when great and exceptional monstrosity disappears: at the end of the nineteenth century. Foucault's genealogy of the monster in *Abnormal* begins when the human monster, defined by its physical deviance from nature (including sexual monstrosity), becomes a moral monster, defined first through political and subsequently through criminal deviance. At the start of this genealogy, Foucault argues that, 'the first moral monster to appear is the political monster'.[39] The moral monster emerges in relation to the social compact, a figure for the limit of law (of and as the absolute sovereign) that defines the law (as the vehicle of political subjects/the people). In the political domain, the 'first monster is the king' who exacts sovereignty over the people rather than manifesting their collective will.[40] Following the age of revolution, we find:

> two figures of the monster: the monster from below and the monster from above, the cannibalistic monster represented above all by the figure of the people in revolt, and the incestuous monster represented above all by the figure of the king.[41]

Foucault argues that these 'great exceptional monstrosities' are 'at the very heart of the juridico-medical theme of the monster' that emerges in the later eighteenth and nineteenth century.[42] On one hand, the incestuous monster is disqualified from state power (as king) and miniaturised in the fictive sovereignty of the father, himself a mere deputy in the regimes of governance. On the other hand, the cannibalistic monster is disqualified from state power (as the people in revolt) and miniaturised in the fictive revolutionary of the criminal.

This is where our story of the abnormal individual begins. Ultimately both the human and the moral monster combine to become a mere pale monster underlying everyday abnormalities. Across the eighteenth and nineteenth centuries, a new mode of power replaces 'the species of great exceptional monstrosity' with a 'host of little abnormalities, of both abnormal and familiar characters'.[43] This 'domain of abnormality' is produced by combining three key figures: the human monster (the monster), the individual to be corrected (the incorrigible), and the masturbating child (the masturbator).[44] The new figure of the 'abnormal individual' emerges when the three specific 'frames of reference' for the monster, the incorrigible and the masturbator are related to one another through a new mode of power.[45] The monster's initial frame of reference is 'nature and society': the human 'monster appears and functions precisely at the point where nature and law are joined'.[46] The incorrigible's frame of reference is in contrast 'the family and its entourage'.[47] Here the individual to be corrected provides the family with its primary mechanism for 'exercising its internal power or managing its economy, or even more, in its relations with the institutions adjoining or supporting it'.[48] Finally, the masturbator's frame of reference is 'the bedroom, the bed, the body'.[49] This figure, the latest arriving of the three, creates 'a kind of microcell around the individual and his body'.[50] Each of these three figures refers to specific domains and in so doing creates a relay or relation between them: nature and society, family and entourage, individual and its body. When these three frames of reference are brought together, they produce the abnormal individual as 'the object of a specific technology' connecting and reconfiguring medical and courtroom power across institutions.[51] This is the 'emergence of the power of normalisation' that operates 'without ever resting on a single institution but by establishing interactions between different institutions'.[52]

This new mode of power emerges through its regularisation of the 'paradox' that each figure introduces into its frame of reference. The human monster at first appears as a paradox in the relay between nature and society: 'the monster is, so to speak, the spontaneous, brutal, but consequently natural form of the unnatural'.[53] But the 'natural' monster who appears as paradox also has the power of paradox when it enters the law. Thus the monster 'violates the law while leaving it with nothing to say'.[54] This is the primary reason that, according to Foucault, the monster remains a central element of the abnormal individual and its new modes of power. The monster introduces a paradox into the law's frame of reference and enables new techniques of power that depend upon the law but deny the law's exclusive sovereign authority over its objects. The individual to be corrected then introduces the paradox of a regular irregularity, here a regularity that depends upon the family but that denies the family's authority. This paradox introduces the 'rectifiable incorrigibility' of the abnormal individual that will make him the 'centre of an apparatus of correction'.[55] Finally, the universal pathology of the masturbator leads to 'aetiological paradox'; this in turn becomes the 'axiomatic form' of the abnormal individual that depends upon bodily pleasure but denies its authority.[56] These three paradoxes combine to create the abnormal individual who retains an element of minor monstrosity even as it elaborates the new relations of power associated with normalisation. The monster does not go away, but rather provides the 'major model of every little deviation' that becomes 'the principle of intelligibility of all the forms that circulate as the small change of abnormality'.[57]

The most unique contribution of *Abnormal* lies in its account of how precisely the monster is maintained and yet diminished in the new mechanisms and objects of power. Foucault argues that a 'technology of human abnormality' – linked to conduct rather than nature – only appears when 'a regular network of knowledge and power has been established that brings these three figures together or, at any rate, invests them with the same system of regularities'.[58] This is what Foucault calls a new juridico-medical field of power that links the 'infracriminal and parapathological' in 'a kind of region of juridical indiscernibility'.[59] The regular irregularity and the aetiological paradox are regularised in a system that depends upon the monster's ability to 'violate the law while leaving it with nothing to say'.[60] This occurs by introducing mechanisms that work through the disqualification of the authority that they produce and depend upon. In *Abnormal*, Foucault calls this 'grotesque sovereignty' or the 'mechanism of grotesque power, of vile sovereignty'.[61] Here the expert acts as a 'switch-point' in which, 'by virtue of their status, a discourse or an individual can have effects of power that their intrinsic qualities should disqualify them from having'.[62] Foucault's example is the psychiatric expert in legal proceedings: through this switch-point the criminal monster and abnormal individual are brought together and redivided, yielding new domains of knowledge/power at a distance from psychiatry or law. As Foucault explains, the monster introduces a 'tautological intelligibility' that lies 'at the heart of analyses of abnormality'.[63] This means that the switch-point operates through and as a monstrous paradox: the monster provides 'a principle of intelligibility in spite of its limit position as both the impossible and the forbidden', which enables 'analyses of abnormality' to accrue intelligibility without giving the analyst impartial sovereign authority.[64]

Criminal monsters

In order to understand how monstrous paradox will appear in neo-liberalism – and why it appears in the figure of the paedophile and its peculiar double, the state – we must briefly explore the criminal monster's capacity to remake the relation between nature and society by disqualifying the law and, via the abnormal individual, psychiatry. Here we return to Foucault's genealogy of monsters but dwell at greater length on the sexual monster, the peculiar figure whose relation to nature (rather than society) will become the basis for the paedophilic monster of the later twentieth century. Prior to the moral monster

Foucault describes a monster purely of nature, the sexual monster. His example is as usual the hermaphrodite.[65] The eighteenth-century hermaphrodite, or 'monstrosity as the mix of sexes', provides the form for those 'eccentricities, kinds of imperfection, errors of nature' that become 'the source or pretext for a number of forms of criminal conduct'.[66] In the aftermath of the hermaphrodite, we find the emergence of 'a monstrosity of conduct rather than the monstrosity of nature', or of a 'criminal monster'.[67] This is the paradox introduced when the moral monster and the sexual monster meet in the switch-point of psychiatry and law. The 'monstrous nature of criminality' – the domain of psychiatric analysis and judgment – 'takes effect in the domain of conduct' – the domain of legal analysis and judgment.[68] The moral monster becomes criminal, rather than political, through the switch-point of sexuality.

The switch-points between conduct and nature appear in *Abnormal* as interest and instinct, the same terms that reappear as through a camera obscura in *The Birth of Biopolitics*. From 1765 to around 1830, Foucault points to the emergence of a new 'problem of monstrous conduct, of monstrous criminality' related to the idea of 'interest'.[69] Foucault suggests that broader political and economic conditions precipitate changes in the condition of monstrosity. In particular, he argues that changes in the 'economy of the power to punish' can be directly linked to the emergence of monstrous conduct, rather than monstrous nature, as a focus of juridico-medical power.[70] Punitive power moved from older models of political economy (related to the state and the family, as described earlier) to a European political economy in which the 'unit of measurement of the new technology of punitive power' was 'interest'.[71] This required a new system of calculation and knowledge. The subject of interest, or *homo economicus*, was used to calculate and quantify the difference between normal, rational interest and conduct with tainted, perverse or seemingly inexplicable interest. Experts could now evaluate the interest that motivated criminal conduct: 'the crime's rationality' would become 'the decipherable mechanism of interest [...] required by the new economy of punitive power'.[72] But this approach also introduced a new problem: the interest of the criminal seemed quite paradoxical. Criminality exhibits a paradoxical interest, a natural impulse to go against self-interest as defined by society.[73] The criminal seems 'a character who is the return of nature within a social body that has given up the state of nature through the pact and obedience to the laws'.[74] The criminal was presumed to have a motive or 'interest' that seems 'blind to its own ends' because it risks punishment, because it 'fails to calculate its consequences and cannot see beyond itself'.[75] This is how the criminal becomes intelligible as a monster:

> Is not an interest that does not conform to the nature of all interests an irregular, deviant interest? [...] And will not this natural individual be quite paradoxical, since he ignores the natural development of interest? [...] In short, is not the criminal precisely nature against nature? Is this not the monster?[76]

We find the rise of psychiatry in its proclaimed expertise over such a criminal as a monster (of nature but a departure from the laws of nature). The aim of such expertise is to understand the 'immanent rationality of criminal conduct, its natural intelligibility'.[77] The criminal was a creature whose interest, however monstrous, could be made intelligible through psychiatric protocols. Psychiatry would then lend itself to law to make criminal conduct regularised, measurable and punishable according to the new system. Problems arose when this criminal monster exhibited seemingly irrational or inexplicable conduct only in the brief event of the crime. The juridico-medical evaluation of criminal interest foundered on the paradox of 'a type of derangement which manifested itself only in the moment and in the guise of the crime, a derangement which would have no symptom other than the crime itself, and which could disappear once the crime had been committed'.[78] We see this in Foucault's treatment of the Henriette Cornier case of 1826, which he argues 'crystallized the problem of criminal monstrosity' because it could not be easily interpreted as either reasonable (justified by interest) or mad (justified by a pattern a conduct).[79] Cornier cut the head off of a neighbour's daughter in 'seemingly a motiveless act' and gave as her reason only 'an idea',[80] provoking confusion about how a 'certain instinct that is monstrous, sick, and pathological [...] passes through conduct like a meteor' without seeming to participate in a rationale of either interest or pleasure.[81] Such conduct demanded new rationales of evaluation and prediction, new mechanisms through which criminal guilt or insane innocence could be evaluated consistently (according to a reproducible rationale with both retroactive and predictive accuracy).

To explain such conduct, at first 'monstrosity is systematically suspected of being behind all criminality',[82] and the aim of psychiatry is to develop mechanisms to disclose the potential criminal before or perhaps even without the act of the crime itself. Here we see the emergence of the domain of abnormality, in which the pale monster becomes a universal instinct (desire) that must be regularised and normalised by disciplines. In his 1978 essay 'About the concept of the "dangerous individual" in nineteenth-century legal psychiatry', Foucault describes how a new criminal individual emerges through legal psychiatric knowledge, 'first a pale phantom', then gradually 'more substantial, more solid and more real', 'until finally it is the crime which seems nothing but a shadow hovering about the criminal, a shadow which must be drawn aside in order to reveal the only thing which is now of importance, the criminal'.[83] This 'pale phantom' of criminality (as an unintelligible paradox of instinct and interest) is slowly incorporated into nineteenth-century psychiatry as the potential criminality haunting all individuals: abnormality as an intelligible trajectory of instinct. As Foucault succinctly summarises this shift:

> the great monsters who loom up at the limit of the judicial apparatus can be reduced, dispersed, analysed, rendered commonplace, and given toned-down profiles within family relationships and the little masturbators who warm up in the family nest can become, through geneses, enlargements, and successive slippages, the mad criminals who rape, cut up, and devour their victims.[84]

Even as the sexual monster seems to disappear and be subsumed into the 'abnormal individual', the moral monster shadows such an individual as a virtual criminality embedded in its nature. Moral monstrosity is increasingly attributed to sexual abnormality, produced in childhood (and its 'family nest') and arrested as 'instinct' that requires successful discipline to acclimate to social mechanisms of 'interest'.

This new economy of punitive power (defined by rational interest) required the discipline of psychiatry to be routed through law in order to establish mechanisms for distinguishing between punishable (governed by interest) and treatable (ungoverned instinct) conduct. While the abnormal individual is merely a 'little masturbator' arrested in development, the moral monster looms within as a potentiality only intelligible to psychiatric experts trained in grotesque reason. This requires 'permanent mechanisms of surveillance and control', even as it renders the discourse of expertise itself somewhat irrational, paranoid and moralistic.[85] Thus the ambiguity of the interest/instinct nexus introduced into psychiatric knowledge its own paradoxical monstrosity – it used the discourse of reason and morality at the same time, often potentially disqualifying one of its discourses through the use of the other. Foucault describes this as 'grotesque sovereignty' or 'vile sovereignty', which operates through a discourse that is ridiculous but that yet proliferates a range of powerful effects.[86] Such discourse operates differently from that of incest; it does not produce 'the caesura that indicates access to the symbolic, but [...] the coercive synthesis that ensures the transmission of power and the indefinite displacement of its effects'.[87] This discourse is produced by the vile sovereignty of the psychiatric criminal expert, that which disqualifies itself as the sole authority over psychological meaning when it interfaces with law, even as it induces a 'coercive synthesis' with 'indefinite displacement of its effects'.

At the close of *Abnormal* (and again briefly in *The History of Sexuality, Volume 1*), Foucault turns to a case of adult–child sex to demonstrate the expansive capacities of vile sovereignty as it treats figures located in the 'region of juridical indiscernibility'. In the 1867 case of Charles Jouy, procedures of psychiatric and legal judgment work to enfold new geographic and social domains into the purview of social security. The forty-year-old Jouy is a liminal social figure cast by Foucault as the 'village idiot', who first has a 'little girl' named Sophie Adam masturbate him in front of another girl and later appears to have had some type of penetrative sexual contact with her (alluded to and evidenced by some sign noticed by the mother on the girl's clothes).[88] The girl's family calls in experts, an unusual turn to external mechanisms to resolve what Foucault calls an otherwise insignificant 'everyday offense' in 'the depths of the countryside'.[89] Like the 1826 Cornier case, legal and psychiatric experts debated the offender's responsibility for his conduct (sexual contact with a higher status child in the village). Unlike the Cornier case, however, in 1867, Jouy is rationalised through the new regular irregularities of the abnormal individual. Jouy is attributed a 'permanent stigmata that brand the individual structurally'; his pleasure becomes a reasonable interest in gratification, even as such interest is dubbed 'deficient' in moral sense and morphology (his interest is guided by undeveloped instinct).[90] This is the unexceptional 'pale monster' who lurks beneath or in the arrested childhood of the abnormal individual: in Jouy we find the 'immobilisation of life, conduct, and performance around childhood' demanded of the abnormal by psychiatric discourse.[91]

Foucault points to the expansion of power through the case; the family calls in outside experts to assess the conduct of Jouy, an 'internal immigrant' who performs low-status wage work. What would otherwise be an 'offense against public decency' case turns into a forum for legal psychiatry to extend its reach into new geographic and socioeconomic spaces of 'juridical indiscernibility'.[92] Foucault argues that Jouy would have been a routine part of village life, providing necessary labour while remaining on the outskirts of the social transactions of the village. He would, however, have participated in sub-economies of sexual and economic exchange with other peripheral denizens – children. Foucault suggests that the entrance of Jouy into this 'infracriminal and parapathological' realm brings the 'peripheral, floating sexuality that brings children and marginal adults together' into the observation of the courts.[93] Thus adult–child sex is a key object for transformations in the power of normalisation and discipline that operates through the family but that in effect denies the family's authority over children and public space. Equally denied is the exclusive sovereignty of either law or psychiatry. What we find instead is a 'coercive synthesis that ensures the transmission of power and the indefinite displacement of its effects' (previously quoted on p. 98 here).

Paedophilic monsters

Foucault's account of vile sovereignty helps us read the monstrous paradox of the paedophile that emerges in 1886 (when Richard von Krafft-Ebing first coined the term in his taxonomy of legal psychiatry). Foucault argues that after 1865 'technological advances',[94] including new connections between psychiatry, neurology and biology, create the 'syndrome' not as illness but as 'a partial and stable configuration referring to a general condition of abnormality'.[95] Foucault mentions Krafft-Ebing's diagnosis of 'agoraphobia' here as part of a new 'syndrome of abnormalities', but he does not treat Krafft-Ebing's discourse on paedophilia.[96] It is intriguing that Foucault does not treat the paedophile as a key figure in his genealogy; Foucault does not in fact provide an extensive genealogy linking the 1867 Jouy case to his efforts to decriminalise adult–child sex in 1978. For Foucault, the problematisation of adult–child sex is an exemplary stage in the universalisation of childhood sexuality. It is in childhood that the latent potential for abnormality must be disciplined, lest instinct emerge as aberrant interest (criminality) or as syndrome (illness). But Foucault does not take up the figure of the paedophile itself as key to this problematisation. Here we might productively turn to Krafft-Ebing's 1886 account of the paedophile, which introduces adult–child sex as a unique problem for medico-forensic psychiatry. Krafft-Ebing produces a new expert discourse on morality through which to differentiate between syndrome and criminality, providing an important missing link between the abnormal individuality of Charles Jouy and the predatory monstrosity of the late twentieth-century paedophile.

Krafft-Ebing coined '*paedophilia erotica*' as a specific psycho-sexual type in *Psychopathia Sexualis: With Especial Reference to the Antipathic Sexual Instinct: A Medico-Forensic Study* (first published in German in 1886). The term is defined in 'Pathological sexuality in its legal aspects' under the subsection 'Notes on the question of responsibility in sexual offences caused by delusion'. In this section, Krafft-Ebing argues that pathological sexualities – such as sadism, exhibition and fetishism – are an illness rather than a crime and should be treated by incarceration on the grounds of mental health ('confinement in insane asylum').[97] But paedophilia is distinguished from these other forms of pathological sexuality since, in Krafft-Ebing's understanding, it poses a rather unique set of problems for determinations of legal responsibility. In the section on 'Violation of individuals under the age of fourteen', Krafft-Ebing ponders the problem of moral responsibility for those who are suffering from sexual pathology, a case presented by adults who seek out sex with children (which the law defines as a violation).[98] Krafft-Ebing seems at first to provide a rational and regularised taxonomy of types. On the one hand, we find:

> cases in which the sexually needy subject is drawn to children not in consequence of degenerated morality or psychical or physical impotence, but rather by a morbid disposition, a *psycho-sexual perversion*, which may at present be named erotic paedophilia (love of children).[99]

The first set of cases differentiate erotic paedophilia from adult moral and physical failure as a 'psycho-sexual perversion', a form of erotic love (love of children) that marks a 'morbid disposition' and should therefore be treated like other psycho-pathologies. This is the paedophile as an abnormal individual. On the other hand, we find non-psychopathological cases, in which legal responsibility should fall on the older party. And yet these latter cases introduce a paradox for psychiatric reason where it interfaces with law: 'it is psychologically incomprehensible that an adult of full virility and mentally sound should indulge in sexual abuses with children'.[100]

Here Krafft-Ebing reintroduces the term 'monster' to describe the paradox that psychiatrists confront when a 'normal' adult has sex with children: 'The finer feelings of man revolt at the thought of counting the monsters among the psychically normal members of human society.'[101] While Krafft-Ebing speculates that such a monstrous normalcy may be the result of some 'injury in the sphere of morality and potency', this does not 'preclude the moral responsibility of the perpetrator'.[102] Moralisation becomes a key mechanism of power and punishment when both interest and instinct fail to explain (or diagnose) adult sexual conduct with children. Moralisation ties the 'psychically normal' adult who has sex with children, or the absence of a syndrome, to the transgression of 'nature': 'judgment of the act should ever be guided by the monstrosity and the degree in which it psychically and physically differs from the natural act'.[103] Monstrosity has come full circle – it is not nature erupting into the unnatural domain of society and its norms (the instinct interrupting rational interest), but rather a seemingly deliberate departure from nature at the level of conduct. This is the responsibility of the normal adult, who is capable of disciplined conduct but who for some reason chooses to pursue morally unnatural acts. The 'monstrosity' of the 'act' – which can be measured psychically as well as physically – is its degree of difference from nature. Sexual monstrosity returns, not as a naturally two-sexed body (the hermaphrodite) but as an immoral interest in unnatural sexual conduct.

It is through this problematisation that the adult who has sex with children becomes a major figure for twentieth-century expansions of power/knowledge. After Krafft-Ebing, new paradoxes are introduced into later nineteenth-century systems of regularities and quantifiable rationalities. How does an expert know whether an adult who has sex with children has a perverse instinct (the erotic paedophile) or a perverse interest (the sexual monster)? The first individual is abnormal; the second is immoral and unnatural. This distinction between psychopathology and sex crime was negotiated across the rapidly urbanising zones of Europe, England and the United States. In the late nineteenth century, the adult who has sex with children was associated with the disease of urban industrialisation and mass migration/displacement of populations. In England, 1880s moral activism cited the city's anonymous public spaces and displaced labour forces as a recipe for sexual exploitation called 'white slavery'. In the United States, the 1890s witnessed an explosion of concern about children's vulnerability to sexual predation from dangerous strangers passing among new urban populations. In 1893 alone, Charlton Edholm's tract *Traffic in Girls* echoed British concerns about white slavery, von Krafft-Ebing's work was translated and circulated in English and the American discipline of criminology was founded. Such 'technological advances' worked to bring the 'peripheral, floating sexuality that brings children and marginal adults together' into the observation of courts even as it expanded the realm of surveillance for potential sexual predation. Over the course of the twentieth century, the possibility that adults would seek out sex with children became the object of moral panic, regardless of whether or not actual sexual conduct took place.

Additional cases of adult–child sex flourished most conspicuously in the United States over what historian Philip Jenkins describes as five major phases of moral panic: the 1890s to 1910s age of the 'white slaver'; the 1920s to 1930s rise of the 'sexual delinquent'; the 1940s to 1950s period of the 'sexual psychopath'; the late 1960s to early 1970s short era of 'liberalisation and/or tolerance'; and the late 1970s to 2000s long era of the 'predatory paedophile'.[104] Jenkins's timeline suggests that Foucault's late 1970s activism can be located at the tail end of the era in which broader 'liberalisation' of sex law was being achieved by women's and gay/lesbian liberation movements. Within the context of these movements, some activists took up children's sexual rights as a key element of broader sexual liberation. Others focused on the rights of all people to participate in consensual relations regardless of age or status. But efforts to liberalise adult–child sex rapidly became segregated from movements focused on consent as the *sine qua non* of sexual freedom (a legal term limited to specific rational and responsible subjects, excluding children and those deemed mentally deficient). The North American Man Boy Love Association NAMBLA) was founded in 1978 in order to resist the perceived persecution of adult men who have consensual sex with underage boys; an early ally of gay and lesbian liberation movements, it was ostracised from sexual liberalisation strategies by the mid 1980s.[105] Foucault's engagement with adult–child sex decriminalisation movements was part of this broader 1970s liberationist agenda, and while he himself seemed sceptical that 'liberalisation' or liberation were political strategies necessarily appropriate to a broader vision of 'revolution' in this era, he was certainly interested in how revolution might be engaged in both legal and governmental arenas – including the arena of the child's eroticism.

We can now return to the paradox of adult–child sex introduced by Foucault in 1978. On the one hand, adult–child sex appears through the lens of abnormality (Foucault does after all include cases from the period up to 1974 in *Abnormal*). The adult who has sex with children is a 'paedophile' in Krafft-Ebing's sense of the term, an adult whose love of children is deemed abnormal (but not monstrous). This abnormal individual, once himself an incorrigible little masturbator, now seeks out incorrigible children whose desire exceeds their discipline. For normalisation to be achieved, the little masturbator must be disciplined by the family (or its extensive apparatuses of correction); otherwise the erotic child is in danger of serving the ends of or ending up a criminal (as his instincts come to depart from their natural form and objects). Thus the paedophile serves a crucial function in maintaining familial discipline even as it yokes the family to broader domains of diagnosis and correction. Activism for and against paedophilia treats it as a stigmatised practice (or abnormal syndrome) rather than a form of monstrosity. On the other hand, in his 1978 interviews Foucault suggests that a new deployment of sexuality is afoot, one focused on marketisation and securitisation (more than discipline and correction). Within this deployment the adult who has sex with children is more like Krafft-Ebing's immoral and unnatural monster. This individual presents a monstrous paradox for disciplinary and regulatory governance, creating new syntheses and effects expanding power into new domains. In place of regularisation and rationalisation, we find paranoiac discourse about a 'roaming danger' that exceeds all disciplinary locales. This monster is a 'phantom' whose imminent threat requires new mechanisms of governance, including 'systems of information carried out in the press' and mass moralisation against monsters large and small. His victims are intrinsic innocents, children who require surveillance and protection against immoral contamination.

In 1978, Foucault encounters in other words the monstrous paradox of the paedophile, a figure whose genealogy he has only partially traced through *Abnormal* and whose emerging significance for neoliberalism is barely intelligible to the 1978 historian of the present. In 1978, the idea that all adults who have sex with children are paedophiles and that all paedophiles are moral predators, was barely emerging. Only a decade later, all adults who have sex with children would become popularly (and at times legally) defined as paedophiles, all paedophiles would be depicted as predatory and 'children' considered naturally vulnerable might be as old as eighteen. How did this transformation happen? How did we move so decisively from the pale monster of abnormality, visible as late as 1978, to the monstrous predator of 1989?

To complete this genealogy, I turn in closing to Foucault's lectures on neoliberalism and self-interest in *The Birth of Biopolitics* (1978–79). Here Foucault argues that the neoliberal subject is defined by interest, rather than instinct, and that competition replaces the commodity as the key to valorisation. This expands the zone of commercial conduct to all spheres of human activity, including child-rearing, and relegates all nature to market models. The paradox within neoliberalism lies therefore in the relation between nature and the market, a relation in which the paedophilic monster will play an important role. What we see in

The Birth of Biopolitics are the emergence of new mechanisms of power that deny the value of governance and yet rely upon it to ensure 'moral' maximisation of value through markets, mechanisms deeply dependent upon the effects of vile sovereignty. These mechanisms will make the state itself into a sovereign reviled by those seeking more 'rational' mechanisms of governance and liberty – the market, whose reason is not that of nature but that of the moral good.[106] This new political economic complex expands new realms of power through the moralisation of the child's potentiality.

Vile neoliberalism

This brings us to the final monster of the piece, the monstrous state of neoliberal discourse, what Foucault citing Nietzsche calls a 'cold monster' in *Security, Territory, Population* and explicates as a shadow or phantom in *The Birth of Biopolitics*.[107] In *The Birth of Biopolitics*, Foucault analyses the emergence of neoliberal discourse from the 1930s onwards as attacking the 'cold monster' of the state. At its core, neoliberal discourse seeks to 'adopt the free market as the organising and regulating principle of the state'.[108] The aim is to create a political economy in which we find 'a state under the supervision of the market rather than a market supervised by the state'.[109] Neoliberal discourse proposes competition as the new model of sociality and subjectivity; the market will foster competition and all forms of relation will be modelled on the maximisation of interest and the accumulation of capital (human, social and economic).[110] And yet neoliberal discourse does not consider competition a natural condition, and so it requires governance to ensure it: 'competition is therefore an historical objective of governmental art and not a natural given that must be respected'.[111] This means that neoliberal discourse – which claims that it is antagonistic to the state – actually requires particular modes of governance in order to secure the aim of competition. As a result, 'there will thus be a sort of complete superimposition of market mechanisms, indexed to competition, and governmental policy'.[112]

Many critics concur that neoliberal discourse exhibits a state phobia; while neoliberal policy and practices rely heavily on state expansion in domains of militarisation and incarceration, neoliberal discourse emphasises the need for a small and ever-shrinking state, the sole purpose of which is to enable marketisation and maximisation of capital.[113] If *Abnormal* notes that 'the first monster is the king', *The Birth of Biopolitics* suggests that the most recent one is the state.[114] Thus the neoliberal discourse of the state conjures it as a monster in order to institute the neoliberal 'event' of biopolitics:

> the moment when that which does not exist is inscribed in reality, and when that which does not exist comes under a legitimate regime of the true and false, marks the birth of this dissymmetrical bipolarity of politics and the economy.[115]

According to Foucault, neoliberal doctrine (1935) and policy (1952) introduce a new event into reality – 'let's ask the market economy itself to be the principle, not of the state's limitation, but of its internal regulation from start to finish of its existence and action'.[116] As a result, Foucault explains that neoliberal discourse relies on 'something like the fantastical profile of the state and there is no longer any need to analyse actuality'.[117] This 'cold monster' is neither actual nor real, but a virtuality that enables new domains of power expressed through competition and interest.

Thus we might consider neoliberal discourse on the state as another effect of vile sovereignty. It operates through the regularisation of new systems of knowledge in which the seeming disqualification of experts, by virtue of their role within the institutions that they critique, only increases the range and impact of their discursive effects. This mode of power enacts the 'nullification of the person holding power by the very ritual that displays this power and the person holding it'. One might think here of neoliberal economists who work for the Federal Reserve System, or neoliberal politicians who become president or prime minister. The state is disqualified (as a cold monster) even as it acts as a switch-point between new domains and new mechanisms. For neoliberal modes of power to operate, 'government must not form a counterpoint or a screen, as it were, between society and economic processes. It has to intervene in society as such, in its fabric and depth'.[118] Governance must intervene in society in a way that constitutes its fundamental reality; governance must not take representational form (counterpoint or screen) but in effect become society, even as it maintains the capacity to regulate it. This requires the disqualification of the state (represented in the form of the cold monster) and the economic rationalisation of governance and society where they meet – interest – such that 'competitive mechanisms can play a regulatory role at every moment and every point in society'.[119]

Through its incorporation of such modes of vile sovereignty, neoliberalism takes up longer traditions of liberal state-phobia and incorporates them as a new governmental rationale. These old themes manifest in a new 'switch-point', one that Foucault argues does not seek resolution in a society 'oriented towards the commodity and the uniformity of the commodity' but rather in 'the multiplicity and differentiation of enterprises'.[120] This places older models of discipline and regulation, such as the family, in relation to new modes of expertise on the subject of human capital. In place of prohibitions, we find multiplications that demand new modes of regulation in the service of maximisation. This requires in turn new mechanisms of power:

> as soon as society poses itself the problem of its improvement of human capital in general, it is inevitable that the problem of the control, screening, and improvement of the human capital of individuals, as a function of unions and consequent reproduction, will become actual, or at any rate, called for.[121]

Here the older theme of family life and co-ownership (collectivity/kinship as commons) becomes the problem of 'unions and consequent reproduction'.[122] This problem requires new mechanisms of powers that 'involves only the marginal transfer from a maximum to a minimum; it is absolutely not the establishment of or regulation around an average'.[123] This shift away from the society of the norm (and the abnormal individual as a key social mechanism dependent upon the family) produces a need for new mechanisms of interest focused on the 'control, screening, and improvement' of human capital.[124]

Foucault argues that in this period the 'individual becomes governmentalisable, that power gets a hold of him to the extent, and only to the extent, that he is a homo economicus'.[125] While this sounds like an echo of Foucault's analysis of liberal interest in *Abnormal*, here Foucault argues that the twentieth-century resurgence of liberalism (Ordo- and neoliberalism) makes *homo economicus* the *only* zone of governance. This is a shift in rationalisation of political economy, in which economics 'is no longer the analysis of the historical logic of processes; it is the analysis of the internal rationality, the strategic programming of individuals' activity'.[126] This constitutes a new model of interest and conduct:

> Homo economicus is someone who accepts reality. Rational conduct is any conduct which is sensitive to modifications in the variables of the environment and which responds to this in a non-random way, in a systematic way, and economics can therefore be defined as

the science of the systematic nature of responses to environmental variables.[127]

In this system the child represents the reservoir of potentiality through which internal and external rationalisation become one, the individual whose interest is the actualisation of governance. Thus the child becomes a key form for this redefinition of reality via the event of biopolitics.[128] Foucault suggests that the United States is where we see this logic in its fullest development as of 1978, creating 'a whole environmental analysis, as the Americans say, of the child's life which it will be possible to calculate, and to a certain extent quantify, or at any rate measure, in terms of the possibilities of investment in human capital'.[129]

This is the making of an enterprise society at every level, including human 'nature'. Human nature is made into interest (rather than instinct), which is mobilised by competition rather than moulded by discipline: 'the principle of an irreducible, non-transferable, atomistic individual choice which is unconditionally referred to the subject himself is what is called interest'.[130] Neoliberalism constitutes as its zone of governance life capacities, or life itself as a reservoir of potentiality.[131] Biopolitics in this text names a new political rationality – an art of governance – founded on an economic logic of competition (and risk), in which human subjects are constituted by their capitalisation of and on their life's potentiality. This creates the need for new mechanisms of judgement:

> the more you multiply enterprises, you multiply frictions, environmental effects, and consequently, to the extent that you free economic subjects and allow them to play their game, then at the same time the more you detach them from their status as virtual functionaries of a plan, and you inevitably multiply judges.[132]

Disciplinary subjects conformed to a virtual plan beyond their design; neoliberal discourses define subjects through their maximisation of human capital without a plan. This is not the crossroads where an anatamo-politics of the body (discipline) and a biopolitics of the population (regulation) meet, as described at the end of *History of Sexuality, Volume 1*. Rather, this is a crossroads that demands new mechanisms for the control, screening and improvement of human capitalisation.

This is where monstrous paradox emerges – unnatural competition must appear as competitive nature, which requires regulation that appears as society itself. In order to manage the potentiality of human subjects, we find new switch-points akin to those of daily and criminal psychiatry in their nineteenth-century interface with law, switch-points through which 'an enterprise society and a judicial society, a society oriented towards the enterprise and a society framed by a multiplicity of judicial institutions, are two faces of a single phenomenon'.[133] This creates a multiplication of 'actual' mechanisms that regulate the potentiality of human capital (which is virtual but subject to control, screening and maximisation as actual value). Foucault therefore describes human capital as a new juridico-natural complex. And this is where we might return to the other Foucault of 1978, the Foucault who notes an efflorescence of sexual moralisation in the law and the press as he engages in efforts to change laws against adult–child sex. In this context Foucault points out what seems like a paradoxical tactic in the economic rationalisation of governance and society. On the one hand, the aim is to rationalise government economically, including the economic rationalisation of all modes of human life. On the other hand, the aim is to regulate society moralistically, introducing new protections of life seemingly without economic basis.

Enter the sexual monster, with his immoral interest in unnatural conduct. While the switch-point of vile sovereignty can occur at any site of monstrous paradox, the paedophile constitutes a particular genealogical figure through which the moral monster of political governance meets the sexual monster of unnatural interest. American lawyer and crime novelist Andrew Vachss can help us see the imminent connections between the discourse of predatory paedophilia and that of neoliberalism. In 1989, Vachss coined the term 'predatory paedophile', becoming a key spokesperson for new 'technological innovations' of expert knowledge.[134] Vachss is an important example of the new switch-point introduced among domains of expertise in this period: a prominent lawyer, child advocate and crime novelist, Vachss has written numerous popular articles on the problem of paedophilia. In his 1990 *Parade* article 'Today's victim could be tomorrow's predator', Vacchs explains the shift from an abnormal instinct to an immoral interest: 'Criminals are made, not born – there is no biogenetic code that produces a violent rapist, a child molester or a serial killer.'[135] This fits in with the broader emphasis defining rational conduct as 'any conduct which is sensitive to modifications in the variables of the environment and which responds to this in a non-random way'. The paedophile is a product of environment, not nature, and his particular pathology is his failure to respond systematically to changing conditions. His monstrous conduct results from an interest that does not respond to changes in market conditions. He is fixated, his conduct is not rational as per *homo economicus* but instead has only one object of value: the child.

Vachss summarises the post-1970s understanding of the difference between an abnormal instinct and a monstrous interest quite clearly in his 2002 *Parade* article 'The difference between "sick" and "evil"': 'Sickness is a condition. / Evil is a behavior. / Evil is always a matter of choice. Evil is not thought; it is conduct. And that conduct is always volitional. / And just as evil is always a choice, sickness is always the absence of choice. Sickness happens. Evil is inflicted.'[136] Monstrous interest is 'evil' behaviour, defined as a choice in conduct. It is evil because it is a choice; paedophilia is the absolute perversion of interest because it operates as a rational choice to do moral wrong. Because it is not responsive to environmental change, it is not rational conduct but rather immoral conduct. Here immoral conduct is a symptom of non-market rationality, which is always culpable. This conduct contrasts to responsible behaviour maximised in the *homo economicus*, whose sexual and civil behaviour exhibit rational responsiveness to market conditions. This is how the pale monster of the paedophile turns into a moral monster (like the state) that enables new switchpoints or relays between emergent domains of power. The paedophile as sex predator emerges as part of the new relays enabled by the vile sovereignty of neoliberal discourse. If neoliberal discourse yields the monstrous paradox of the state, which disqualifies its authority even as it regulates competition through its governmental mechanisms, it also yields the monstrous paradox of the predatory paedophile. Both the paedophile and the state are attributed monstrous sovereignty – they will steal the potentiality of the child.

The child capitalises on its potential by becoming a responsible consumer and entrepreneur; contact with the paedophile (or the state) robs it of its developmental autonomy, its capacity to adapt to environmental conditions and develop proper neoliberal subjectivity. Protection against these monsters requires 'moralisation' as a mechanism of power, a discourse of vile sovereignty that refers to the family and the law even as it disqualifies them from having sole authority over managing or regulating its effects. Thus we see the radical resurgence of the discourse of family and the law from the 1980s onwards, even as both domains have weaker sovereignty over their traditional domains. For the family, education, consumption, sexuality and reproduction are increasingly subject to marketisation (education, consumption) and moralisation (sexuality, reproduction). The family remains the boundary of the social, but not the adequate training ground of childhood potentiality. Children are increasingly opened to the market for training in proper consumption and entrepreneurial competition. In contrast, childhood eroticism is subject to moralisation that uses the family as the limit of marketisation: moralisation trains the monstrous interest within – the child – and the one without – the paedophile. Security is needed, and now dangerous sexuality begins to be on the move. Prison cannot be far away, and indeed the need to secure the child leads to increased penality for those suspected of dangerous potentialities (including placing the child in the veritable 'prison' of sex).

The predatory paedophile thus moves beyond the regime of normalisation described in Foucault's 1978 essay 'About the concept of the "dangerous individual" in nineteenth-century legal psychiatry': the paedophile creates a mode of criminality that does not need an actual criminal. What in the nineteenth century was a 'shadow hovering about the criminal' becomes a shadow hovering around the whole of society. The paedophile is not the only such monster; neoliberalism has the capacity to produce a range of virtual predators who require the state for security, even as the state is disqualified from securing the citizenry. These predatory monsters appear as the 'intrinsic virtualities of the state'.[137] Foucault explains that the 'people in revolt', those earlier cannibalistic monsters, first appeared in liberal political discourse as 'sedition and riot'.[138] In neoliberal discourse, these monsters are the 'paedophile', the 'illegal alien' and the 'terrorist'. This is a powerful trio: the paedophile is a sexual monster attributed a 'peripheral, floating sexuality that brings children and marginal adults together'; the illegal alien is an economic monster attributed a peripheral, floating labour capacity that brings surplus and monopoly together; and the terrorist is a political monster attributed a peripheral, floating radicalism that brings violence and the state together. Each figure requires new regimes of expertise and technologies of detection and detention within and, most importantly, across these three domains (sex, economic, politics). Together, these figures haunt the borders of biopower as 'phantoms', making governance itself into an '"infracriminal and parapathological" realm' in need of ever expanding modes of expertise.

The paedophile in particular creates an important switch-point between liberal and neoliberal modes of power, enabling the 'abnormal' to become a virtual monster (incorporeal materiality), a sexual chiasma (like scarcity), that which might exist 'naturally' (like monopoly) but that neoliberalism has the unique governmentality to master and manage in order to ensure the achievement of an unnatural but morally desirable condition – 'free' market competition.[139] The predatory paedophile figures the threat of interrupting or diverting the otherwise unregulated process of human capitalisation, which would ruin the child's potentiality for 'free' competition. But it also provides the rationale for regulating human capitalisation when it appears as sexuality. Because sexual conduct is a rational choice, it is subject to moralisation in order to ensure that it does not impede other modes of subjective capitalisation.[140] Together marketisation and moralisation route through but exceed the state; this is where the vile sovereignty of neoliberal discourse relies on the very monsters that it seems to revile. Civil society must intervene to regulate these monsters, installing experts within the state (think now of the FBI profiling of sex predators, or the Federal regulation of Wall Street allegedly attached to the bailout) who yet routinely fail in their efforts at surveillance and entrapment. Because of this productive yet disqualifying circuit of neoliberal discourse, the population becomes an apparatus of security – the multiplication of judges described earlier – trained on the threat of virtual predators. In this way the twin monsters of the paedophile and the state together offer up the lure of the erotic child perpetually to extend neoliberal governance. They do so by virtualising the sexual monster, making it everywhere and nowhere, a potentiality that must be managed through specifically neoliberal 'economies of punishment' and biopolitical measurements.

Permanent criticism

At the beginning of this chapter, I suggested that Foucault treats the child as a site of erotic potentiality that might interrupt the 'roaming danger' of sexuality and serve as a vanguard counter-conduct in the era of biopolitical security. Resituated in this genealogy of the monster, Foucault's effort to decriminalise adult–child sex seems inadequate to the task of dismantling sexual security in the era of neoliberalism. His effort to locate potentiality in the realm of erotic childhood touches on the problem of control, screening and improvement of human capitalisation. But the child with its potential pleasures had even in the late 1970s already begun its transformation into potential human capital; in the United States in particular, this process was already well underway as Foucault notes. While it is possible that a successful 1970s decriminalisation effort might in fact have transformed the terrain of struggle in interesting ways, it seems unlikely that legal 'liberalisation' would have enabled the child's erotic potential to realise revolutionary aims. More likely the child's eroticism would be incorporated (as it already has been within the limits placed on actual sexual conduct) into new markets for the child's maximisation of potential.[141] This might limit the role of the family in the moralisation of childhood sexuality. But it is unlikely to provoke a radical revolution in childhood eroticism given the context of a broader market rationality and moralisation of non-capitalist conduct in civil society.

This brings me back to the problem of the intellectual posed at the start. In an interview with Didier Eribon given in 1981, entitled 'Is it really important to think?', Foucault says that 'deep transformation' requires 'permanent criticism', such that 'modes of thought' are understood as 'modes of action'.[142] It is in the spirit of permanent criticism that I have undertaken this chapter. I have turned to Foucault to explore how targeting a moralistic discourse rationalised as *raison d'état* obscures the limits of decriminalisation and the problems posed by locating revolutionary potential in erotic childhood. Such a critique of moralistic discourse too often dominates critical work on adult–child sex; here I have read Foucault for paradox rather than as a 'unitary discourse' to help us open up alternative modes of thought.[143] This effort is in keeping with Foucault's own account of the work of the present-day historian, in which he challenges us to develop a genealogical sensibility defined by its encounter with paradox. As Foucault explains in the 1981 Eribon interview:

> You know, to say that we are much more recent than we think isn't a way of taking the whole weight of history on our shoulders. It's rather to place at the disposal of the work that we can do ourselves the greatest possible share of what is presented to us as inaccessible.[144]

Notes

1. Michel Foucault, PAO, xv.
2. Foucault signed a 1977 petition to Parliament to change articles in the law regarding the age of sexual majority along with Louis Althusser, Roland Barthes, Simone de Beauvoir, Jean Danet, Jacques Derrida, André Glucksmann, Guy Hocquenghem, Alain Robbe-Grillet, Jean-Paul Sartre, Philippe Sollers and others. This coincides with broader activity to protect specific adults from prosecution under age of consent and statutory rape laws, including an open letter published in *Le Monde* on 26 January 1977 (not signed by Foucault) defending Bernard Dejager, Jean-Claude Gallien and Jean Burckhardt against prosecution for having sex with twelve- and thirteen-year-old boys and girls, and a 1979 *Libération* letter defending 'Gérard R.' on similar charges with younger partners.
3. See Didier Eribon, *Michel Foucault*, Betsy Wing (trans.) (Cambridge, MA: Harvard University Press, 1991); David Macey, *The Lives of Michel Foucault* (New York: Vintage, 1993); David Halperin, *Saint Foucault: Towards a Gay Hagiography* (Oxford: Oxford University Press, 1995). On Foucault in Iran, see Janet Afaray and Kevin B. Anderson, *Foucault and the Iranian*

Revolution: Gender and the Seductions of Islamism (Chicago, IL: University of Chicago Press, 2005).
4. Gilles Deleuze argues that Foucault's work with the GIP between 1971 and 1973 maintained a post-1968 decentred left practice of linking 'prison struggle and other struggles' through a concept of power, at a time when broader left approaches became more centralised (including a return to Marxism). See Gilles Deleuze, *Foucault*, Seán Hand (trans. and ed.) (Minneapolis, MN: University of Minnesota Press, 1988 [1986]), 24. Gayatri Chakravorty Spivak criticises Foucault and Deleuze for opposing power to ideology/interest (rather than thinking about their interrelationship), symptomatic of Western/metropolitan intellectual interests in the era of neocolonial international capitalism. See Gayatri Chakravorty Spivak, 'Can the subaltern speak?', in Cary Nelson and Lawrence Grossberg (eds), *Marxism and the Interpretation of Culture* (Urbana, IL: University of Illinois Press, 1988), 271–313.
5. Foucault, ABN, 56.
6. Michel Foucault with David Cooper, Jean-Pierre Faye, Marie-Odile Faye and Marine Zecca, 'Confinement, psychiatry, prison', PPC, 209; originally published as 'Enfermement, psychiatrie, prison', in *Change*, 32–3 (1977), 76–110.
7. Foucault, 'Social security', PPC, 166.
8. Foucault, 'Power and sex', ibid., 121. This discussion with Bernard-Henri Lévy was originally published as 'Foucault: Non au sexe roi', in *Le Nouvel Observateur* (12 March 1977).
9. See Wendy Brown, *Politics out of History* (Princeton, NJ: Princeton University Press, 2001).
10. On 'pale monster', see Foucault, ABN, 57. On 'cold monster', see STP, 144. This phrase is adapted from Friedrich Nietzsche, *Thus Spoke Zarathustra*, R. J. Hollingdale (trans.) (London: Penguin, 1969), 75: 'The state is the coldest of all cold monsters [*das kälteste aller kalten Ungeheuer*]. Coldly it lies, too; and this lie creeps from its mouth: "I, the state, am the people."'
11. Foucault, 'Sexual morality and the law', PPC, 271. Originally broadcast as 'Dialogues', produced by Roger Pillaudin, the French transcript was published as 'La loi de la pudeur', in *Recherches*, 37 (April 1979), 69–82.
12. Foucault argues that the Penal Code of 1810 in France did not stipulate specific sexual offences and that laws of sexuality only came into existence later in the nineteenth and twentieth centuries, pointing specifically to the Mirguet Amendment of 1960. See Foucault, 'Sexual morality and the law', PPC, 271–2.
13. The United States mobilisations by Anita Bryant are explicitly named. Ibid., 272.
14. Ibid., 272.
15. Foucault, HS1, 45.
16. Foucault, STP, 103.
17. Ibid.
18. Ibid., 104.
19. Ibid.
20. Foucault, BOB, 149.
21. Ibid., 148.

22. Ibid., 149.
23. Ibid.
24. Foucault, 'Sexual morality and the law', PPC, 281.
25. Ibid.
26. Foucault, 'Power and sex', PPC, 117.
27. Ibid.
28. Ibid., 120.
29. Ibid.
30. Ibid., 121.
31. See Vikki Bell, *Interrogating Incest: Feminism, Foucault and the Law* (London: Routledge, 1993); and Linda Alcoff, 'Dangerous pleasures: Foucault and the politics of paedophilia', in Susan J. Hekman (ed.), *Feminist Interpretations of Michel Foucault* (University Park, PA: Penn State University Press, 1996), 99–135.
32. See Wendy Brown, *Walled States, Waning Sovereignty* (New York: Zone Books, 2010).
33. Roger N. Lancaster, *Sex Panic and the Punitive State* (Berkeley, CA: University of California Press, 2011). This book came to my attention only in the final revision of this chapter.
34. According to the *Oxford English Dictionary*, the term enters the English language in the fifteenth century from the French 'paradoxe'.
35. See Foucault, DOL, 215–37; originally published as *L'Ordre du discours* (Paris: Gallimard, 1971). Here Foucault traces the changing paradoxes of intellectual work, from those of the sophists to those of commentary. Foucault suggests that the contemporary intellectual work must re-engage paradox in order to break free of humanist and structuralist approaches to truth. In contrast to such studies of 'consciousness and continuity (with their correlative problems of liberty and causality)' or 'sign and structure' (Foucault, DOL, 230), Foucault proposes 'the philosophy of the event' (ibid., 231).
36. Gillian Harkins, *Everybody's Family Romance: Reading Incest in Neoliberal America* (Minneapolis, MN: University of Minnesota Press, 2009). See chapter 1, 'Laying down the law: the modernisation of American incest', 26–68.
37. Foucault, ABN, 56.
38. James Kincaid, *Child-Loving: The Erotic Child and Victorian Culture* (London: Routledge, 1992), 3.
39. Foucault, ABN, 92.
40. Ibid., 94.
41. Ibid., 101.
42. Ibid.
43. Ibid., 110.
44. Ibid., 56.
45. Ibid., 59.
46. Ibid., 59 and 65.
47. Ibid., 59.
48. Ibid., 57.
49. Ibid., 60.
50. Ibid., 59.
51. Ibid., 21.

52. Ibid., 26.
53. Ibid., 56.
54. Ibid. See also Giorgio Agamben, *Homo Sacer: Sovereign Power and Bare Life*, Daniel Heller-Roazen (trans.) (Stanford, CA: Stanford University Press, 1998).
55. Foucault, ABN, 58–9.
56. Ibid., 60.
57. Ibid., 56.
58. Ibid., 61.
59. Ibid., 21.
60. Ibid., 56.
61. Ibid., 12.
62. Ibid., 35 and 11.
63. Ibid., 57.
64. Ibid.
65. Andrew N. Sharpe contests Foucault's privileged focus on the hermaphrodite in *Foucault's Monsters and the Challenge of Law* (London: Routledge, 2010).
66. Foucault, ABN, 72–3.
67. Ibid., 73–5.
68. Ibid., 74.
69. Ibid.
70. Ibid., 75.
71. Ibid., 89.
72. Ibid., 114.
73. Ibid., 82.
74. Ibid., 90–1.
75. Ibid., 90.
76. Ibid., 90–1.
77. Ibid., 89–90.
78. Ibid., 132.
79. Ibid., 111.
80. Ibid., 112.
81. Ibid., 297.
82. Ibid., 82.
83. Foucault, 'About the concept of the "dangerous individual" in nineteenth-century legal psychiatry', PPC, 127–8.
84. Foucault, ABN, 277.
85. Ibid., 87.
86. Ibid., 12. Foucault describes this as 'Ubu-esque', ibid., 28 n. 20.
87. Ibid., 15.
88. Ibid., 292.
89. Ibid., 293.
90. Ibid., 297.
91. Ibid., 301.
92. Ibid., 293.
93. Ibid., 296.
94. Ibid., 310.
95. Ibid., 311.
96. Ibid., 310.

97. Richard von Krafft-Ebing, *Psychopathia Sexualis: With Especial Reference to the Antipathic Sexual Instinct: A Medico-Forensic Study*, Franklin S. Klaf (trans. from 12th German edn, original 1st German edn published in 1886) (New York: Arcade Publishing, 1965), 369.

98. Ibid., 369. On the same page, Krafft-Ebing defines legal violation as 'the most horrible perversions and acts, which are possible only to a man who is a slave to lust and morally weak, and, as is usually the case, lacking in sexual power'.

99. Ibid., 371.

100. Ibid., 369.

101. Ibid., 370.

102. Ibid.

103. Ibid.

104. Philip Jenkins, *Moral Panic: Changing Concepts of the Child Molester in Modern America* (New Haven, CT: Yale University Press, 1998).

105. For a popular history of NAMBLA, see Benoit Denizet-Lewis, 'Boy crazy', *Boston Magazine* (May 2001), available at: http://www.bostonmagazine. com/articles/boy_crazy/ (last accessed 1 March 2012). The Paedophile Information Exchange (PIE) was a United Kingdom group founded in 1974 and ended in 1984. *Paidika: The Journal of Paedophilia* was published from 1987–95.

106. See Bernard E. Harcourt, *The Illusion of Free Markets: Punishment and the Myth of Natural Order* (Cambridge, MA: Harvard University Press, 2011). Harcourt's account draws attention to the changing meaning of 'nature' in discourses of order, including the rationalisation of the economy and the turn to markets to rationalise life. Foucault's statement that free markets are not natural but rather require order is a limited reading of the relation between nature and order (better explored by Harcourt).

107. Foucault, STP, 109.

108. Foucault, BOB, 116.

109. Ibid.

110. Ibid., 118–19.

111. Ibid., 120.

112. Ibid., 121.

113. Lisa Duggan, *The Twilight of Equality? Neo-Liberalism, Cultural Politics, and the Attack on Democracy* (Boston, MA: Beacon Press, 2003); David Harvey, *A Brief History of Neoliberalism* (Oxford: Oxford University Press, 2005); Nikolas Rose, *Powers of Freedom: Reframing Political Thought* (Cambridge: Cambridge University Press, 1999).

114. Foucault, ABN, 94.

115. Foucault, BOB, 20.

116. Ibid., 116.

117. Ibid., 188.

118. Ibid., 145.

119. Ibid.

120. Ibid., 149.

121. Ibid., 228.

122. Ibid.

123. Ibid., 143.

124. Ibid., 228.
125. Ibid., 252.
126. Foucault, SMD, 223.
127. Foucault, BOB, 269.
128. See Lauren Berlant, *The Queen of America Goes to Washington City: Essays on Sex and Citizenship* (Durham, NC: Duke University Press, 1997).
129. Foucault, SMD, 230.
130. Foucault, BOB, 272.
131. Nikolas Rose, *The Politics of Life Itself: Biomedicine, Power, and Subjectivity in the Twenty-First Century* (Princeton, NJ: Princeton University Press, 2006).
132. Foucault, BOB, 175.
133. Ibid., 150.
134. Andrew Vachss, 'How we can fight child abuse', *Parade* (20 August 1989).
135. Andrew Vachss, 'Today's victim could be tomorrow's predator', *Parade* (3 June 2000).
136. Andrew Vachss, 'The difference between "sick" and "evil"', *Parade* (14 July 2002).
137. Foucault, SMD, 271.
138. Ibid.
139. Harcourt, *The Illusion of Free Markets*, 46–7; again contesting such a static contrast of 'nature' to order.
140. See Pamela Haag, *Consent: Sexual Rights and the Transformation of American Liberalism* (Ithaca, NY: Cornell University Press, 1999).
141. See The Scottish Report on the Sexualisation of Young People 4.2, *Identities and Consumption*, available at: http://www.scottish.parliament.uk/s3/committees/equal/reports-10/eor10-02.html (last accessed 1 March 2012). My thanks to Robbie Duschinsky for drawing my attention to this report.
142. Foucault, 'Practising criticism', PPC, 155–6.
143. Foucault, SMD, 11.
144. Foucault, 'Practising criticism', PPC, 156.

Part II
Evaluations

5
Jacques Donzelot's *The Policing of Families* (1977) in Context

José Luis Moreno Pestaña

The Policing of Families (first published in French in 1977 [English edition, 1979]) is Jacques Donzelot's best-known book and a crucial point of reference in studies on the family, social work and social policy. Nikolas Rose has highly praised *The Policing of Families* as 'pathbreaking', and as 'the best account' of 'the whole range of technologies that were invented that would enable the family to do its public duty without destroying its private authority'.[1] The text stands in an interesting relationship with the analysis of the family in Foucault's Collège de France lectures, which the *History of Sexuality, Volume 1* only presents in brief. Donzelot's text has been available to Anglophone scholars for decades longer than Foucault's lectures, and has long appeared to stand as the Foucauldean paradigm on 'the family'. Jaimey Fisher, for instance, notes that 'Foucault's generalisations' in the *History of Sexuality, Volume 1* 'have been filled out to a large degree by Donzelot',[2] while Michael J. Shapiro states that 'to exemplify the Foucauldean discursive event, we can revisit Jacques Donzelot's Foucauldean history of modernity's emerging surveillance of the family'.[3]

Chris Philo has argued that '*The Policing of Families* represents a sustained out-working of themes from the *Psychiatric Power* and *Abnormal* lecture series.'[4] But rather than an 'out-working' of Foucault's lectures, *The Policing of Families* is perhaps best understood as a discursive act shaped by the interrelation between the academic, professional and political fields. This interaction between fields was also important for Foucault's work and its reception; Donzelot should be understood in terms of his positioning within the academic field, with Foucault as a predecessor. In its account of social work practice, *The Policing of Families* followed the tracks of Foucauldean theory of the relationship between psychiatry and the family. Yet, although Donzelot's work agrees with

Foucault's chronology of the family, it departs from his methodological caution regarding the need to trace differences and tensions in forms of normalisation rather than treat them as a totalising system. This chapter first proposes to reconstruct the field of discourses on social work in France after the political upheaval of May 1968. Jacques Donzelot is then situated, as a scholar, within his political, professional and intellectual generation. The last section is a critical analysis of *The Policing of Families* that examines the content of the book, its methodology and the philosophical assumptions on which Donzelot's analysis of the family rested.

The intellectual and professional vanguard

Before the 1970s, little specific expertise was needed to engage in social work in France. Social workers used 'culture' to mask the regulation of their clientele's morals behind scientific jargon. The appeal to the representatives of the 'noble' fields of knowledge was a mere pretext for legitimising the professionals' stance, as shown in Jeannine Verdès-Leroux's study that included a historical survey of the presentations by academics at the congresses of the Association Nationale des Assistants de Service Social (ANAS).[5] The interventions of the intellectuals in these congresses did not address the practice of social work and its problems. Intellectuals – normally linked to political powers and the institutional powers of the academic world – granted professionals a measure of neutrality and rigour; given their weaker academic backgrounds, professionals offered intellectuals a devoted, undemanding market that enhanced the speakers' social prestige.

After the upheavals of May 1968, social workers in the 1970s demanded new forms of theoretical discourse. More rigour was called for; in response to this demand, an important group of aspiring intellectuals produced new kinds of discourses. The recipients in the world of social work would use these discourses to stand out from their less innovative colleagues.[6] This situation was also reflected in issue 107 of *La Revue française de service social*. An anonymous article announced the 1974 congress in Versailles on 'Social Service and Political Life', and this indicated the conflicts that were buffeting professional life. A group of social workers apparently called the very foundations of social service into question during the 1972 congress in Toulouse, and at the congress in Strasbourg in the following year, a sociological perspective that was at once reflective and critical was demanded with respect to social work. And the 1974 congress in Versailles aimed to extend this self-flagellating dynamic, albeit always being careful that the critique was not too harsh. Discovering the ideological structures of professional practice, the sociologists insisted, ought not to be at odds with belief in the professionals' creativity.[7]

Yet, there were professional sectors that experienced the crisis as a personal, professional and intellectual opportunity. To a large extent, they constituted the 'home front' of revolt that had played a major role in triggering the crisis. According to Francine Muel-Dreyfus' characterisation, these professional sectors had properties that differentiated them from the more traditional sectors. Although choosing the profession of social work ran counter to family hopes of social advancement in more traditional sectors, a demographic of a young, male population from a more diverse social background entered the profession. They used the ambiguous areas of the social space – the barely encoded, easy-to-redefine areas – for a range of projects to reclassify the profession of social work that, until then, each professional could define according to his or her own resources.[8] In particular, an orientation towards critical discourses helped this population distance itself from the public's image of social work as a conservative female profession. Moreover, the number of social workers in France exploded during this period: there were 199,800 social workers in 1975, compared with 94,600 in 1968.[9] Under these conditions, an audience arose that was sensitive to the new discourses that questioned professional identity; the social conditions were met for a critical prophecy that broke with old, conservative moulds.[10]

Political activism, nourished and strong in the years after 1968, provided many young social workers with a series of 'improbable encounters' with representatives of the Parisian philosophical culture. A harsh critique commenced of how institutional work propagated social norms, and this was in line with the new orientations of a section of Parisian intellectuals – Michel Foucault, Gilles Deleuze and so forth. A Social Workers' Information Group (Groupe d'Information des Travailleurs Sociaux (GITS)) was established, in line with the model of Michel Foucault's Prison Information Group (Groupe d'Information sur les Prisons (GIP)). According to sociologist Michel Autès, May 1972 was a kind of 'May 1968' in social work.[11] Various conflicts with institutions shook up professional practice. In December 1971, Josette d'Escrivan, a social worker at the prison of Fresnes, raised the alarm about the poor sanitary conditions of a detained American citizen. D'Escrivan was dismissed from her post. In a letter published by *Esprit* addressed to the ANAS, the social worker referred to her professional obligations to defend her work. A whole range of conflicts in reformatories – in Nantes, in Caen, in the centre in l'Espélidou – attracted collective attention and stimulated professional activism.[12]

The term 'social work' referred to very different practices and practitioners: those working as specialised and kindergarten educators, social assistants, sociocultural motivators, family social workers, service staff. These professions had an array of tasks and enjoy different kinds of prestige. Those with more concrete obligations recruited staff from more humble social backgrounds and aimed their work at working-class populations. By contrast, the professions with more 'relational' tasks had more theoretical support and greater symbolic prestige and recruited agents from more varied social backgrounds.[13] 'Social work' served to describe a varied and poorly understood environment, denounced as the setting for practices of social control.[14] Yet this also made social work a legitimate subject of intellectual reflection, following an issue of *Esprit* magazine published in April–May 1972. Jacques Donzelot's *The Policing of Families* must be situated within this context.

The first generation of 'Foucauldeans': the specific intellectual, the activist and the theorist

Social work, or the group of professions that would be encompassed under that name, was a locus of activist participation in France after the events of May 1968. This section presents three profiles that enable us to understand the features of the different worlds that intersected and collaborated in the political project: this first was an agent who would begin to theorise about social work; the second, a professional who was a key actor of the process, but did not take advantage of it in order to find a different professional and intellectual scope; and the third was Jacques Donzelot himself, someone who had achieved major intellectual renown through the springboard of social work. It was a time, as Donzelot explained, in which being 'in the margins was not synonymous with exclusion, but rather opportunity'.[15]

Michel Chauvière: social work connects trajectories

Michel Chauvière, currently a directeur de recherche at the Centre national de la recherche scientifique (CNRS), was born in Laval in 1946 and graduated in psychopathology. 'Afterwards, I changed my perspective quite radically and realised I would never be a clinician, that I didn't like it.' He studied sociology and linguistics at Rennes. Chauvière arrived in Paris in 1970, because:

> I found a job as an instructor at a teaching college through a friend who had studied psychology. In short, because of contacts. But I was

not very involved in social work, not 100%. Through colleagues, I gave some courses at Paris VIII in Vincennes. I had one foot inside and one outside the university. At the teaching college, I was introduced to *Esprit* magazine and Philippe Meyer [who was close to Foucault at that time and a member of the GIP]. Yet, I was not Parisian, but rather very provincial. As Bourdieu later said about himself, I had that suspicious, provincial class neurosis, which was protective of all those Parisian intellectuals. Because Philippe Meyer and Jacques Donzelot were in their element in that environment, the environment of critical leftist Parisian intellectuals.[16]

The testimony of Chauvière, a contributor to the April–May 1972 issue of *Esprit*, was indicative of the conflicts that existed. On the one hand, Chauvière was working in an institution inspired by the personalist philosophy of *Esprit*'s founder Emmanuel Mounier. He then attempted to fashion a 'Marxist view of social work' that was mostly at odds with the incumbent paradigm of personal Christianity as the underpinning ethics of social work.[17] On the other hand, he was welcomed at *Esprit* – alongside Jacques Donzelot, Michel Foucault, Michel Meyer, Paul Virilio and others – to expound upon his critical view of social work. Reading this issue of *Esprit*, the coalition of leftist critics and progressive Catholics is not so surprising. The articles propose very few concrete analyses of professional reality and have the aroma of a global critique of civilisation that was able to serve as a meeting point for Catholics and leftists at that time.[18]

According to Chauvière, it was the place where 'the first generation of Foucauldeans' was consecrated. And this encounter between Michel Foucault and *Esprit* would have a significant impact on the French intellectual space. Young intellectuals inspired by Foucault such as Jacques Donzelot and Philippe Meyer greatly increased in the intellectual scene. In Chauvière's opinion:

> *Esprit* offered a space where anything could be said, things that would not be uttered in other areas. Social workers talked about their problems; then people such as Foucault and others who saw things from above attempted to define the nature of the issue of social work from the top down, but without knowing anything about what was actually happening. The two worlds were there: the people who came from above with all their theories of social control and the grassroots people. Yet, the conjunction between the two logics did not take place.[19]

Jean-Michel Courtois: a perfect audience for the 'great ones'

Jean-Michel Courtois was born in Poitiers. He was the son of a barber, who became the commercial director of a large company, and a Banque de France employee. Courtois studied at the Saint-Stanislas school ('a school that famous people such as Marshal Jean de Lattre de Tassigny and [...] Michel Foucault had attended'). Although Courtois was a very precocious reader, he had a difficult academic career. After some time in scouting, he secured a post at an observatory for young offenders. After four years of work during which he secured his diploma as an educator, he left Poitiers: 'I came to Paris in 1971. It was already the post-'68 period. I left in 1977 after a family, political and professional rupture.'[20]

Courtois was working as a street educator and founded the GITS. Its founding manifesto was published in the aforementioned 1972 issue of *Esprit* devoted to social work – in short, he was the model of conjunction between professional and activist practice and the vocation of a self-taught man.[21] Contact with the intellectual field allowed him to teach courses in Vincennes – at Jacques Donzelot's invitation – and to become the founder of *Champ Social*, an organ of critical leftist thought in social work:

> I put the people with whom I worked into the van and took them to hear Michel Foucault [...] He gave us a good deal of guidance on how to conceive social work differently and also how to apply it. Yet, we are the ones who must use his writings as a starting point for ascertaining what to extract from our own tradition.[22]

At the time of my interview with Jean-Michel Courtois in January 2002, he was still a creator of social work institutions and an active writer. During the existence of *Champ Social*, he wrote many articles in which he attempted to apply Foucault's 'toolbox' to social work. Like many self-taught people, Courtois despised academics as much as he appreciated the true 'haute' intellectual:

> I am especially proud of being self-taught. I love it when I come across an intellectual, a university graduate, and we start talking about general culture and the fellow has no idea of anything. It's a kind of bliss! Yet, at the same time, I was always attracted by great intellectuals, attracted if they are intellectuals in the Greek sense of the term. But with one condition: that they be great. At the same time that I have that admiration – because it cannot be expressed otherwise, that transference, those processes of identification, if you

like – for people like Foucault and Sartre, I have only contempt for everything academic.[23]

Jacques Donzelot: between sociology and critical philosophy

Jacques Donzelot's assessment later confirmed Michel Chauvière's description. For him, social work was a space of knowledge that fell short of his initial expectations. Regarding social work, he said:

> I knew nothing. Even now, I know nothing. The year 1972 was preceded by people like Foucault, the GIP and me. Deleuze was also involved. In 1969, I had begun working on a text about the birth of prisons based on *History of Madness*. Foucault took that problem off my hands. And he did it well, very well [...] My problem was somewhat like Foucault's, because I am not a sociologist! I am a historian and philosopher by training.[24] I began teaching sociology and found that object strange. What was the use of that discourse? Because there is a grouping that consists in sociology and social work; all this forms a magma, one sole ensemble. Which caused me to distance myself and made me yearn for theorising.[25]

After passing through the Centre d'études sociologique (which was influenced by American positivism), Donzelot, who was not at ease in that environment, was hired as an instructor at the Université de Paris VIII Vincennes à Saint-Denis through Daniel Defert. Given the difficulties of finding a space at that university, which he said was dominated by an alliance between sociologists who were Bourdieu's disciples and Althusser's disciples, Donzelot ended up at the University of Nanterre.[26] His doctoral thesis, 'La Police des familles', was supervised by Jean-Claude Passeron, who had begun to distance himself from Pierre Bourdieu in the early 1970s.[27] Passeron, who was personally very close to Foucault, described the atmosphere of militant leftism and its relationship to sociological research with this anecdote:

> Foucault, who had brought me with him to one of his political acts in 1971, one with the GIP (Groupe d'Information sur les Prisons), decided that a statistical analysis that he had extracted from encrypted documents his friends had stolen from the Ministry of Justice – and that, moreover, he found interesting as a measure of the opportunities for imprisonment depending on the offenders' social status and type of crime – would not have been good publicity for his line of intellectual ferment of opinion.[28]

In a text that was a homage to Robert Castel – a philosopher by training and a sociologist close to both Bourdieu and Foucault at the time – Donzelot said about himself:

> Robert was my initiator to a certain degree in the two domains that matter here: the university domain – since I became a university instructor in Vincennes in 1969 thanks to him – and the domain of written production, because he was the one who asked me for my first article [...] I was the leftist at Robert's service, the one who needled him by calling him a 'naive humanist'.[29]

Since the time of its establishment in February 1971, Donzelot was part of the GIP.[30] In Issue 12 of *Esprit* in 1972, Donzelot commented on Gilles Deleuze and Félix Guattari's *Anti-Oedipus* (2004 [1972]), citing Robert Castel's *Le Psychanalisme* (which was not published until 1973) and Jean Baudrillard's *For a Critique of the Political Economy of the Sign* (1972). Donzelot's comments display the same desire as these works to safeguard the philosopher's privilege over the social sciences, without impeding their practice by others. In his opinion, Deleuze and Guattari's book was an alternative to sociology that was incapable of conceiving marginal struggles and studying the problem of the state in all of its complexity.[31] According to Donzelot, Foucault privately had little regard for *Anti-Oedipus* and thanked him for being the one to review it: 'Foucault did not like *Anti-Oedipus* and told me so quite often.'[32] Deleuze would write a foreword to *The Policing of Families*; Foucault was disappointed by this because he thought that it was inappropriate for a recognised author to intervene with the work of a junior researcher.[33]

The professional space and its poles

To have an understanding of the audience that received the message of the 'critical intellectuals', it is worth discussing briefly the reactions of some of the social work professionals published in *Champ Social*, the journal founded by Jean-Michel Courtois. A reader, who signed as 'Social Worker since 1946', placed the entire discourse of social control in relation to certain difficult professional situations (prisons, hospitals, crime prevention, psychologists): 'I don't venture into that field, said the social worker, because I know of others where one can breathe.'[34] Despite its critical content, the letter confirmed the editors' cultural capital: 'Although I often dislike the vocabulary because it is too vulgar, the French is nonetheless perfect.'[35] Another reader wrote: 'It is a super-intellectualised journal. I have no dictionary large enough in order to read it.'[36]

Jean-Michel Courtois and the participants in GITS and *Champ Social* were the most receptive audience to the intellectuals' engagement with social work. The discourse on 'relationships of power' – a new symbolic asset compared with a Marxism that was regarded as simplistic – meant that each professional choice, even the most banal, was viewed as a political decision. Within such an account, social work was devoid of any logic of its own and was merely politics in disguise. It was impossible not to criticise social work if the aim was to produce a discourse of prestige, winning political capital. The following poles of discourses on social work in the field during the incipient period can thus be distinguished: on the one hand, the old professional world attempted to read in a technical mode the problems posed by the theoretical and professional vanguards. The oldest professional groups had been aware of the crisis for some time and turned to the social sciences to give them a new technical legitimacy. This turn towards the social sciences, Jacques Donzelot suggested, served to make social workers 'believe that people's problems have to do with professional knowledge rather than power'.[37] This pole's prestige was very weak at a time during which political capital was a condition of intellectual recognition, after 'leftism' became a driving force in the theoretical field. On the other hand, there was the discourse fashioned by young intellectuals – or activists who aspired to be like them – who specialised in rummaging the 'toolboxes' of renowned thinkers, especially Michel Foucault. This pole did not believe that the social scientists were promoting a solution to social problems.

A 'mutual admiration society' was established at the meeting point between activists and theorists: the 'philosophers engaged in the struggle' were consecrated, and they in turn consecrated 'specific intellectuals' who revealed the workings of power by adapting their daily reality to theoretical schemes.[38] From his viewpoint as a social worker, Jean-Yves Barreyre – the second and last director of *Champ Social* – believed that the symbolic exchange was experienced as follows:

> Activism will allow professionals to make a place for themselves; they attempt to theorise to provide an analysis of society. And they also completely selfishly attempt to find a place in the field of action and the field of concepts.[39]

Robert Castel represented another position in the debate, between the critical and technicist poles. There were two features of this position: first, it expressed itself in a language that was 'critical', yet committed to real social work; and second, this language could be assimilated by specialised journals and understood by their readers. Given the political criticism of their work, most social workers exercised their profession on the basis of a guilty conscience and excessive demands. Robert Castel recalls being invited along with a young analyst of social work to an audience of professionals who were harshly scolded by that young intellectual. Castel said:

> I was a little upset. I think they were fascinated by intellectual speculation, since their theory was non-existent and they tended to admire theory. They saw someone like Foucault and said that what he told them had to be true, because great men said so. Yet, they ended up realising that it was unfair. Specifically in social work, people did what they could. What they did was not always glorious, but they were generally people of good will.[40]

Castel's disgust at that hypercritical attitude was accompanied by a scathing critique of leftist excesses, which he clearly expressed in *Champ Social*: 'My analysis may not be very radical. Yet, if the psychiatrist is a "cop", why are there psychiatrists and "cops"? Social work is more finely divided and all practices are not identical.'[41]

As we have seen, therefore, there was no consensus among the new generations on the value of certain critical discourses. Some agreed with them and were the audience for the discourses that Foucault inspired. Others deemed them reductionist and too violent towards grassroots social workers. Robert Castel and others represented a third position, between these two poles. Donzelot's *The Policing of Families*, towards the critical pole of the professional field, followed the tracks of Foucauldean discourses.

A historical sociology of the family and social work

Whereas in *Abnormal*, the 1974–75 lectures at the Collège de France, Foucault explored the role of psychiatric power in the constitution of the family, Donzelot's project was to explore the role played by social work. Yet, Foucault's *Abnormal* and Donzelot's *The Policing of Families* have much in common. First, both of them are studies of the transition between two forms of the family, which Donzelot would describe as the passage from a 'government of the family' to a 'government through the family'.[42] In the ancien régime, the head of the family ruled the family financially (controlling children's work) and socially (through marriage alliances) in order to safeguard the family honour (for which it would resort to the state in times of difficulty, for example when an illegitimate child was born or when denouncing a child's improper behaviour). At the same time, the head of the household was ruled by higher hierarchical structures and had to respond to them regarding his family's behaviour. Yet, this regime would enter into a crisis. Foucault and Donzelot both argued that during the seventeenth century, philanthropy attempted to contain illegitimate children because of the large public expenditure that they entailed. Professional expertise and philanthropy provided home aid for families in need, coupled with an investigation into the reality of their needs.[43] Working-class families were subjected to inspection and tighter control.

These professional and philanthropic interventions found an essential support from women, whose role within the family they attempted to strengthen. Many women were sent to convents to prevent them from sullying the family honour. Philanthropy attempted to bring them back home. An alliance was forged between feminism and philanthropy, of which its overriding objective was to control working-class customs. In the second half of the nineteenth century, the two attempted to extricate men from the bar culture. Armed with medical legitimacy, bourgeois women rushed to moralise the lives of working-class women, who were held responsible for ensuring that their husbands and children remained at home, a home that would be consolidated by single-family housing imposed on working families in order to control political insubordination through an orderly life.[44]

Donzelot argued that during the nineteenth century, physicians, in competition with priests, attempted to manage family sexuality in the name of science. One pole of medical discourse situated the family as an instrument of population growth to serve the needs of imperialism; the other progressive pole supported abortion and contraception, in line with the discourses of socialists and feminists.[45] The futuristic speculation of Dr Ernest Tarbouriech, who imagined a society supervised by medical science in *La Cité future* (1902), allowed Donzelot to accuse the progressive pole of totalitarianism. At that time, in the mid 1970s, the assimilation of socialism and fascism was becoming fashionable among many French intellectuals, which Foucault's 1975–76 Collège de France lectures *Society Must Be Defended* demonstrated.[46] According to Foucault, socialism has not resorted to racism, in that it has been limited to seeking economic transformations. Yet, each time that socialism has framed the class struggle as the elimination of an adversary, it has slid towards racism.[47] In keeping with the 'anti-totalitarian' turn of many French leftists, Donzelot combined conservative and progressive currents and conceptualised them as two permutations of a single totalitarian enterprise.[48] From a limited sample of writings, Donzelot concluded that:

> The maintenance of a strong family structure and the preservation of social privileges went by way of *social fascism*, while the dissolution of organic moorings and the social and medical annulment of inequalities were manifested in a *social-sector fascism*.[49]

Foucault and Donzelot agreed that these professional and philanthropic interventions had two components. The first component was a *welfare apparatus*. Within this welfare apparatus, for example, counselling served to privatise social problems by turning them into the responsibility of those affected; the promotion of individual savings was also used to ensure individuals' autonomy against the state and charities. The second component was a *medical-hygienist apparatus* that would regulate working-class birth rates and introduce norms of civilised life, sustained by children and women. Public schools, in competition with religious schools (in the same way that philanthropy competed with Christian charity), were the core of a series of laws to protect the public health of housing or children. Donzelot considered them invariably tools to destroy autonomous working-class culture: if mothers were recognised as having the right to say whether their child was going to reform school or not (previously, the father's consent sufficed), it was in order for them to confront fathers and allow for greater administrative intervention in controlling children. The promotion of marriage among workers would allow them to adapt to the demands of a decent, industrious life. Within marriage, Foucault explained, activity in the name of the prevention of incest allowed family behaviours to be medically regulated.[50] Mobilising subjects against patriarchal power, allowing divorce and meeting the needs of women and children all justified outside intervention in the family. Donzelot considered that the family, subjected to academic, health and welfare mechanisms, lost its autonomy:

> A wonderful mechanism, since it enables the social body to deal with marginality through a near-total dispossession of private rights and to encourage positive integration, the renunciation of the question of political right, through the private pursuit of well-being.[51]

Thus, Foucault and Donzelot share two assumptions in their analyses. On the one hand, they regard the family as a space of intervention for various social institutions. To Donzelot and Foucault, the family is a privileged place for modulating individuals' most private behaviour and in this sense, for controlling the forms of family within a social formation; it is a basic issue for political order. This control assumes the family's relationship with different socialisation systems: Foucault in *Abnormal* especially emphasises the relationship within the psychiatric apparatus, while Donzelot shows the family's relationship with social work institutions. Donzelot's ethnographical work allows him to construct more closely fitted typologies of the relationship between families and institutions. On the other hand, Foucault and Donzelot insisted on family autonomy towards these systems and apparatuses. This autonomy allows for forms of resistance to the institutions. This resistance does not have an explicit political formulation, but it is fundamental to the stability of the social order. In this sense, understanding the action towards the family and the bourgeois or proletarian forms of family towards the institutions is a basic political issue.

An ethnography of social work

Following an analysis on these changes in the family considered above, Donzelot's book focused on social workers. Donzelot set himself against discourses that positioned social work as a progressive, scientific response to social problems. Yet he also argued against those forms of critical discourse that reduced social work to an instrument that represses deviant behaviour, equivalent to the judicial system. While firmly at the critical pole of academic discourse, Donzelot followed Foucault in attempting to analyse the specific forms of power operating within social work discourse and practice. In 1977, Foucault would give an elegy of Donzelot's work:

[Donzelot] shows how the absolutely specific forms of power exerted within the family have been penetrated, as a result of the development and expansion of the school system, by more general mechanisms of State power, but also how State and familial forms of power have each retained their specificity and have only been able to interlock so long as the specific ways in which they each operate have been respected.[52]

Donzelot developed an ethnography in the cities of Lille, Valenciennes and Bobigny, exploring social work professional practice. He turned his attentions to the institution of the juvenile court. Donzelot set out to show that it had little to do with the operation of legal justice, which was not applicable to minors. Instead, the evaluation of risks posed by minors replaced the application of legal sentences, and individuals were evaluated for what they were and not by what they did. Who could appeal sentences that were tempered by the judge? How could one resist the normalising authorities that evaluate daily behaviour?[53] To illustrate his findings, Donzelot resorted to a single case – which presumably had exemplary value – that narrated the measures taken against an individual who had clearly not committed any crime or there was reasonable doubt as to whether the individual committed a crime. The fourteen-year-old adolescent could have been acquitted and in not being so, Donzelot believed that this proved that justice was essentially normalising.[54] I shall return to this particular use of ethnography, which manifests the hyper-politicised critical view of social work to which I referred earlier.

Social work institutions fundamentally serve to achieve normalising outcomes, according to Donzelot. A crucial part of this operation is through the classification of service-users. First, the social inquiry is an 'inquisitorial' type of knowledge that attempts to monitor complaints from the family.[55] The social inquiry endeavoured to control all the knowledge about the family that existed in social, educational or prison administrations. Thereafter, the family members are 'interrogated' separately and the different versions contrasted. Finally, home visits allow for verification of precisely how the family lives: 'A technique that mobilises a minimum of coercion to obtain a maximum of verified information.'[56]

The social investigation must generally be supplemented by a medical diagnosis. Child psychiatry aims to identify a child's future adult pathologies. In the nineteenth century, school became the favourite place to identify children with 'problems'. Later, psychiatry would penetrate juvenile justice, but at the cost of modifying its own theoretical discourse. Psychiatry, which formerly classified children rigidly as ill or well, ended up with the idea that they could be changed through education. Psychiatrists focused on disorders that come from the environment, forgetting the notion of the perverse, incurable child. The category of 'maladjusted children', which groups together children with welfare problems (poverty, abandonment and so on) and those with judicial problems (young offenders), is related to the increasing presence of psychoanalysis in psychiatric practice. Social workers were to identify 'families at risk'. The notion of risk assumed that opportunities for deviant behaviour could be predicted within a given set of correlations – violence and social background, crime and dropping out of school – and allowed the normalising intervention to be modulated with more or less educational or coercive measures.

Critique of a methodology

Jean-Claude Passeron was the supervisor of Jacques Donzelot's thesis, on which *The Policing of Families* was based. Passeron went on to use Donzelot's work as an example of the idyllic interpretation of working-class cultures, which turned family poverty and unhealthiness into a symbol of autonomous working-class life. According to him, this is a sterile sociological model that ignores the fact that marginalised and dominated cultures idealise their conditions of existence – and in this sense, they are *counter-cultures* – yet at the cost of concealing how much of it is due to deprivation and domination and in that sense, they are *subcultures*.[57] Pierre Bourdieu stated that *The Policing of Families*:

> brings together all the conditions for high symbolic yield on the market of cultural products: the incessant to-and-fro between complicitous references to the present – tending to produce the effect of a 'radical critique' – and disconnected, decontextualised references to the past – tending to lend an air of 'scholarship' – and the consequent confusion of demands dispenses the author both from any systematic inquiry into the present.[58]

Criticising Donzelot's theoretical narrative, Bourdieu asserts that:

> to ground the objectivist overview which completely evacuates study of the agents [...] one only has to hand over to that kind of negative finalism which reduces history to the mechanical process of timeless, impersonal agencies with allegorical names [...] [such as] 'the judicial, the psychiatric, and the educative.[59]

A true history, Bourdieu argued, would begin 'by resituating institutions and practices in the system from which they receive their meaning and their sociological necessity, would constitute the past as past and nullify the object of retrospective indignation'.[60]

My critique here is less severe. Jacques Donzelot's work, which combines historical research in the archives and an ethnography, is the pioneer of a model for fashioning a sociological history of social work. Through empirical surveys, Donzelot's work develops, in the only concrete way possible, the requirement of studying the effective functioning of the relationships of power and their link to forms of knowledge. Thanks to this perspective, Donzelot shows how certain apparently technical solutions to social problems are in fact solutions based on complex political relationships. For example, the turning cradle in which children born of illegitimate unions were deposited could only operate within the framework of the strategic relationships that linked the state and the families in the ancien régime. Families did not want to besmirch their honour; the state did not want to lose its strength and population. The turning cradle, which preserved children and obliterated any trace of their origin, was a perfect solution. Another example – working-class housing – helps us grasp how urban transformation involved complex industrial and familial policies. Lastly, *The Policing of Families* provides an interesting principle of the sociology of knowledge, which arises from discussions on science and ideology: 'To understand the social fortune of a knowledge [*un savoir*], one has to locate the reasons favouring its acceptance, find the existing link between its discursive properties and the problems posed by the functioning of institutions.'[61]

However, it is true that *The Policing of Families* leaves much to be desired at the ethnographic level. First, the devices analysed are described without examining how agents put them into practice. Donzelot's social workers have no biography or customs, or the capacity for surprise and the modification of the structures: they simply act within the power systems that employ them. This is an intellectual problem that is more understandable when working on historical records since records on how agents relate to their functions are sometimes missing – but not in an ethnography. Donzelot does not describe even one social worker beyond a random picturesque detail such as the fact that educators in juvenile court sported beards to look more serious and mask their facial expressions.[62] Why does Donzelot not tell us anything more about them, for instance about their academic careers or family backgrounds? Because he is only interested in what serves their normalising function, such that educators are simply the 'manifestation of the tutelary agencies in the lives of young people'.[63] Donzelot's description of psychological services plays with the same rhetoric: as if from one example, we could read the characteristics of the whole; in short, as if the systems analysed were the expression of one sole logic that would be imposed on all agents. Of course, any description handpicks some aspects that describe and others that do not. Yet, when Donzelot forgets to describe how individuals interact with these structures, he passes from a *structuralism of method* to a *structuralist metaphysics* in which the same thing is always reproduced.[64]

This conversion of reality into a monolithic logic ends up distorting the historical narrative by the very worst form of functionalism. X's contribution to the Y dynamic becomes X's (hidden) *raison d'être*. If attempts are made to diminish parental authority, it is to extend social control over the family; if social workers try to act through agreements, they are attempting to *seduce* and *entice* families.[65] If the juvenile justice system modulates sentences for minors, it appears to be expanding a totalitarian normalising control over emergent subjects. Donzelot's attempt to follow Foucault in exploring the specific form of power of social work, rather than treating all state institutions as operating the same form of normalisation, is so unsuccessful that it has not even been noticed by commentators. At times, the argument surreptitiously approximates two different realities that, unfortunately, coincide in some points. As we have seen, population control is identified with fascism and socialism or anarchist feminism and Malthusianism.[66] Or, since psychoanalysis preserves the family, it appears to extend part of the work of Philippe Pétain, the Chief of State of Vichy France.[67] It is never clear whether these are unwanted effects, the results of complex strategies guided by coincidences, or random intentions transformed by Donzelot's imagination into continuities.

At times, the interpretation clearly raises ethical and epistemological problems. Bourdieu spoke of the general contempt for social workers: indeed, although they help children whose parents are in prison or protect girls who suffer sexual violence, they cannot expect any positive justification for their work, still described as simply 'normalising'.[68] The symbolic violence of intellectuals with respect to social workers, which Robert Castel addressed, is evident. To Donzelot, liberty is the absence of state intervention and in this sense Passeron was absolutely right in saying that with all this, Donzelot idealised misery and violence as if they stood for some kind of popular autonomy. In his next work, Donzelot himself would level a radical critique of such philosophical assumptions – ironically without ever acknowledging that he had held the same assumptions in *The Policing of Families*.[69] These assumptions rest on the belief that the sovereign freedom of subjects is the condition of institutions, and that when they interfere with these subjects, these institutions automatically become illegitimate. This is what Isaiah Berlin called 'negative liberty'. Thus the existence of forms of interference in the lives of subjects that enhance and do not diminish their freedom – in short that improve their capabilities – is ignored.[70] We need theoretical work that is critical but committed to real social work, navigating in reflexive awareness of the tendency of the sociology of social work towards either a critical or a technicist pole. And, like the research of Robert Castel, this work should be available to social work journals and their readers. For from this perspective, new tools could be created for understanding, evaluating and supporting the operation of social work. Yet, in this analysis, Jacques Donzelot would still have much to teach us.

Notes

The text was written as part of R+D project FFI2010-15196. It was translated from Spanish by Judith Glueck.

1. Nikolas Rose, *Powers of Freedom: Reframing Political Thought* (Cambridge: Cambridge University Press, 1999), 74.
2. Jaimey Fisher, *Disciplining Germany: Youth, Re-education, and Reconstruction After the Second World War* (Detroit, MI: Wayne State University Press, 2007), 279.
3. Michael J. Shapiro, *For Moral Ambiguity: National Culture and the Politics of the Family* (Minneapolis, MN: University of Minnesota Press, 2001), 175.
4. Chris Philo, 'Foucault's children', in Louise Holt (ed.), *Geographies of Children, Youth and Families: An International Perspective* (London: Routledge, 2011), 48.
5. Jeannine Verdès-Leroux, *Le Travail social* (Paris: Minuit, 1978), 68–82.
6. This situation was described by Jacques Donzelot in one of his first articles: a social worker appeared at the university to study the elemental structures of kinship in marginal neighbourhoods. See Jacques Donzelot, 'Travail social et lutte politique', *Esprit*, 4–5 (1972), 654–73, reprinted in Philippe Meyer (ed.), *Normalisation et contrôle social (pourquoi le travail social?)* (Paris: Seuil, 1976), 99–120.
7. See the articles in *La Revue français de service social*, 107 (1973); Verdès-Leroux, *Le Travail social*, 82.
8. Francine Muel-Dreyfus, *Le Métier d'éducateur: Les instituteurs de 1900, les éducateurs spécialisés de 1968* (Paris: Minut, 1983), 145–98.
9. Murielle Monrose, 'Une lecture statistique de l'histoire des travailleurs sociaux', in Jean-Noël Chopart (ed.), *Les Mutations du travail social: Dynamiques d'un champ professionnel* (Paris: Dunod, 2000), 13–21 at 17.
10. Cf. Pierre Bourdieu, *The Rules of Art: Genesis and Structure of the Literary Field*, Susan Emanuel (trans.) (Stanford, CA: Stanford University Press, 1996), 380 n. 54 on the demand of 'prophecy': 'A more complete understanding of the "Sartre effect" would require an analysis of the social conditions of the appearance of the social demand for a prophecy for intellectuals: conjunctural conditions, such as the experiences of rupture, tragedy and anguish associated with the collective and individual crises produced by the war (the Occupation, the Resistance and the Liberation); structural conditions, such

as the existence of an autonomous intellectual field endowed with its own institutions of reproduction (the École Normale Supérieure) and legitimation (journals, circles, publishers, academies, etc.), and hence able to sustain the independent existence of an "aristocracy of intelligence" which was separated from power, if not against all powers, and able to impose and sanction a particular definition of intellectual accomplishment.'

11. Michel Autès, *Les Paradoxes du travail social* (Paris: Dunod, 1999), 49.
12. Josette d'Escrivan, 'Peut-on ne pas dénoncer l'inacceptable?' *Esprit*, 4–5 (1972), 33–7. See also Autès, *Les Paradoxes du travail social*, 51 and José Luis Moreno Pestaña, *Foucault, la gauche et la politique* (Paris: Textuel, 2011), 81–6.
13. See Verdès-Leroux, *Le Travail social*, 142. On the imposition of the label 'social work', as of the 1972 issue of *Esprit*, see Robert Castel, 'Du travail social à la gestion sociale du non-travail', *Esprit*, 3–4 (1988), 28–47.
14. Autès, *Les Paradoxes du travail social*, 50.
15. Jacques Donzelot, 'Devenir sociologue en 1968: Petite topographie physique et morale de la sociologie en ce temps-là', *Esprit*, 344 (2008): 47–53 at 50.
16. Author's interview with Michel Chauvière, February 2002.
17. Anne Bessaguet, Michel Chauvière and Annick Ohayon, *Les socio-clercs: Bienfaisance ou travail social* (Paris: Maspero, 1976), 30.
18. On the conflicts in the conception of the work by the GIP between the Christian factions (*Esprit* and those tending towards reformism) and the young activists associated with Michel Foucault, see Daniel Defert, 'L'émergence d'un nouveau front: les prisons', in Philippe Artières, Laurent Quéro and Michelle Zancarini-Fournel (eds), *Le Groupe d'information sur les prisons: Archives d'une lutte, 1970–1972* (Paris: Éditions de l'IMEC, 2003), 315–26 at 321.
19. Author's interview with Michel Chauvière, February 2002.
20. Author's interview with Jean-Michel Courtois, January 2002.
21. Every symbolic message adapts to an audience – always with peculiar properties – to which it provides a certain response to its specific needs for meaning. See Jean-Claude Passeron, 'Le sociologue en politique et *vice versa*: Enquêtes sociologiques et réformes pédagogiques dans les années 1960', in Jacques Bouveresse and Daniel Roche (eds), *La Liberté par la connaissance: Pierre Bourdieu (1930–2002)* (Paris: Odile Jacob, 2004), 15–104 at 38. On the mutual adaptation of demand and the production of discourses between theoreticians and recipients of the theories of social control, see Robert Castel, 'De l'intégration sociale à l'éclatement du social: l'émergence, l'apogée et le départ à la retraite du contrôle social,' *Revue internationale d'action communautaire*, 20 (1988), 67–78 at 74.
22. Author's interview with Jean-Michel Courtois, January 2002.
23. Ibid.
24. In his own words, Donzelot was studying history, but was attracted by Foucault's philosophy and studied under Raymond Aron at the Sorbonne. See Donzelot, 'Devenir sociologue en 1968', 48.
25. Author's interview with Jacques Donzelot, February 2002.
26. Donzelot, 'Devenir sociologue en 1968', 50–1.
27. François Dosse, *Gilles Deleuze and Félix Guattari: Intersecting Lives*, Deborah Glassman (trans.) (New York: Columbia University Press, 2011), 311.

28. Raymond Moulin and Paul Veyne, 'Entretien avec Jean-Claude Passeron: Un itinéraire de sociologue', *Revue européenne des sciences socials*, 34 (1996), 275–354 at 303.

29. Christian Bachmann, *Autour de Robert Castel* (Paris: Cedias-Musée Social, 1992), 12.

30. Philippe Artières, Laurent Quéro and Michelle Zancarini-Fournel (eds), *Le Groupe d'information sur les prisons*, 30.

31. Jacques Donzelot, 'Une anti-sociologie', *Esprit*, 12 (1972), 835–55.

32. Dosse, *Gilles Deleuze and Félix Guattari*, 316.

33. Ibid., 311.

34. Letter printed in *Champ Social*, 8 (1974), 4.

35. Ibid.

36. Letter printed in *Champ Social*, 21 (1976), section 'Débat sur les luttes'.

37. Donzelot, 'Travail social et lutte politique', reprinted in Meyer (ed.), *Normalisation et contrôle social*, 99–120 at 108–9.

38. See Pierre Bourdieu, 'Champ intellectuel et projet créateur,' *Les Temps modernes*, 246 (1966), 865–906 at 872.

39. Author's interview with Jean-Yves Barreyre, January 2002.

40. Author's interview with Robert Castel, February 2002.

41. Robert Castel, '*Champ Social* a rencontré Robert Castel', *Champ Social*, 21 (1976), 4–5 at 5.

42. See Jacques Donzelot, *The Policing of Families*, Robert Hurley (trans.) (Baltimore, MD: Johns Hopkins University Press, 1979 [first published in French in 1977]), 48–95, section entitled 'Government through the family'.

43. Ibid., 33–4.

44. Ibid., 34–6.

45. Ibid., 181.

46. See the final lecture in Foucault, SMD, 239–64.

47. On this question, see Moreno Pestaña, *Foucault, la gauche et la politique*, 104–7. Donzelot would go on and theorise totalitarian, Bolshevik and fascist unity in his next work, published in 1984, conceived as a settling of scores with the leftism to which he belonged. See Jacques Donzelot, *L'Invention du social: Essai sur le déclin des passions politiques* (Paris: Seuil, 1984). On the ideological shift of Foucault's circle: Jacques Donzelot, 'Misère de la culture politique', *Critique*, 34 (1978), 572–86, available at: http://donzelot.org/articles/Misere%20de%20la%20culture%20politique.pdf (last accessed 1 March 2012); Jacques Donzelot, 'À propos de la gouvernmentalité: Une discussion avec Colin Gordon' (2005), available at: http://donzelot.org/articles/gouvernementalitecolingordon.pdf (last accessed 1 March 2012).

48. See Michael Scott Christofferson, *French Intellectuals Against the Left: The Anti-Totalitarian Moment of the 1970s* (Oxford: Berghahn Books, 2004), 184–228.

49. Donzelot, *The Policing of Families*, 187.

50. Foucault, ABN, 269–71.

51. Donzelot, *The Policing of Families*, 94.

52. See Foucault, 'Les rapports de pouvoir passent à l'intérieur du corps', DE2, 228–36 at 233. In the course summary of *Psychiatric Power*, Foucault's lecture series at the Collège de France for the 1973–74 academic year, Foucault demanded an 'ethno-epistemology', an account of the figure of the physician in his specificity that would take into consideration both his knowledge

and the way in which it was reflected in his daily activities (in his body, relationships with patients and professional work), Foucault, PSP, 337.

53. Donzelot, *The Policing of Families*, 111.
54. Ibid., 115.
55. Ibid., 117.
56. Ibid., 124.
57. Claude Grignon and Jean-Claude Passeron, *Le Savant et le populaire: Misérabilisme et populisme en sociologie et en littérature* (Paris: Gallimard, 1989), 93.
58. Pierre Bourdieu, *The Bachelors' Ball: The Crisis of Peasant Society in Béarn*, Richard Nice (trans.) (Cambridge: Polity, 2008), 196.
59. Ibid., citing Donzelot, *The Policing of Families*, 99.
60. Bourdieu, *The Bachelors' Ball*, 196.
61. Donzelot, *The Policing of Families*, 135–6. This is a creative appropriation of Foucault's proposals in *Archaeology of Knowledge*.
62. Donzelot, *The Policing of Families*, 102.
63. Ibid.
64. Jean-Claude Passeron, *Le Raisonnement sociologique: Un espace non poppérien de l'argumentation* (Paris: Albin Michel, 2006), 306.
65. Donzelot, *The Policing of Families*, 90.
66. Ibid., 174–5. For Donzelot, 'the construction (or the historical reconstruction) of the policing discourse coincided perfectly with historical reality. I wonder whether anything could be further removed from Foucault's own convictions in that matter.' See Willem Frijhoff, 'Foucault reformed by Certeau', in John Neubauer (ed.), *Cultural History after Foucault* (New York: Walter de Gruyter, 1999), 83–91.
67. Donzelot, *The Policing of Families*, 197–8.
68. Bourdieu, *The Batchelors' Ball*, 195.
69. Donzelot, *L'Invention du social*, 118 and 240–2.
70. Philip Pettit, *Republicanism: A Theory of Freedom and Government* (Oxford: Oxford University Press, 1997), 51–80.

6
Gender, Reproductive Politics and the Liberal State:
Beyond Foucault

Véronique Mottier

In this chapter, I shall explore some of the ways in which Foucault's theorisation of sexuality and power thematised the family, especially through the concept of biopower developed in his later thought. In doing so, I shall move away from a focus on the family itself, to shift the analysis instead to family politics. More precisely, I propose to reflect upon Foucault's ideas on biopower and sexuality in the context of a specific area of politics of the family in modern liberal states: eugenic policy-making, which aimed at improving the biological 'quality' of the national population.

I do not wish to suggest that eugenic state intervention was particularly representative of family policy more generally. Rather, I shall deliberately focus on some of the most extreme practices of state intervention in citizens' bodies and subjectivities in the history of modern liberal states as a way of exploring what the social theorist Zygmunt Bauman (in characteristically Foucauldean overtones) would call the 'dark side' of Western liberal states. I shall thus draw on a few historical examples of eugenic practices in various Western countries (1920s–1960s) as a basis for highlighting the role of the state in regulating and policing the reproductive sexualities, sexual practices, sexual identities and future families of its citizens. In doing so, I shall both draw upon Foucault and attempt to go beyond some of the blind spots in his work. Among these blind spots, I shall point in particular to his under-theorisation of the gendered nature of biopower and his relative lack of interest in the institutional design of the modern state. In contrast, this chapter will emphasise the importance of gender for exploring the complex links between gender, reproductive politics and the liberal state. It will also suggest that the notion of the state itself needs conceptual unpacking, if we wish to grasp the subtle ways in which biopower operates in particular domains. In other words, I shall argue that gender matters in the analysis of the power relations linking the normative family to the state, as does the architecture of state institutions.

Biopolitics and the liberal state

In the closing chapter of the first volume of *History of Sexuality* (first published in French in 1976), titled 'Right of Death and Power over Life', Foucault revisited the central argument of the book that had immediately preceded it, *Discipline and Punish*. Published just a year earlier in 1975, *Discipline and Punish* had been a *succès de scandale*, triggering public acclaim as well as outrage. Its provocative central thesis questioned the liberal achievements of modern society, arguing that the exercise of power had undergone a fundamental shift in the transition from pre-modern to modern society that should not be seen as a history of ever-greater individual freedom, as depicted by conventional Enlightenment narratives of progress, but rather, as the rise of ever more pervasive techniques of surveillance and disciplinarisation of citizens. Through a rather sketchy history of punishment and prison reforms in the West (especially in France), Foucault developed an analysis (in his own words, 'analytics') of power, which influentially depicted modern forms of power as omnipresent, decentralised and targeting citizens' bodies as well as their minds. This contrasted with the workings of power until the late eighteenth century, Foucault argued, when power remained strongly concentrated in the figure of the sovereign. The latter had absolute power over his or her subjects, including that of putting them to death. The public torture and execution of subjects who had committed crimes (especially of *lèse-majesté*) thus served, Foucault suggested, to display the sovereign's absolute power over their subjects.

The final chapter of *History of Sexuality, Volume 1* returned to this idea of the pre-modern sovereign having power of life and death over his or her subjects to make a somewhat different point about modern forms of power. The latter, Foucault wrote, rests upon the capacity to 'manage life'. 'The ancient right to *take* life or *let* live', he wrote, 'was replaced by a power to *make* live or to throw life back into death.'[1] This power over the biological properties of the population developed, Foucault argued, along two poles: first, that of an 'anatomo-politics of the human body', which involved the disciplinary powers that turn individuals into well-trained, obedient, docile bodies. However, to this first form of power, which had been the central theme of *Discipline and Punish*, Foucault now added a second type that, he suggested, emerged a little later than disciplinary power, around the middle of the eighteenth century: a 'biopolitics of the population', which targets the 'human species' and involves the regulation of features of the national body such as its health levels or birth rates. Whereas disciplinary power operates in an individualising way, 'biopolitics' produces population policies that manage collective levels of migration, public health or birth rates. The twin rise of these two types of modern power signalled the advent of 'the age of biopower', as Foucault put it; when 'life entered history', or more precisely, when the management of the biological properties of the population became part of the field of new political technologies deployed by social institutions including the family (as well as the army, schools, the police, medicine and public administration).[2] The two types of power at first emerged independently from each other and in different domains of social life. By the nineteenth century, however, they came to be intertwined in concrete deployments of power – especially within the domain of sexuality, which Foucault considered as one of its most important deployments (dispositifs).[3]

Foucault had tried out the notions of biopower or biopolitics for the first time in the 1975–76 Collège de France lecture series *Society Must Be Defended*, specifically in the 10 March 1976 lecture,[4] reusing the concepts in the first volume of *History of Sexuality* that came out that same year. Initially and rather unhelpfully, he defined biopolitics in *History of Sexuality, Volume 1* in only the vaguest of terms, as 'what brought life and its mechanisms into the realm of explicit calculations and made knowledge-power an agent of transformation of human life'.[5] After a sabbatical year (1976–77) in which he did not give any lectures at the Collège de France, Foucault had planned to flesh out further the theme of biopolitics in his lectures for the 1977–78 academic year, as he suggested in his two opening lectures that year. However, he rapidly shifted the focus to an analysis of the changing nature of forms of governmental techniques instead.

More precisely, Foucault further developed the argument (already raised in *Discipline and Punish*) that the modern state twins the exercise of disciplinary power with relations of care for its citizens. On the one hand, modern disciplinary techniques, including mechanisms of surveillance and normalisation within state and para-state institutions such as educational establishments and prisons, aim to produce orderly and docile subjects. On the other hand, the population is cared for and protected by new welfare policies, which in turn involve both relations of care and the establishment of further technologies of scrutiny, surveillance and disciplinarisation, Foucault argued. These modern techniques of government, which Foucault came to call 'governmentality' in the course of his 1977–78 Collège de France lectures, however, are not limited to action by the governmental structures of the central state.[6] They include, more generally, all ways of directing and regulating the conduct of citizens, as he was putting it in his lectures by the spring of 1979, thereby further stretching the concept of governmentality.

In his 1977–78 lectures, *Security, Territory, Population*, Foucault came to argue that an understanding of biopolitics required an exploration of modern governmentality since the eighteenth century. Whereas his 1977–78 lectures thus got sidetracked from their intended focus on bio-politics to analyses of governmental techniques and relations of pastoral care of citizens since the early centuries of Christianity, he announced to the audience of his first lecture of *The Birth of Biopolitics* (1978–79) that that year's programme would renew the focus on the theme of biopolitics.[7] However, he went on to echo the argument of his 1977–78 lectures that the analysis of biopolitics needed to be pursued against the backdrop of a wider account of modern 'governmental reason'.[8] Given the importance of liberalism in particular in shaping modern forms of governmentality, Foucault now argued that an account of liberalism and its relationship to the state was particularly crucial for the under-standing of biopolitics. Consequently, he would start with liberalism 'for some weeks' before reaching the theme of biopolitics.[9] In the end, Foucault again never quite got around to the theme of biopolitics that year. Instead, he spent most of the year discussing two particularly influential versions of neoliberalism in the twentieth century: German Ordo-liberalism (1948–62), and the American neoliberalism developed by the Chicago School. More precisely, his lectures focused not on the ideology of neoliberalism as such, but rather, explored neoliberalism as a set of techniques of government, founded on an ideologically driven hostility towards the state.

The 1979 lectures on different strands of neoliberalism are remark-able, in that they represent the only moment in all of his lectures at the Collège de France in which he focused on themes in recent twentieth-century history.[10] They demonstrate the importance of the theme of governmentality to Foucault's later thought, but also, I would argue, operate an important break with his earlier analytical neglect of the state. Indeed, neither *Discipline and Punish*, nor *History of Sexuality* paid sustained analytical attention to the role of the state in the workings of disciplinary or biopower, a flaw for which his work had been severely criticised. To the extent that the state appears at all, it is in scattered comments, for example when Foucault refers in the most general of terms to the *'étatisation illimitée'* (unrestricted state control) of the ever-expanding reach of micro-powers into the most intimate relations of private life in Nazi Germany in the context of eugenic ordering of society by the Nazi regime, towards the end of *History of Sexuality, Volume 1*.[11] In contrast, Foucault's lectures on liberalism were meant to act as a foundation for exploring the ways in which micro-powers operate in the context of regimes of power that, in contrast to totalitarian regimes, are characterised instead by the explicit desire to limit the scope of state intervention in citizens' lives, while at the same time targeting citizens and their bodies as objects of biopolitical interventions. And yet, by the time that this foundation had been laid, Foucault's lectures and writings again shifted the focus away from biopolitics, to explore instead the notion of 'governing oneself', the relationship of individuals to themselves and to others: themes that would run through his lectures of the early 1980s, and would also constitute the central theme of his final books, *History of Sexuality, Volume 2* and *Volume 3* (both first published in French in 1984). Against this backdrop, and despite the repeated invocation of the theme of biopolitics in Foucault's lectures, his most sustained comments on biopolitics are still to be found in the context of his analyses of sexuality in *History of Sexuality, Volume 1*.

The biopolitics of eugenics

In the final chapter of *History of Sexuality, Volume 1*, Foucault made a point about historical preoccupations with 'blood' and 'sex'. Premodern society was primarily characterised by a 'symbolics of blood', where social rank depended on birth or, Foucault added, on the willingness to spill one's blood for one's sovereign.[12] Modern society, he argued, saw a move away from the societal importance of 'blood', privileging instead an 'analytics of sexuality' that reflected the shift of focus of technologies of power to the management of 'life'. As he pointed out, the first eugenic thinkers who emerged in the second half of the nineteenth century reflected this shift from 'blood' to 'sexuality', while also illustrating that there was not a simple historical transition of one to the other.[13] Rather, the old symbolics of blood came to be redeployed within the new management of sexuality, particularly through the rise of biological notions of 'race'. Indeed, modern understandings of race recast the old notions of superior, aristocratic 'blood' in the context of discourses on 'racial purity', where 'superior' blood now came to mean 'racially pure' blood.

Foucault's point is tellingly illustrated in the definition of eugenics coined in 1883 by Sir Francis Galton, a British pioneer of modern statistics and genetics and the cousin of Charles Darwin. As Galton saw it, the term 'eugenics' referred to collective efforts to genetically improve the national 'stock' on the basis of the scientific study of 'all influences that tend, in however remote a degree, to give to the more suitable races or strains of blood a better chance of prevailing speedily over the less suitable than they otherwise would have had'.[14] The new eugenic science aimed to assist governments in implementing social policies that would improve the quality of the national 'breed'. Eugenicists advocated active social engineering, arguing that the individual had a patriotic duty to contribute to the improvement of the national community through what Galton's student Karl Pearson called a 'conscious race-culture'.[15] Eugenics was thus from its origins deeply intertwined with social and political aims. It emerged as both a science and a social movement. The term caught on rapidly, and numerous eugenics societies were established in Great Britain as well as in other countries, to be followed by the creation of International and World Leagues. Through such social reform societies, as well as scientific disciplines such as psychiatry, anthropology, biology and sexology, eugenicist discourses acquired institutional support.

Eugenics was thus from the start a (self-declared) science with political ambitions.[16] The aim of eugenics was to assist governments in formulating social policies that would improve the 'quality' of the population. Policy propositions centred in particular on the rational management of reproductive sexuality. Reproductive politics thus became a central matrix of the political technology of life that eugenicists promoted. Eugenic biopolitics of life, heavily intertwined with notions of race and racial purity, involved both types of power distinguished by Foucault: at the micro-level, bodily disciplines such as the medical scrutiny of individual bodily characteristics were twinned with the surveillance of citizens' sexual practices; at the macro-level, statistical studies of the hereditary transmission of population 'defects' formed the basis for state interventions targeting entire groups rather than isolated individuals. Examples of such collective regulations included practices that eugenicists described as 'positive' eugenics, that is to say measures that encouraged those categories of citizens who were deemed to be of 'superior' quality to have more children. They also included 'negative' eugenics, referring to ways of preventing 'inferior' citizens from reproducing, for example by refusing to deliver administrative 'authorisation to marry' certificates or by coercive measures such as coerced sterilisation.

Nowadays, eugenics tends to be associated with the sinister large-scale experiments in social engineering of Nazi Germany. It is important to remember, however, that eugenic ideas found support across the entire political spectrum at the time. In Europe, social-democrat reformers were among the pioneers of eugenic 'science' as well as policy practices. Eugenic policies such as coerced sterilisation of 'degenerates' were strongly promoted by the left, and first applied by liberal governments in countries such as Sweden and Switzerland several years before Nazi Germany, as we shall see. The growth of modern health and social policies from the turn of the twentieth century onwards provided the institutional conditions for translating eugenic rhetoric into a policy programme. The emerging welfare state also added an additional motive to that of preventing degeneracy: limiting public expenditure. Indeed, the 'inferior' categories of the national population were soon constructed as the main recipients of the expanding welfare institutions. Limiting the numbers of indigents in the (future) nation therefore appeared as a rational means of reducing welfare costs.

The construction of the nation as an ordered system of exclusion and disciplinary regulation is central to the workings of modern welfare. As Foucault argued in his 1978 lectures, the practices of care and normalisation involved in pastoral power are internalised by individuals as contributing to the common good. In this respect, pastoral power involves a normative articulation of collective identity as well. The national order of the welfare state is founded on the notions of community and solidarity – even though entitlement to welfare provisions is always conditional and was initially restricted to a very limited number of specific categories of the population. Pastoral power thus contributes to the forging of a collective identity that is based on exclusion of those categories of the population that do not 'fit in'.[17]

The eugenicist concern with the improvement of the population through the political regulation of reproductive sexuality reflected the emergence of a wider preoccupation among Western industrialising nation-states with the underclasses. In the context of accelerating industrialisation, the rapidly growing urban population appeared as an unruly, potentially destabilising force, while an orderly, healthy and prolific population came to be seen as a source of wealth, as Foucault described in *History of Sexuality, Volume 1*. Against this backdrop, the political aim of eugenicists was to create an orderly society through the twin reign of science and reason. The rational management of reproductive sexuality was at the heart of this political project, turning reproductive sexuality into a concern of the state.

As Foucault put it in his discussion with Bernard-Henri Lévy, 'Non au sexe roi' (Refusing the reign of sexuality): 'Sex has always been the forum where both the future of our species and our "truth" as human subjects are decided.'[18] Consequently, sexuality became a prime target of 'biopower', and subjected to processes of disciplinarisation, normalisation and marginalisation, as Foucault had outlined in *History of Sexuality, Volume 1*.

Foucault suggested that biopower invests women in particular ways, highlighting the ways in which medical discourses and interventions pathologise women by reducing them to their reproductive functions.[19] In doing so, he depicted the workings of power on women's bodies primarily in individualising terms, however, as producing the 'hysterisation' of individual women. He failed to acknowledge (and consequently, I would argue, under-theorised) the ways in which women's reproductive bodies became particular targets of population policies such as eugenic policy-making, despite his own use of eugenics as an illustration of biopolitics in modern times at the end of *History of Sexuality, Volume 1*. This analytical neglect partly results, I believe, from the fact that, although the notion of biopolitics emphasises the importance of concrete practices (a theme that Foucault's understanding of governmentality as a set of governmental practices would also echo), Foucault's scattered comments on eugenics in the final chapter of *History of Sexuality, Volume 1* refer to eugenics primarily as a set of ideas (on racial purity, on the population as a resource and so on), without engaging in any depth with concrete eugenic practices. To his defence, most of the research exploring eugenic practices rather than eugenic science or movements, and the debates on the differences between these two levels of analysis, only became available well after his death, intensifying over the past fifteen years or so.

Indeed, the eugenic preoccupation with the unruly underclasses took deeply gendered forms, in that female reproductive sexuality became a particular target of eugenic intervention. This reflects the fact that reproduction and parenting are conventionally coded as particularly female domains, while female bodies and 'respectable' female sexuality more generally act as the 'gatekeepers' of the moral and biological boundaries of the nation, as Nira Yuval-Davis and other feminist scholars have pointed out.[20] While male citizens are expected to sacrifice their lives for the nation when called upon to do so, the primary duty of female citizens towards the nation is to engage in its biological reproduction – a point that suggests that Foucault's earlier quoted comments on citizens' willingness to shed their blood needs gendering. Female citizens and their reproductive bodies thus became of particular interest in the eugenic ordering of the nation.

Against this backdrop, the next section examines some of the ways in which biopolitical relations of power around gender and reproductive sexuality operated in the context of the eugenic management of reproductive sexuality that various Western states engaged in between the 1920s and 1960s.

Gendering biopolitics

In the European context, countries such as Switzerland and Sweden were at the forefront on both the theoretical and practical levels of eugenics. Swiss and Swedish eugenicists made significant contributions to the international 'science' of eugenics, while important eugenicist practices and policies (including coerced sterilisation) were pioneered in these countries. In 1928, the Swiss canton (that is to say, province) of Vaud adopted the first European eugenic sterilisation law that was only abrogated in 1985, although the number of interventions that were legitimised by eugenic arguments seems to have fizzled out by the 1960s. It was followed by similar legislation in Denmark in 1929, Germany in 1933, Sweden and Norway in 1934 and Finland in 1935. The Vaud canton's Criminal Code of 1931 additionally included a clause allowing for eugenically motivated abortions. The notorious 1928 Law allowed for the sterilisation of the 'mentally ill' or 'feebleminded' on eugenic grounds, without requiring (or even explicitly against) the consent of the targeted individuals. It is important to emphasise that the general categories of mental illness and feeblemindedness were notoriously vague at the time. To take an example, the famous Swiss psychiatrist (and eugenicist) Eugen Bleuler (1857–1939), a student of Charcot who coined the term 'schizophrenia' in 1908, included in mental illness 'anything that deviates from the norm' in his influential *Textbook of Psychiatry*, published in 1916.[21] His student Hans W. Maier's 1908 dissertation on the term 'moral idiocy' reflected prevalent views at the time when he extended mental instability to include moral flaws. As Foucault also pointed out in his lectures and writings on the history of psychiatry, 'madness' was thus routinely diagnosed by referring to the 'abnormality' of individuals whose behaviours deviated from socially and historically defined normative models.

The Swiss government (called the Federal Council) reported to Parliament in 1944 that its family policies pursued three aims: demographic, pedagogic and eugenic. Concerning the eugenic dimension of its family protection measures, the Federal Council declared that: 'the state must help to prevent the founding of families which would produce hereditarily diseased offspring, and encourage the founding and stability of families who are hereditarily healthy'.[22] However, both Parliament and Council agreed that a federal law was 'unnecessary', since sterilisation practices were in reality already common at the time. Against this background, doctors' lobbies feared that a national law would introduce unwelcome scrutiny of doctors' practices and no doubt curtail current sterilisation practices (a fear that was borne out by the example of Vaud, where the number of sterilisations indeed dropped following the introduction of the eugenic sterilisation law). Consequently, no other Swiss canton besides Vaud ever adopted a sterilisation law, preferring local administrative guidelines or informal agreements between local authorities and doctors.

In practice, the main targets for eugenic sterilisations were those categories of the population who were thought to be carriers of degenerate hereditarily transmissible characteristics: the mentally ill, the physically disabled and those members of the underclasses whose behaviour had transgressed social norms, such as unproductive 'vagrants' or unmarried mothers. Denmark, Norway, Sweden, Finland, Iceland and Estonia all passed eugenic sterilisation laws in the late 1920s and early 1930s. (In non-liberal contexts, eugenic sterilisation was applied on a particularly large scale by Nazi Germany that sterilised an estimated 400,000 citizens following the passing of the notorious 1933 Sterilisation Law, which introduced compulsory sterilisation on eugenic grounds.)

Eugenic sterilisation practices were deeply gendered. First, in many (though not all) national contexts, the vast majority of those subjected to coerced sterilisation were women from the underclasses. In Sweden, for example, the number of sterilisations performed on eugenic/social grounds between 1935 and 1975 is currently estimated at about 18,600, over 90 per cent of which were performed on women, a gender proportion that is echoed in many other countries for which data are available.[23] Second, eugenic policies in turn 'produced gender', strengthening normative models of femininity and masculinity. Indeed, since the categories of mental illness and feeblemindedness, which were invoked in eugenic sterilisation laws, could include any kind of behaviour that deviated from social norms, the justifications for eugenic sterilisation routinely portrayed women as deviating from the social norms of female respectability, in particular in terms of their sexual morality. Underclass women who had had children out of wedlock (thereby demonstrating 'loose' sexual morals as well as the risk of welfare dependency) represented the vast majority of coerced sterilisations in liberal contexts. Additionally, women whose behaviour deviated from respectable femininity in other ways were targeted on the grounds of 'promiscuity', 'nymphomania', 'disorderly housekeeping' or 'the inability to financially support children'. Men who were subjected to sterilisation or castration (representing small numbers in Switzerland and Sweden, but half of all sterilisations in the United States of the 1920 to 1940s) were often already institutionalised in psychiatric or penal institutions on the grounds of sexual 'abnormality' such as homosexuality or exhibitionism. Not all of these interventions were eugenically driven, however. They also reflected the therapeutic aim of moderating 'deviant' sex drives, or were accepted 'voluntarily' (with the pressure of long-term internment offered as the only alternative). More generally, the original eugenic emphasis on the prevention of the hereditary transmission of 'defective' characteristics became diluted in wider state measures against antisocial behaviours that were not necessarily attributed to strictly hereditary factors. This further blurred the boundaries between eugenic scientific rhetoric and its translation into concrete biopolitical practices.

Figures on the total number of sterilisations in the whole of Switzerland are not available to date. New archival research carried out in recent years by Swiss historians, however, allows us to understand practices in major urban centres and demonstrate significant regional differences in the sterilisation practices.[24] Sterilisation practices seem to have been relatively common in the canton of Zurich for example, where in the 1930s alone, between 1700 and 3600 sterilisations were carried out after approval from the local psychiatric policlinic.[25] As in the United States, women who requested permission for an abortion were only granted one if they consented to sterilisation (a practice that demonstrates the historical distance from contemporary understandings of 'informed consent'). The justifications for sterilisation used in Zurich were primarily of a social and psychiatric nature, including sexual promiscuity, the inability to support children financially or illegitimacy of the children, while hereditary arguments appeared in about 30 percent of recommendations for sterilisation.[26] In contrast, in the canton of Bern, doctors tended to apply explicit hereditary criteria, reflecting the preference of a key actor in the implementation of sterilisations, the director of the Bernese Women's Clinic, Hans Guggisberg, who refused to accept social justifications for sterilisation.[27] More generally, arguments for sterilisation reflected the legal frameworks at the time. For example, from 1931, local guidelines in Bern required psychiatric examination and no longer accepted either eugenic or social indications alone as grounds for sterilisation. Psychiatrists often amalgamated psychiatric, social and hereditary arguments to justify sterilisation with or without consent, including the prevention of pregnancies for 'morally deficient' or 'sexually pathological' women, welfare dependency of future children or a family history of mental illness, suicide or epilepsy; recommending an average of 25 women per year for sterilisation in the years 1935–53.[28] As these examples illustrate, sterilisation practices varied quite widely between different federal cantons, reflecting differences in local administrative and legal frameworks, but also in the scope for individual agency on the part of key officials in the implementation of such measures.

Concluding comments

My aim in this chapter was not primarily to provide a detailed historical analysis of eugenics, but rather to discuss some historical examples of eugenic practices as a way of exploring the workings of biopolitics in the rational management of reproductive sexuality. I have thus been concerned with a wider question: how can we use eugenics as a way of thinking about the links between gender, reproductive politics and the liberal state? In this light, I shall make two sets of concluding comments: first, two points about gender; second, two points about the nature of the liberal state.

Whereas eugenic concerns with racial purity emerged in Britain and Germany against the backdrop of empire and the encounter with colonial 'others', in non-colonial nations such as Switzerland and the Scandinavian countries, eugenic preoccupations with the purity of the national blood turned primarily towards 'internal others'. The national order was seen to be under threat from various categories of 'disorderly' citizens, including the mentally ill, the physically disabled, the 'morally defective' or 'anti-social' citizens and 'vagrants' or travellers (who were sometimes racialised, as in the case of the 'Tattare' in Sweden). The rational management of citizens' reproductive sexuality thus became a central focus of the eugenic efforts to eradicate the 'degenerates' from the national gardens. What Foucault failed to recognise, or at least paid insufficient theoretical and empirical attention to, however, was the deeply gendered nature of such collective practices targeting citizens' reproductive sexuality. As we have seen, the eugenic politics of life was heavily gendering and targeted female sexual morality and practices especially. However, recognising the importance of gender for the workings of the modern state is not to say that the state exercises male power over its female citizens in any straightforward way. Women were often important agents in the implementation of eugenic measures, while men were sometimes its victims. Furthermore, gender was not the only category around which eugenic interventions were structured; some practices were linked to racialised differences and disability, while social class was a strongly differentiating factor in the application of eugenic measures, illustrating the importance of taking into account what Patricia Hill Collins has described as the intersectionalities between gender, sexuality, class and other identity markers.

My second point about gender is that eugenic practices were not only applied differently to female and male citizens; they also, in the process, produced normative femininities (orderly women, who are not promiscuous) and normative masculinities (heterosexual men, whose masculinity was confirmed rather than challenged by promiscuity unless the latter included 'perverted' sexual practices). In other words, eugenic practices also helped to *produce* gender, in the sense that they produced normative models of masculinity and femininity.

The specific institutional design of states affected both the ways in which eugenic policies were implemented and the incentives for doing so. In other terms, the type of state 'matters'. In Sweden, for example, eugenic sterilisation of 'asocial' and 'work-shy' citizens (terms that are currently experiencing something of a revival) such as prostitutes and vagrants, the mentally ill and the mentally 'retarded' came to be seen as a way of strengthening the social-democratic welfare state, since it limited the number of future welfare dependents. In turn, the presence of a strong centralised welfare state was seen as a guarantee against the risk of arbitrariness in the implementation of such measures, administered under the responsibility of the Swedish National Board of Health. In contrast, federalism led to variations in policy frameworks and practices between cantons or states. In the federalist system of the United States, important differences occurred in the scope of the application of eugenic measures between different states, as studies by Wendy Kline, Johanna Schoen and Alexandra Stern have revealed. In the case of Switzerland, also a federal state, similar differences can be observed between the different cantons. The main dividing line seems to have been religion: while Protestant cantons tended to engage in sterilisation practices, Catholic cantons, on the whole, did not, reflecting more general differences in attitudes towards poverty, illness and disability within Protestant and Catholic doctrines. Indeed, for Catholics, any form of life, no matter how 'defective' or 'flawed', is worthy of preservation (in liberal contexts, sterilisation laws were introduced exclusively in Protestant countries, such as the Swiss canton of Vaud, Denmark, Norway, Sweden, Finland, Iceland and Estonia).

Differences in institutional design of states produced further variations in policy implementation, depending on how welfare provision was organised. The Swiss state, again, constitutes a good example of this: local authorities, rather than the federal state, were responsible for the financial support of indigent members of local communes. This factor increased the appeal of the argument of cost reduction since limiting the number of future dependents would have a direct effect on local budgets that were modest compared to that of the federal state. Local authorities' financial responsibility for 'their' citizens also led to differences in welfare practices between local authorities with regard to measures such as issuing marriage licenses or sterilisation. The implementation of eugenic policies was thus shaped by the specific design of political institutions, in particular federalism and its attendant levels of autonomy of local agencies and authorities. Many eugenic practices, including coerced sterilisation, were not carried out by the central state at all, but implemented by cantonal and local authorities as well as para-state actors such as psychiatric clinics on the basis of local legislation and administrative measures. Psychiatric clinics in particular acted as eugenic playgrounds. They offered practical opportunities for applying eugenic ideas and technologies to citizens who were often already under tutelage or guardianship orders.

More generally, the notion of the state itself thus needs unpacking. Comparative analysis of the connections between welfare, politics and the state demonstrates that states have not always acted in coherent, homogeneous ways, but in ways that were at times non-systematic and contradictory.[29] Whereas eugenic ideologues often promoted ambitious national and international visions, concrete eugenic policies within liberal states did not, generally, reflect any grand 'masterplan' on the part of the state, but were more often the product of accidental political opportunities and local compromise. Numerous, frequently incoherent, sometimes contradictory, eugenic discourses and practices sprang up from various institutional settings at the micro-level, and cross-cut with other disciplinary motivations and practices that were not always intentionally eugenic. In other words, the institutional design of states matters for the analysis of biopolitical practices – as does gender. Exploring their role in the politics of life allows us to think both with, and beyond, Foucault.

Notes

1. Foucault, HS1, 138. Author's modification of the translation.
2. Ibid., 141.
3. Ibid., 140.
4. Foucault, SMD, 215–38.
5. Foucault, HS1, 143.
6. The term first emerges in his lecture of 1 February 1978, see Foucault, STP, 144; see also Michel Senellart's comments at the end of the lectures of 1977–78. Ibid., 503–7.
7. Foucault, BOB, 21.
8. Ibid., 20–2.
9. Ibid., 22.
10. See also Senellart's comments at the end of *The Birth of Biopolitics*. Foucault, BOB, 327–31.
11. Foucault, HS1, 150.
12. Ibid., 148.
13. Ibid., 149–50.
14. Francis Galton, *Inquiries into Human Faculty and its Development*, 1st edn (London: Macmillan, 1883), 25.
15. Karl Pearson, 'The scope and importance to the state of the science of national eugenics', in Lucy Bland and Laura Doan (eds), *Sexology Uncensored: The Documents of Sexual Science* (Cambridge: Polity Press, 1998 [1909]), 176–7 at 177.
16. My arguments on eugenics in these sections of this chapter are developed at greater length elsewhere: on gender and sexuality in Swiss eugenics, see Véronique Mottier, 'Narratives of national identity: sexuality, race, and the Swiss "Dream of Order"', *Swiss Journal of Sociology*, 26 (2000), 533–58; and Véronique Mottier, 'Eugenics and the Swiss gender regime: women's bodies and the struggle against "difference"', *Swiss Journal of Sociology*, 32 (2006), 253–67. On eugenics and social-democratic thought, see Véronique Mottier and Natalia Gerodetti, 'Eugenics and social democracy: or, how the European left tried to eliminate the "weeds" from its national gardens', *New Formations*, 20 (2007), 35–49. On theorising the state in eugenic policy-making, see Véronique Mottier, 'Eugenics, politics and the state: social-democracy and the Swiss gardening state', *Studies in History and Philosophy of Biological and Biomedical Sciences*, 39 (2008), 263–9; and Véronique Mottier, 'Eugenics and the state: policy-making in comparative perspective', in Alison Bashford and Philippa Levine (eds), *The Oxford Handbook of the History of Eugenics* (Oxford: Oxford University Press, 2010), 134–53.
17. See also Véronique Mottier, 'From welfare to social exclusion: eugenic social policies and the Swiss national order', in David Howarth and Jacob Torfing (eds), *Discourse Theory in European Politics: Identity, Policy, Governance* (London: Palgrave MacMillan, 2005), 255–74.
18. This discussion with Bernard-Henri Lévy was originally published as 'Foucault: Non au sexe roi', in *Le Nouvel Observateur* (12 March 1977), and printed in PPC, 110–24, quotation on 111.
19. Foucault, HS1, 153.

20. See Nira Yuval-Davis and Floya Anthias (eds), *Woman–Nation–State* (London: Macmillan, 1989).

21. Eugen Bleuler, *Lehrbuch der Psychiatrie* (Berlin: Julius Springer, 1916), 476.

22. Bericht des Bundesrates an die Bundesversammlung über das Volksbegehren, 'Für die Familie', *Bundesblatt*, 96 (10 October 1944), 868.

23. Gunnar Broberg and Mattias Tydén, 'Eugenics in Sweden: efficient care', in Gunnar Broberg and Nils Roll-Hansen (eds), *Eugenics and the Welfare State: Sterilisation Policy in Denmark, Sweden, Norway, and Finland* (East Lansing, MI: Michigan State University Press, 2005), 77–149 at 109.

24. These Swiss historians include: Geneviève Heller, Gilles Jeanmonod, Regina Wecker, Jacob Tanner, Roswitha Dubach, Beatrice Ziegler and Gisela Hauss. Much of their work is collected in Véronique Mottier and Laura von Mandach (eds), *Pflege, Stigmatisierung und Eugenik: Integration und Ausschluss in Medizin, Psychiatrie und Sozialhilfe* (Zurich: Seismo, 2007).

25. Regina Wecker, 'Vom Verbot, Kinder zu haben, und dem Recht, keine Kinder zu haben: Zu Geschichte und Gegenwart der Sterilisation in Schweden, Deutschland und der Schweiz', *Figurationen*, 02/03 (2003), 101–9 at 108.

26. Roswitha Dubach, 'Zur "Sozialisierung einer medizinischen Massnahme": Sterilisationspraxis der Psychiatrischen Poliklinik Zürich in den 1930er-Jahen', in Marietta Meier, Brigitta Bernet, Roswitha Dubach and Urs Germann (eds), *Zwang zur Ordnung: Psychiatrie im Kanton Zürich, 1870–1970* (Zurich: Chronos, 2007), 155–92 at 191.

27. Béatrice Ziegler, 'Frauen zwischen sozialer und eugenischer Indikation: Abtreibung und Sterilisation in Bern', in Veronika Aegerter, Nicole Graf, Natalie Imboden, Thea Rytz and Rita Stöckli (eds), *Geschlecht hat Methode: Ansätze und Perspektiven in der Frauen- und Geschlechtergeschichte* (Zurich: Chronos, 1999), 293–301.

28. Gisela Hauss and Béatrice Ziegler, 'Norm und Ausschluss in Vormundschaft und Psychiatrie: Zum institutionellen Umgang mit jungen Frauen', in Mottier and Mandach (eds), *Pflege, Stigmatisierung und Eugenik*, 63–75.

29. Mottier, 'Eugenics, politics and the state', 263–9.

7
Foucault, the Family and History:
'Imaginary Landscape and Real Social Structure'

Deborah Thom

Foucault wrote that each of his works represented a new project that developed on the previous ones, but showed him thinking through new theories or new narratives:

> I would like my books to be a kind of tool-box which others can rummage through to find a tool which they can use however they wish in their own area [...] I only write a book because I don't know exactly what to think about this thing that I so much want to think about, so that the book transforms me and transforms what I think. Each book transforms what I was thinking when I finished the previous book. I am an experimenter, not a theorist.[1]

Family was not the central subject of any of Foucault's own books and, of all of the intimate relations based inside the family as a social institution, only sexuality received sustained discussion. However, one can describe elements of the toolkit for ways of thinking about the family. A chronology of Foucault's writings shows changes in the theory of family over his career. He wrote about the family early on in his first books, using it as a metaphor for care and power when he sought to understand subjection – the process of making people both disciplined citizens and productive workers. His analysis did not offer substantial surprises in suggesting that the family was a site of regulation, as any history of social work, philanthropy or policing would indicate. The family is very different from his favoured type of social institution, which is either a system of ideas (like psychiatry or criminology) or a physical entity (like a prison or an asylum), and has, historically, often been analysed with an eye to its repressive as well as its emancipatory activities. Marxists, following Engels, have seen the family as a general regulatory system integral to the reproduction of social values, based around economic relationships but also containing a potential to develop and restrict the regulation of social norms.[2] Foucault saw it rather as a site of intervention, the place where surveillance was most dramatically visible and, far from being private, a place of intense public attention after the French Revolution.

In *Madness and Civilisation* (1967), Foucault insightfully described the family as 'imagined landscape and real social structure'.[3] Yet Foucault appeared to move away from this recognition of the importance of imagination and the society in which families operated, towards an increasing concern with systems of thought and the work of professionals. This culminated in concepts such as governmentality and biopolitics, but something seemed to have been lost along the way: the feelings and emotions of the family members themselves, embedded within economic and cultural structures and relations of power. As a result, Foucault's histories neglected issues of great importance, such as gender, mutual aid and love. He also neglected the contributions that psychoanalysis made to the study of affect. Throughout his career, Foucault offered brilliant insights into historical change, even if sometimes it appeared that there was no comprehensive narrative of when exactly change happened and who was affected. However, the field of experience itself appeared from time to time in Foucault's use of history to illustrate his arguments. Building with and beyond Foucault in addressing the family, this chapter also explores the work of Pierre Bourdieu, whose concerns with contemporary social practices in families offer a productive, alternative view.

Traces of the family in the Foucauldean corpus

In his early work, Foucault described the family as an 'imaginary landscape and real social structure'[4] – a brilliant description that could still be productively used, because it includes the imagination and the idea of fiction, as well as the objective material facts of physical objects. But the family was also the site and the metaphor for patterns of institutional care in the late eighteenth century. In *History of Madness*, Foucault wrote:

> The liberal economy tended to place the onus on the family rather than the State when it came to assistance of the poor and the sick,

so the family became the place of social responsibility. But if a sick patient could be entrusted to a family, a madman could not, as he was too foreign and inhuman. Tuke's innovation was to create a simulacrum of the family around the mad, an institutional parody that was nonetheless a real psychological situation. Where family is lacking, he substituted a fictitious familial décor through signs and attitudes [...] long after the sickness of the poor had again become an affair of the State, asylums maintained the insane in a fictional family imperative. The mad remained minors, and for a long while to come reason bore for them the attributes of a Father.[5]

He spelt out the idea of patriarchal power and its relation to reason on the next page, describing Tuke's asylum:

Tuke's intention was to create a milieu that imitates the most ancient, pure, and natural forms of coexistence: the milieu was to be as human as possible, while remaining as un-social as possible. What he did in practice was to cut out the structure of a bourgeois family, symbolically recreate it inside the asylum and set it adrift in history.[6]

He went on to argue that this dialectic of family life, half-real and half-imagined, was seen in its modern form, not transformed but developed and extended in psychoanalysis.

As Rémi Lenoir and Robbie Duschinsky describe in their chapter, in the 1970s Foucault attempted to correct this account of *History of Madness*. In doing so, however, he sacrificed an account of the imaginary landscape and real social structure of the family to a concern with the peculiar rationality of power that operates within the family and that links it up with other institutions. In *Psychiatric Power*, Foucault directly rejected the earlier argument of *History of Madness* about the family as the paradigm for disciplinary power. The family now became a completely different sort of institution:

I do not think it is true that the family served as the model for the asylum, school, barracks, or workshop. Actually, it seems to me that nothing in the way the family functions enables us to see any continuity between the family and the institutions, the disciplinary apparatuses, I am talking about. Instead, what do we see in the family if not a function of maximum individualisation on the side of the person who exercises power, that is to say, on the father's side?[7]

This set of lectures saw the replacement of the hospital by the clinic as the mechanism that made the family the place where discipline was learned and produced:

> [T]he family, while retaining the specific heterogeneity of sovereign power, begins to function like a little school: the strange category of student parents appear, home duties begin to appear, the control of the school discipline by the family; the family becomes a micro-clinic which controls the normality or abnormality of the body, of the soul; it becomes a small-scale barracks, and maybe it becomes [...] the place where sexuality circulates.[8]

Foucault used two mechanical metaphors for the family's place in society – it was 'the hinge, the interlocking point [...] absolutely indispensable to the very functioning of all the disciplinary systems' but it was also 'the switch-point, the junction ensuring passage from one disciplinary system to another'.[9] Here the metaphor was physical or mechanical and became very functionalist indeed. Foucault left the varied activities within families out of the discussion except to the extent that they served to smooth the functioning of the disciplines – schooling, psychiatry, labour and so forth.[10] Something important and almost totally missing in this account is how children were made into housekeepers and mothers. One reason for this, I would argue, is Foucault's focus on prescriptive texts at the expense of the theoretical problem of the affections or the emotions in the exercise of power, given that affects are so crucial in the process of gendered subjectivation. Key questions are flattened by the neatness of the model of the family as a hinge and switch-point for the disciplines. One wonders: how far is family life part of a network of relationships with institutional forms designed to socialise and normalise individuals? Is the emotional division of labour of contemporary and past family relationships regulatory in any simple way? Moreover, Foucault's attention to 'alliance' obscures the operation of affection, solidarity, mutual support and the real problems of power within the history of the affections. Foucault stated that the family was 'an obligatory locus of affects, feelings, love' but much of his account was about control – going on, for example, to cite Jean-Martin Charcot's emphasis on removing the patient from the family in order to ensure successful treatment.[11]

Omitting the subjectivation of mothers and daughters is clearly a problem, as Katherine Logan's chapter in the present volume touches upon. Had Foucault stuck with his initial plan for the *History of Sexuality* series, the volume on 'the woman, the mother, and the hysteric' might have addressed this question.[12] The four moments of his historical enquiry into sexuality in *History of Sexuality, Volume 1* were the hysterical woman, the masturbating child, the Malthusian couple and the perverse adult.[13] That list alone demonstrates the high valuation of discourses created by the educated middle-class about the uneducated working-class or about themselves, but ignores the multiple voices influencing family life during the period – the eighteenth and nineteenth centuries. Mothers were not only viewed through the lens of reproduction but viewed themselves with an eye to autonomy and self-regulation in an area of social commentary totally missing from Foucault – feminism. Some self-regulation came out of the demands and claims of the subordinated but in the process new norms of femaleness radically affected the concept of gender itself, both as an analytical category and a term in political debate.[14]

Another significant issue is that this omission of the potentially complex power dynamics that attend the subjectivation of women and children undergirds Foucault's theoretical reduction of familial power to sovereign power, operating from the head to the rest. In *Psychiatric Power*, Foucault described it thus:

Instead, what we do see in the family if not a function of maximum individualisation on the side of the person who exercises power, that is to say, on the father's side? The anonymity of power, the ribbon of undifferentiated power which unwinds indefinitely in a panoptic system, is utterly foreign to the constitution of the family in which the father, as bearer of the name, and insofar as he exercises power in his name, is the most intense pole of individualisation, much more intense than the wife or children. So, in the family you have individualisation at the top, which recalls and is of the very same type as the power of sovereignty, the complete opposite of disciplinary power.[15]

A case that appears at first sight to support this model, but in fact renders Foucault's own analysis problematic through the detail that it provides on the interplay of power within the family is *'I, Pierre Rivière, Having Slaughtered My Mother, My Sister, and My Brother': A Case of Parricide in the Nineteenth Century*, which was first published in French in 1973, a year before the *Psychiatric Power* lectures began.[16] Pierre Rivière described his own motive as 'to preserve the honour of a family'.[17] But actually he specifies that his real motive was to preserve the honour of his father with whom he lived. Rivière senior had married in order to escape military service and separated from his wife after several unhappy years. It sounds as if she was a manipulative bully and the father was ill-equipped to deal with her cruelty. Rivière junior wanted a return to the sovereign, patriarchal power of the Romans even though he recognised that times had changed: 'I knew the rules of man and the rules of ordered society, but I deemed myself wiser than they.'[18]

This peasant, who articulated his own social theory and his fears of the feminine, then became a construct of the medico-legal system, a test case for new ideas of criminal responsibility and madness. Foucault regarded this as a demonstration of the battle of discourses. What is remarkable and rare about the text is the voice of the peasant himself, the person at the centre of the discursive battle. But the picture of the family is only about control in this example, based on the difficulties of masculinity rather than family life altogether. The women of the family did not speak or act in Rivière's account and they were only present as an imaginary landscape of hostility and cruelty. To follow the model of *Psychiatric Power* here and attribute the operation of sovereign power would be problematic in that it functions more as a fantasy of Rivière's than as an accurate or incisive characterisation of his family life.

Following the *Psychiatric Power* lectures, Foucault continued giving his attention to the family in the 1974–75 lectures entitled *Abnormal*. Here he described how parents monitored the sexualised body of the child, and masturbation became the central concern of middle-class parents, the way in which the family was opened up to professional scrutiny. This is what Foucault elsewhere referred to as 'parental pedagogy', explaining how the middle-class family became a place of instruction.[19] Masturbation became the channel through which children appeared in Foucault's accounts of family because it was the most troubling aspect of the new scientific description of abnormal development. Middle-class families feared the sexual power of masturbation to distract or undermine healthy children. They scrutinised their bodies and monitored their behaviour in order to detect its presence. One of the most interesting things about this account is that, for the first time, Foucault described the agency of children. But this was not a very dialectical account. Children's bodies were constructed through the gaze of the parents, who feared the power of the children's sexual desire and turned to the social sciences to resist it. But we do not know what this description could mean to the children themselves.

However, the working-class family operated, according to Foucault's account, in a very different way. Working-class families were disciplined through the social institution of marriage rather than the obsessive monitoring of the child's body. And the history happened at a different time, around 1760 for the masturbation panic, and around 1820 to 1840 for the insistence on marriage as the social glue that enabled the family to socialise its children. Because, Foucault argued, free unions no longer served the mobility of labour, marriage was encouraged and enforced by a 'matchmaking' campaign. But this, too, created anxieties according to Foucault, leading to the ideal of 'one bed per person'. Unlike the middle class, which got closer to their children and observed their bodies, the working class were told to 'distribute bodies with the greatest possible distance between them'.[20] Foucault's account of the working class almost implies their passivity in his near exclusive attention to professional discourses; he does not explore their experience of, interest in or engagement with these changes in family life.

Foucault ended *Abnormal* with an account of the criminalisation of a man called Charles Jouy, who might have raped a child known as Sophie Adam:

> Jouy dragged young Sophie Adam (unless it was Sophie Adam who dragged Charles Jouy) into the ditch alongside the road to Nancy. There, something happened: almost rape, perhaps. Anyway, Jouy very decently gives four *sous* to the little girl who immediately runs to the fair to buy some roasted almonds.[21]

Sophie's contribution to the story was different from Jouy's. Foucault seemed to imply that she might have been selling sex for money, rather than being forced against her will.[22] In Foucault's reiteration of this episode in *History of Sexuality, Volume 1*, published a year after the *Abnormal* lectures, Sophie Adam was not named at all and the emphasis was not on the incident itself, nor on the narrative of the story with its games of power involving the different participants. Instead, emphasis was placed on the abstract constitution of Jouy as an object of medical and legal concern. In this second version of the tale, the family as well as the girl herself completely vanished, leaving only Jouy and the psychiatrists.[23] Famously, Foucault theorised that power flowed in no particular direction and there was not a simple or single hierarchy of subordination and domination. Yet the family, in his account, remained a deeply hierarchical place in Foucauldean theory in the period of the 1970s, even as his case material exceeded the bounds of this theory.

A shift occurs, however, in Foucault's attention to family life in the early 1980s. Foucault and the historian Arlette Farge edited selections of *lettres de cachet* and other documents dated from 1728 to 1758, deposited at the archives of the Bastille; they published this in 1982 as *Le Désordre des familles*.[24] Their introduction – translated by Thibaud Harrois and Leon Antonio Rocha into English for this volume – explained the history of these documents, which offered great insight into the domestic life of French citizens of the eighteenth century. Most of those documented were manual workers, and in the first section about married life we can see households torn apart by drunkenness, promiscuity and problems of money. In these documents, one spouse petitioned the king to have the other removed to hospital. Quite often, we have included the report of a police official on the relative merits of the complaint, supporting the request by detailing the debauchery, fecklessness and, frequently, the sale of domestic property to fund drinking, gambling and fornication. A frequent complaint about the individual whose confinement was requested was the selling of children's beds – the final straw for the spouse because it seemed to strike right at the heart of the family as a place of refuge and support. Both the men and women documented in the first section were likely to be violent as well as spendthrift, and there were clearly conventions about how misbehaviour was reported. Farge and Foucault argued that these documents showed a period in which royal justice was equally available to both men and women, who brought these petitions in roughly equal numbers. It was the abolition of this system that brought families closer to the sovereign model of *Psychiatric Power*. But Farge and Foucault did not explain the psychic effects of these ideas and norms of behaviour, or ask whether concepts of shame and responsibility were equally allocated to the sexes.

The second section of *Le Désordre des familles* explores the family dynamics between parents and children, and the context that led to the petition for the child's removal. The children complained of were nearly all adults in modern legal systems, yet their parents remained morally responsible for their behaviour and interested in their support. Farge and Foucault pointed out that delaying the age of marriage, as people tended to do in all urbanising societies in the late eighteenth century, prolonged dependency and created problems for adult children if they were unable to support themselves. This was one of the few places where Foucault recognised economic constraints both on subjectivity and behaviour, and on the extent to which state authority was increasing in a modernising world. Here Farge and Foucault did observe a gender difference in that girls were more likely to be interned on the request of their parents because of the scandal of concubinage or the birth of illegitimate children:

> There are, between parents and children, young and old, in the interior of families, a surface of confrontations where occur the economic conflicts, physical violence, place in the household, neighbourhood reputation, shocks of character, more than marriage, more than the difference between a 'good' marriage and a 'dishonourable' concubinage. People leave to others the care of locking up their children because they do not marry appropriately or because they bring them shame. People lock them up because they disturb them.[25]

Farge and Foucault explained that this disturbance or disarrangement (dérangement) was particularly created by different spaces – in the household, the street or in the neighbourhood, so that the people who had to be confined were not necessarily connected by blood but by contiguity. They were those who were closest at hand.[26] One of the commonest complaints that led to these adult children being incarcerated was that they were running free, in a state of vagabondage, people out of their 'proper place'.

The materials collected by Farge and Foucault differed from the prescriptive texts that Foucault frequently drew upon. Among the *lettres de cachet* at the Bastille archives, alternative voices could be heard that told of a subjectivity and a reality different from that prescribed by professionals. For example, Magdelaine Blanchet, accused by her father of living in shameful concubinage with a man, riposted that her father had not supported her as he ought to. She lost her liberty because she persisted in living in shame – she only 'demanded her liberty to keep living in libertinage and succeeded in covering her family in ignominy'.[27] She opposed her economic narrative to a construction of her subjectivity in terms of sexual shame and honour. Surveying Farge and Foucault's text, there was a common pattern: male witnesses were more likely to refer to the sexuality of women in their condemnations, than women in their narratives.

These texts make salient the multiplicity of competing narratives of what the family meant. They also highlight the role of the family as an economic site, an emotional resource, and a place where gender relations played out to the disadvantage of women, whose free movement was increasingly curtailed and whose sexuality was constructed as troubling, even for the humblest people, especially if it led to the disadvantage of young children, disturbance of the neighbourhood or damage to family honour. The narrative of Marie Fumet is an example. Her father, a water carrier, said that despite the pains that he took with her education, she did not turn out as he had hoped. His request to send his daughter into confinement was supported by a surgeon, a wine merchant, relations and several other named citizens, demonstrating a multiplicity of intersecting positions of power. Farge and Foucault argued that cases like this represent a real historic shift in the power relations that organise family life. In 1728, when this series of documents started, parents emphasised their tenderness and affection, and a generation later in 1758, they wrote about the good education that they had given their children. Parents came to be seen not as good because they loved their children, but because they brought them up well. Measures and expressions of virtue had changed.[28]

Here Foucault and Farge described real families who lived with an emerging system of state surveillance and instruction, but who themselves engaged in strategies and discourses to navigate, temper and even alter these dynamics. They negotiated with the state and used it to make their lives easier as well as to manage their most troubled members. The members of the family had an imaginary landscape with which they negotiated the real social structure of their lives. Foucault's contribution to *Le Désordre des familles* represented three elements of a wider shift in his thinking about power in the early 1980s, linked to his account of the family (see also Lenoir and Duschinsky in this volume): he was beginning to take care of the voices of historical actors; he was beginning to reject the more mechanical metaphors from *Psychiatric Power* (1973–74); and he was coming to recognise that relations of power could be more open than the disciplinary metaphor implied.[29]

Critique of Foucault and possibilities with Bourdieu

Having now explored the theme of the family in Foucault's texts and lectures, these accounts can be considered in terms of their effectiveness as a history of families. To start off, there is a consistent problem with the chronology in Foucault's writings.[30] Systems of thought do not change universally or simultaneously, as Foucault sometimes implies. When change occurred and what marked that change in Foucault's writings are often fuzzy, and there is often little sense of causation.[31] Foucault has been criticised for imprecision and for the way in which he selectively mobilises historical evidence – examples are treated indiscriminately despite their divergent origins, such that legislation, advice literature and individual histories are mixed up together without any of the standard historical tests of their validity or representativeness.

Sometimes Foucault's comparisons are with world historical systems, in which 'modernity' replaces the ancien régime. This narrative moves between France and occasionally Britain, and certainly rarely, if ever, covers non-European developments.

Gareth Stedman Jones commented critically on the absence in Foucault's writings of recognition of the power of popular protest to transform social institutions. '[A] central feature of Foucault's non-historical appropriation of the past', Stedman Jones argued, 'is that it is disabled from accepting that changing norms of right may occasionally in favourable circumstances provide the most powerful means whereby the weak may be enabled to combine together to defeat the strong'.[32] Yet there were other threads on the question of doing politics in Foucault's work, especially on the family. Foucault wrote about the family and power in his 1977 preface to the American translation of Gilles Deleuze and Félix Guattari's *Anti-Oedipus*, in which he argued against unitary notions of political action:

> Free political action from all unitary and totalising paranoia. Develop action, thought, and desires by proliferation, juxtaposition, and disjunction, and not by subdivision and pyramidal hierarchisation. Withdraw allegiance from the old categories of the Negative (law, limit, castration, lack, lacuna), which Western thought has so long held sacred as a form of power and an access to reality. Prefer what is positive and multiple, difference over uniformity, flows over unities, mobile arrangements over systems. Believe what is productive is not sedentary but nomadic.[33]

This more dynamic account of power would suggest an account of the family that runs counter to the theory in *Psychiatric Power* of the family as an adjunct to the disciplines. In thinking about the family, there is always the problem of its multiple activities and the fact that conceptually so many of them are enshrined in thoroughly concrete institutional discourses – law, taxation and inheritance; architecture with its analysis of everyday life; religious tradition that continues to supply many with their notions of what family life should be. As José Luis Moreno Pestaña's chapter in this volume suggests, in his criticisms of Jacques Donzelot, the agents of social welfare and the psy-disciplines have only a limited power to regulate, change or redirect people's thinking about concepts of family life so thoroughly embedded in various forms of material provision.

Yet feminist scholars have found the recognition of the power of the body in Foucault's texts from the mid 1970s extremely useful.[34] They have used both the idea of disciplinarity and the possibility of resistance, following up the recognition of Foucault's historicism as another way of reflecting upon the unstable categories of sex and gender.[35] Yet feminist scholars, too, have noted that Foucault's theorisation of subjectivation is predominantly an account of subordination, despite his theoretical attention to the polyvalence and malleability of power relations:

> In a sense, for Foucault, as for Nietzsche, cultural values emerge as the result of an inscription on the body, where the body is understood as a medium, indeed, a blank page, an unusual one, to be sure, for it appears to bleed and suffer under the pressure of a writing instrument. In order for this inscription to signify, however, the body-as-medium must itself be destroyed and transvaluated into a sublimated (to use Freud's language) or 'transvaluated' (to use Nietzsche's language) domain of values. Implicit to this description of the creation of cultural values is the notion of history as a relentless writing instrument, and the body as the medium that must be destroyed and transfigured in order for 'culture' to emerge.[36]

This account of subordination, however, is one that detaches concern for subjectivity from its material conditions. Foucault fully acknowledged the complexity of a society of biopolitics, and he wanted to reject a vulgar notion of the market and the pursuit of commodities as the sole sources of society's development:

> A society that is not orientated towards the commodity and the uniformity of the commodity, but towards the multiplicity and differentiation of enterprises [...] An enterprise society and a judicial society, a society orientated towards the enterprise and a society framed by a multiplicity of judicial institutions, are two faces of a single phenomenon.[37]

However, in practice, Foucault often ended up abandoning economic concerns, and this has facilitated feminist theorising along the same lines.

Yet it is possible to offer an account of the family that accommodates emotions and that retains the sense of family relationships as multiple, fluid and dynamic while attending to material inequalities. Pointers towards such an account may be found in some of the later writings of French sociologist Pierre Bourdieu. In Bourdieu's early work, the family was conceived as the site where social capital was reproduced and maintained, and where children would learn their place in the social

hierarchy. The family was a field – an area of specific social processes
with its own environment and cultural activities. This was very much
like Foucault's family as a place of parental pedagogy. Yet the field operated in what Bourdieu called a *habitus*, 'the internalised form of the class
condition and of the conditionings it entails'.[38] This concept allows for
greater specificity than Foucault's approach, as it is more attuned than
Foucault's description of rationalities of power to taking into consideration both interpersonal variation and social change.

In the 1990s, Bourdieu had turned away from seeing people as 'objects
that speak'[39] to letting them speak more for themselves. He reproduced
long, unedited case histories in *La Misère du monde* (translated into
English as *The Weight of the World*), and allowed for the possibility
of affection and happiness in the family.[40] His idea of social taste as
indicative and constructive of social distinction was an attempt to create a picture of the modern world that incorporated mass commercial
culture, which Foucault's picture of the mid-nineteenth century rarely
mentioned. Bourdieu treated mass commercial culture as a key location
where the market affected subjectivity. It was, he argued, 'substituting
seduction for repression, public relations for policing, advertising for
authority, the velvet glove for the iron fist, [pursuing] the symbolic
integration of the dominated classes by imposing needs rather than
inculcating norms'.[41] In this way, Bourdieu developed a less top-down
notion of social life, one in which the experience of subordination did
not entirely deprive people of emotional resource.

Bourdieu's later writings increasingly looked to the family as the
place where capital's immense power might be tempered or somewhat
mitigated, and the world's misery could be more easily fended away.[42]
Terry Lovell has criticised these writings of Bourdieu, for many of the
same reasons that I criticised Foucault's conceptualisation of systems
of thought: Bourdieu omitted and compressed the work of feminist
scholars, overlooked the presence of political mobilisation, ignored the
play of power between individuals and groups and was overly pessimis-
tic about change.[43] Yet while Bourdieu might have been naive about
the inequality within the family between men and women and adult
and child,[44] he did see the family as facing outwards in a different way
compared to other social institutions, not just as another site of control
or a hinge in a technology of power. Bourdieu described the 'family
discourse', the depiction of:

> A world in which the ordinary laws of the economy are suspended, a
> place of trusting and giving – as opposed to the market and its

exchange of equivalent values – or to use Aristotle's term, *philia*, a word that is often translated as 'friendship' but which in fact designates the refusal to calculate: a place where interest, in the narrow sense of the pursuit of equivalence in exchanges, is suspended.[45]

He saw 'family discourse' as a fiction, but a well-founded one. Like all the best fictions this imagined narrative of family motivated and inspired individuals, even if the actual experiences in the family were unhappy or uneven. It turned, he wrote, 'from a nominal fiction into a real group whose members are united by intense affective bonds', and he talked of the practical and symbolic work necessary to maintain 'a "family feeling" that generates devotion, generosity, and solidarity'.[46] This work, Bourdieu pointed out, would often be done by women and he cited contemporary sociological studies of the telephone, the snapshot, gifts and social events as the sites of this labour and the maintenance of the family as *habitus*. This sociology of the family allowed for the political presence of familial relationships as a source of support and mutual aid, and Bourdieu thus escaped to some degree Foucault's tendency to pessimistically theorise the family in terms of its predominant rationality of power.[47]

Putting it quite simply, Bourdieu allowed us to look at the family as a site of love, not just of government. He tends occasionally to imply a separation between love from government. Overall, however, Bourdieu recognises that governance operates through love but that this does not reduce love to governance, such that it would be ethically or sociologically indistinguishable from other forms of power. Thus like Foucault he recognised that love and control were not opposed to each other, but unlike Foucault he did take both into account, and in doing so recognised the emotional labour and gender in the household. It was to some extent a sentimental view, but it cashed out a politics of the family that moved on from nineteenth-century innovations in patriarchal power, to consider the power of women and children as well. One of the developments of this was the idea of 'emotional capital', put forward by Helga Nowotny in 1981; Diane Reay has argued that this concept is a useful way of thinking about emotional labour in the household as an extra, valuable resource that individuals and families might have, alongside bodily, social and cultural capital.[48] Treating Bourdieu as a signpost to a more sensitive account of the family and power, however, is not for a moment to suggest that Foucault's insights do not remain valuable. For instance, in a perfectly Foucauldean moment, the concept of 'emotional capital' was copyrighted in 2004 by the analyst of human resources Bénédicte Gendron.[49]

Concluding thoughts

The bourgeois family of the 1860s was a long way from Foucault's own stifling provincial middle-class milieu of 1940s Poitiers, which was in turn a long way from the liberal family of our time. Although the method of thinking about discourse and practices in the present owes a great deal to Foucault's critical dissection of historical texts, Foucault's theories cannot and should not be seen as a simple template that we can use for thinking about subjectivity and subjection in the 2000s. The idea of surveillance, self-regulation and the integration of attitudes into daily practice in family as well as other social institutions, is one of Foucault's most productive critical insights. Allied to this are the questions that Foucault raises about the space of the family, particularly the challenge of making household and family the same when they may be emotionally and politically very different, as well as the recognition of the public nature of reproduction and sexuality, the importance of law and the professions in effecting cultural and social change. But we should be mindful of Robert Gordon's criticism of those who expect Foucault to cover all of the angles, to be the perfect social theorist who enables us all to make progress. Gordon rightfully argues that too much is being expected of Foucault's texts: 'There is now a burgeoning academic sub-literature of complaint about the things which Foucault left undone, as though he had neglected his duty to write his readers' books as well as his own.'[50]

Jacques Donzelot's development of Foucault – discussed in the chapter by José Luis Moreno Pestaña in this volume – was one way in which the analysis of some of the systems of thought had been extended to the modern family. However, Pestaña expresses concerns about Donzelot similar to those in my chapter about Foucault's too exclusive focus on professional discourses about the family, to the exclusion of the interplay of power relations in organising family life. Foucault's writing from the 1960s to the early 1980s demonstrates the development over time of a new responsiveness to the records of people who spoke. However, he remained dismissive of psychoanalysis as it 'never succeeded in making images speak'.[51] One of the most successful discourses of the affections and emotions was thus excluded from Foucault's account, except along the simple axis of domination and subordination. One cannot expect Foucault to provide the full toolkit in explaining either the 'imaginary landscape' or 'the real social structure' that is the family. From Bourdieu can be added the ways in which the family is a site of difference between the sexes, a sense of the topography of emotional life that is equally historicist, but takes into consideration the influence of markets and commodities as well as professionals. However, Bourdieu should be understood as a signpost rather than a solution to theorising the family, and there remains a need for histories of the present of the family that allow for both affect and institutional change.

My own research on the history of corporal punishment in twentieth-century Britain uses parts of Foucault's toolkit. Ideas of surveillance and the embodied learning of disciplinary practices have been enormously productive in understanding how the home and its architecture moves in and out of public understanding of parenthood, of delinquency and of the significance of the professions in relation to a very specific place and time. The ideas of capital and of emotional labour help a great deal in asking who disciplines the child, and what happens within the family as a place of disciplinary elaboration. Where Foucault does not help is in understanding why professional discourses are resisted by those parents who like to beat their children, nor why that enthusiasm is different within class groups rather than between them. That moment, when discipline and punishment were replaced by attentiveness and social science, could be summed up as the moment of 'child abuse' replacing 'child cruelty' as the prevalent term, roughly in the 1960s for medical and professional groups, in the 1980s for lawyers, the press and the general public. Here the surveillance of one group – social workers, primary school teachers, doctors – is used against the secrecy of another – parents and family. But the iterated return of the loving slap in British public discourse can be seen in the 1890s, 1930s and 1990s. The punishing parent is never simply the patriarchal father even when the law insisted that only he had the power to offer 'reasonable chastisement'.[52] Most oral histories and users of personal accounts suggest that in the working class it was mostly mothers who disciplined children, and in the middle class it was fathers or schoolteachers. Bodily needs were to some extent replaced by psychic needs in the descriptions of managing children, but not quite when Foucault described them as being so replaced in the 1860s, but much later in the 1960s. For Foucault's account was too rooted in the nineteenth century, and while Bourdieu considered television, the popular press and education, he did not offer an adequate methodology to describe those changing practices either.

The gaze and surveillance, the mixed economy of disciplinarity and governmentality, the question of systems of thought have all inspired thinking about the history of the present of the family, but they have come far more from Foucault's general theorisation of power, regulation and systems of thought, than they do from his own narratives of the family. Families remain too unsystematic as institutions to fit neatly into accounts that ignore the changing ways in which families both control and support their members. General histories of change that see reduced masculine domination and call into question professional regulation can be developed from Foucault, but the more precise and nuanced analysis remains something for which we need a bigger toolkit than just Foucault on the family.

Notes

I would like to thank Robbie Duschinsky and Leon Antonio Rocha, the editors of this volume, for their patience, generosity and thoughtful insights; also Martin Thom and Liz Guild for discussing Foucault with me.

1. Michel Foucault, 'Interview with Michel Foucault', EW3, 240.
2. See Mark Poster, *Critical Theory of the Family* (New York: Pluto Press, 1978).
3. Michel Foucault, *Madness and Civilisation: A History of Insanity in the Age of Reason*, Richard Howard (trans.) (London: Routledge, 2001 [1967]), 240.
4. Ibid. Foucault's doctoral thesis was first published as *Folie et déraison: Histoire de la folie à l'âge classique* (Paris: Plon, 1961), and an abridged version was published in 1964 as *Histoire de la folie à l'âge classique* (Paris: Union générale d'éditions, 1964). *Madness and Civilisation* was the English translation of this truncated 1964 edition. The 1961 original was then reissued in expanded form by Gallimard in 1972 with a new preface and two essays as appendices, but the title *Histoire de la folie à l'âge classique* was adopted. The English translation, by Jean Khalfa, was based on this 1972 Gallimard edition and released as *History of Madness* (London: Routledge, 2006). Note that the phrase 'imaginary landscape and real social structure' appears only in *Madness and Civilisation*.
5. Foucault, HOM, 490.
6. Ibid., 491.
7. Foucault, PSP, 80.
8. Ibid., 115.
9. Ibid., 81.
10. He repeated the same functionalist analysis in *History of Sexuality, Volume 1*: 'The [conjugal] family organisation, precisely to the extent that it was insular and heteromorphous with respect to the other power mechanisms was used to support the great "manoeuvres" employed for the Malthusian control of the birth rate, for the populationist incitements, for the medicalisation of sex and the psychiatrisation of its nongenital forms.' See Foucault, HS1, 99.
11. Ibid., 112.
12. Foucault's initial plan for the *History of Sexuality* series could be found on the back cover of the French first edition of the first volume: 1. *La Volonté de savoir* [The Will to Knowledge]; 2. *La Chair et le corps* [The Flesh and the Body]; 3. *La Croisade des enfants* [The Children's Crusade]; 4. *La Femme, la mère et l'hystérique* [The Woman, the Mother and the Hysteric]; 5. *Les Pervers* [The Perverse]; 6.

Populations et races [Populations and Races]. On Foucault's change of direction, see for instance the interview, 'The concern for truth', PPC, 255–70.

13. Foucault, HS1, 105.
14. See Maïté Albistur and Daniel Armogathe, *Histoire du féminisme français, du moyen âge à nos jours* (Paris: Éditions des femmes, 1977); Clara Goldberg Moses, *French Feminism in the Nineteenth Century* (Albany, NY: SUNY Press, 1984); Steven C. Hause and Annie Kenney, *Women's Suffrage and Politics in the French Third Republic* (Princeton, NJ: Princeton University Press, 1984).
15. Foucault, PSP, 80.
16. Another case study in which the family as a place of many activities and forms of power becomes visible is the puzzled family of Michel Foucault, *Herculine Barbin: Being the Recently Discovered Memoirs of a Nineteenth-Century French Hermaphrodite*, Richard McDougall (trans.) (New York: Pantheon, 1980). Barbin was raised as a girl but then kept falling for other girls and was eventually 'identified' as a boy. It had been published in 1872 by one of Herculine's psychiatrists as the case of 'Alexina'. It was then published in French in 1978 by Foucault.
17. Foucault, 'Preface', IPR, xi.
18. Ibid., 105.
19. See Arlette Farge and Michel Foucault, DEF, 172.
20. Foucault, ABN, 268–70.
21. Ibid., 293.
22. See Linda Alcoff, 'Dangerous pleasures: Foucault and the politics of paedophilia', in Susan J. Hekman (ed.), *Feminist Interpretations of Michel Foucault* (University Park, PA: Penn State University Press, 1996), 99–135.
23. Foucault, HS1, 31–2. On a recent critique of Foucault's use of the Jouy story, see Spencer Jackson, 'The subject of time in Foucault's tale of Jouy', *SubStance*, 39 (2010), 39–51.
24. Farge and Foucault, DEF.
25. Ibid., 161, my translation.
26. Ibid., 162, my translation.
27. Ibid., 208, my translation.
28. Ibid., 171.
29. See Michel Foucault and Michael Bess, 'Power, moral values, and the intellectual: an interview with Michel Foucault', *History of the Present*, 4 (1988), 1–2, 11–13, available at: http://www.vanderbilt.edu/historydept/ michaelbess/Foucault%20Interview (last accessed 1 March 2012).
30. Jeffrey Weeks, 'Foucault for historians', *History Workshop Journal*, 14 (1982), 106–19; Allan Megill, 'The reception of Foucault by historians', *Journal of the History of Ideas*, 48 (1987), 117–41; Jan Goldstein, *Foucault and the Writing of History* (Oxford: Wiley-Blackwell, 1994); Colin Gordon, 'Foucault in Britain', in Andrew Barry, Thomas Osborne and Nikolas Rose (eds), *Foucault and Political Reason: Liberalism, Neo-Liberalism, and Rationalities of Government* (Chicago, IL: University of Chicago Press, 1996), 253–70; Michelle Perrot (ed.), *L'Impossible Prison: Recherches sur le système pénitentiaire au XIXe siècle réunies par Michelle Perrot: Débat avec Michel Foucault* (Paris: Seuil, 1980).
31. See, for instance, Charles Taylor, 'Foucault on freedom and truth', in *Philosophy and the Human Sciences: Philosophical Papers 2* (Cambridge: Cambridge University Press, 1985), 152–84. A succinct summary of criticisms

176 *Foucault, the Family and Politics*

and defences of Foucault in the history of psychiatry may be found in Gary Gutting, 'Foucault and the history of madness', in Gary Gutting (ed.), *The Cambridge Companion to Foucault*, 2nd edn (Cambridge: Cambridge University Press, 2005), 49–73.

32. Gareth Stedman Jones, 'The determinist fix: some obstacles to the further development of the linguistic approach to history in the 1990s', *History Workshop Journal*, 42 (1996), 19–35 at 31.

33. Foucault, PAO, xv.

34. For instance, Sandra Lee Bartky, 'Foucault, femininity and the modernisation of psychiatric power', in Irene Diamond and Lee Quinby (eds), *Feminism and Foucault: Reflections on Resistance* (Boston, MA: Northeastern University Press, 1988), 61–86; Jana Sawicki, *Disciplining Foucault: Feminism, Power and the Body* (London: Routledge, 1991); Susan Bordo, 'Feminism, Foucault, and the politics of the body', in Caroline Ramazanoglu (ed.), *Up Against Foucault: Explorations of Some Tensions between Foucault and Feminism* (London: Routledge, 1993), 179–202.

35. Chloë Taylor, 'Foucault and familial power', *Hypatia*, 27 (2012), 201–18 at 215.

36. Judith Butler, 'Foucault and the paradox of bodily inscriptions', *Journal of Philosophy*, 86 (1989), 601–7 at 604. See also Lois McNay, 'The Foucauldean body and the exclusion of experience', *Hypatia*, 6 (1991), 125–37.

37. Foucault, BOB, 149–50.

38. Pierre Bourdieu, *Distinction: A Social Critique of the Judgement of Taste*, Richard Nice (trans.) (Cambridge, MA: Harvard University Press, 1984), 101.

39. Pierre Bourdieu, Jean-Claude Chamboredon and Jean-Claude Passeron, *Le Métier de sociologue: préalables epistémologiques* (Paris-La Haye: Mouton-Bourdas, 1968), 64.

40. Pierre Bourdieu et al., *La Misère du monde* (Paris: Éditions du Seuil, 1993). English edition: *The Weight of the World: Social Suffering in Contemporary Society*, Priscilla Parkhurst Ferguson (trans.) (Cambridge: Polity, 1999).

41. Bourdieu, *Distinction*, 154.

42. Pierre Bourdieu, 'On the family as a realised category', *Theory, Culture and Society*, 13 (1996), 19–26.

43. Terry Lovell, 'Thinking feminism with and against Bourdieu', in Bridget Fowler (ed.), *Reading Bourdieu on Society and Culture* (Oxford: Wiley-Blackwell, 2000), 27–48. But also see Simon Charlesworth's passionate defence of Bourdieu as someone who included happiness and unhappiness in his theorising in the same collection, 'Bourdieu, social suffering and working-class life', 49–64.

44. Pierre Bourdieu, *Masculine Domination*, Richard Nice (trans.) (Stanford, CA: Stanford University Press, 2001), originally published as *La Domination masculine* (Paris: Seuil, 1998); Lovell, 'Thinking feminism', 27–48.

45. Bourdieu, 'On the family as a realised category', 20.

47. See Beverley Skeggs, 'Context and background: Pierre Bourdieu's analysis of class, gender and sexuality', *Sociological Review*, 52 (2004), 19–33.

48. Diane Reay, 'Gendering Bourdieu's concept of capitals? Emotional capital, women and social class', in Lisa Adkins and Beverley Skeggs (eds), *Feminism after Bourdieu* (Oxford: Wiley-Blackwell, 2004), 57–74.

49. Helga Nowotny, 'Women in public life in Austria', in Cynthia Fuchs Epstein and Rose Laub Coser (eds), *Access to Power: Cross-National Studies of Women and Elites* (London: George Allen and Unwin, 1981), 145–58; Bénédicte Gendron, 'Why emotional capital matters in education and in labour? Toward an optimal exploitation of human capital and knowledge management', *Les Cahiers de la Maison des Sciences Economoqies*, série rouge, 113 (Paris: Université Panthéon-Sorbonne, 2004), available at: http://econpapers. repec.org/paper/msewpsorb/r04113.htm (last accessed 1 March 2012).
50. See Robert Gordon's 'Review of Michel Foucault, *History of Madness*, Jean Khalfa (trans.) (London: Routledge, 2006)', *Notre Dame Philosophical Reviews*, 23 February 2007, vailable at: http://ndpr.nd.edu/news/25226-history-of-madness/ (last accessed 1 March 2012).
51. Foucault, DIE, 38. On Foucault and psychoanalysis, see John Forrester, 'Michel Foucault and the history of psychoanalysis', in *The Seductions of Psychoanalysis: Freud, Lacan and Derrida* (Cambridge: Cambridge University Press, 1991), 286–316.
52. This term was only abandoned in the UK in 2004 to be replaced by 'punishment which does no visible damage'.

8

'Présentation', *Le Désordre des familles: Lettres de cachet des Archives de la Bastille au XVIIIe siècle* (1982)

Arlette Farge and Michel Foucault
Translated from French by Leon Antonio Rocha
and Thibaud Harrois

The idea that History is vowed to the 'accuracy of the archive', and philosophy to the 'architecture of ideas', seems nonsensical to us. That is not the way that we work.

One of us had studied street-life in eighteenth-century Paris, and the other the procedures of administrative confinement from the seventeenth century to the French Revolution. We both had to use the so-called *Archives de la Bastille*, deposited at the Bibliothèque de l'Arsenal. These archives are in fact predominantly dossiers concerning police affairs, which were gathered at the Bastille, became dispersed during the Revolution, and were subsequently reunited.

Upon perusing the Archives, both of us were struck by a number of facts. First, a very large number of these dossiers were concerned with *lettres de cachet*,[1] and more precisely, with petitions that were addressed either to the Police Lieutenant, or directly to the *Maison du Roi* to obtain the Sovereign's order to restrict the freedom of an individual (this may be house arrest, exile, but most of the time incarceration). We were also struck by the fact that, in many cases, the requests were made in relation to familial and absolutely private matters: minor conflicts between parents and children, household dissensions, the misconduct of one of the spouses, the disorderly behaviour of a son or a daughter. It was also apparent to us that the vast majority of these requests came from those of modest backgrounds,[2] sometimes from even the very poor – from petty merchants or craftsmen, to market gardeners, second-hand clothes dealers, domestic servants or day-wage labourers. Finally, we could establish that, despite the fragmentary nature of these archives, there was often,

178

alongside a request for internment, a whole collection of other items: the testimonies of neighbours, of the family or close circle; the inquiries of police commissioners; the crown's verdict; requests for release from those who were subjects of these internments, or even from those who had requested their incarceration in the first place.

For all these reasons, we felt that these documents could offer interesting insights into the specificities of daily life of the lower classes in Paris during the era of absolute monarchy – or at least during a certain period of the ancien régime. One would tend to see in the *lettres de cachet* in the archives documents that depict absolutism, illustrating the manner in which the monarch struck at his enemies or assisted rich and powerful families to get rid of a relative.

As it happens, reading these dossiers sent us in a direction that had not so much to do with the Sovereign's ire, but with the passions of the common people, at the centre of which were family relationships – husbands and wives, parents and children.

After a few words on the history of the *lettres de cachet*, the way they worked, and the reasons that guided our choice among this mass of documents, we shall provide, in their entirety, the dossiers that captured our attention: namely those that were concerned with requests for confinement stemming from a husband or a wife against a spouse, or parents against their children, between 1728 and 1758. In the final chapter we shall indicate a number of perspectives that to us seem to emerge from this collection of documents.

The King's orders

One has to look for the history of the *lettres de cachet* beneath the thicket of received ideas, which are often only remembered as something that in fact served His Majesty's Pleasure, used in order to lock up disloyal nobles or disobliging grand vassals. The *lettre de cachet* was a public act, which aimed at eliminating the enemy of power without further recourse. History immortalised it as a symbol for the Storming of the Bastille [...]. Collective memory has forgotten the countless letters from the King that were used for something entirely different from the affairs of the State. In Paris, the establishment of a Police Lieutenancy, responsible for both policing the city and forwarding the *lettres de cachet*, accentuated the phenomenon. The Police Lieutenants were quick to use this flexible, simple, fast, formality-free means to arrest and incarcerate people. Thus they could take control of the accused more quickly. The regular justice system moved so slowly that the accused often fled before the trial could be arranged: it was only by a decree of *prise de corps* that the judge could arrest anyone, unless that person was caught *in flagrante*. Then the investigation would begin and the witnesses would be heard only after the summons were issued. Thus it was not unusual for the general prosecutor quite simply to request imprisonment with a *lettre de cachet*.

Thus the *lettre de cachet* was a very common part of police affairs in Paris. The term 'police affairs' was sufficiently vague and imprecise to allow a great number of cases to be included under this label.

A conflict between a master and an apprentice could quickly become a police affair;[3] crowd-gathering was a *cas royal* and workers' organisations were always prohibited through innumerable arrests, ordinances and decrees that punctuated the sixteenth, seventeenth and eighteenth centuries.[1] To enforce the prohibition of workers' organisations, the King very often used the *lettre de cachet*; and when it concerned a particular conflict between a master and an apprentice, ordinary judges took care of the matter. They had an interest in acting swiftly; the fear of disorder in workshops was far stronger than the desire for the complex regular procedures. The *lettre de cachet* was indeed the easiest instrument for the discreet and secretive incarceration of those hotheads, who on each payday asked for more money from their master or who rarely hesitated to rebel. This obvious use of the *lettre royale* partially explains the lack of labour disputes of which judicial archives have kept a trace, and on the contrary suggests – something that should be proved – that a large number of conflicts were very quickly concealed under the impenetrable opacity of the *lettres de cachet*. The police affair was very convenient indeed.

'Disturbing the peace' was another sufficient ground for issuing a *lettre de cachet*: street prostitution for example was one such disorder, and the *lettres de cachet* would remedy this so-called scandalous debauchery. It was through their use that there were regular roundups of women, who were taken away in tipcarts and sent to the Salpêtrière amid the derision of the crowd. Comedians also felt the force of that so-called jurisdiction: the *ordres du Roi pour faits de théâtre*[4] were employed to send to the prison of For-l'Évêque those who were deemed troublemakers because they were jugglers and street comedians.

The register of Inspector Poussot, which he kept regularly from 1738 to 1754, was preserved at the Archives de la Bastille. It allows one to have a better understanding of how both orders from the King and police decisions were used to clean up the capital.[5] Poussot was in charge of the Halles district and he recorded in alphabetical order the arrests that were made under his authority, and mentioned a good deal of information about the arrested – surname, forename, age, occupation, residence, date of arrest, name of the authority that made the decision, reason for arrest, name of the prison.

Of the 2692 people arrested and recorded in this register, 1468 were arrested on the King's order, that is to say half. The others were put in prison via a police decision. Therefore it was as a direct agent of the King that Inspector Poussot operated and this clearly differentiated him from the Commissioner. Poussot did not act on civil complaints but from royal instructions allowing searches and arrests of persons under suspicion. The Inspector's lists provide an overview of the issues that concerned the monarchy, and the rapid measures taken to deal with them.

Skimming through the pages of Poussot's register that tell so little and so much at the same time, one reads so many names of men and women, and one takes note of their ever so common nicknames, and a picture soon emerges. Almost 3000 names ended up on the register, most of these people were young, and most of them were born far from the capital. They had all sorts of occupations except the most esteemed, they were stranded in Paris after experiencing vagrancy, the insecurity of seasonal work, the heady atmosphere of taverns and traffics, quick alliances with other people whose lives had not been much easier and were as tempted as they were by mischief. Swindles and fraudulent deals that one would accept in haste or through desperate need, the gangs of buddies that one joined in the country, and the loose women that joined this hopelessness and these dishonest ambitions. Crooks, veterans, beggars, women of encounters, accomplished thieves, gang leaders and poor wretches: they were all here; the columns of the register were filled with their fast trajectories, which were suddenly stopped by arrest and imprisonment. Moreover, this was not the end of their journey: they escaped from prison, were released or transferred, were re-arrested later on or wandered about forever, *roulant les campagnes* [roaming around the countryside] to use the expression of the time. Herein lies the paradox of Poussot's register: it suddenly froze people's lives, yet at the same time it suggests a feeling of incessant motion and constant circulation. Not only is the register about these migrants, but the information one can sometimes gather about their pasts shows the extent to which the world was shifting and transient, both there and elsewhere; the bands of ruffians that one so clearly sees in this register reinforce this impression of small and large movements, of fleetingness and elusiveness. Beyond Poussot's neat pictures, there were surges of brigands, and miserable people, immense waves that broke and spread, swelled, and fled or lingered on in order to recover and come back again.

It is also an image of Paris captured in the nighttime: the police searches of boarding houses, of inn rooms, or of closed and disreputable places, revealed what life was like during the night. The Inspector could go anywhere he wanted, waking people from their sleep, surprising lovers and liaisons, asking the motives behind each and everyone's activities. He deliberately waited until the darker hours to harass his prey, certain that time and darkness would work in his favour. Poussot meticulously brought together before our eyes all those beings who were trapped as they doubtlessly naively believed that they were protected by the night. Not a line in the register about thieves arrested in consequence of public clamour, as they were stealing chickens in the market, clothes on stands or on the clotheslines of the laundresses, even though the register did manage to squeeze in those who had stolen handkerchiefs in churches, caught in the act or reported by bystanders. On the contrary, the register gathered mostly a crowd of people who were often known by the police, sought by the police and who had been identified either by small-time informants or by higher authorities. All that was left to do was to pick them up after dusk in forbidden places like gambling dens or cabarets that had not yet pulled their shutters, and in places for sleep such as boarding houses and inns. This was certainly made possible by the records kept by innkeepers and hotel managers, which were closely monitored by the Inspectors who also did not refrain from collecting substantial fees on this occasion.

It was an image of nighttime Paris, sheltering in its innumerable dark dens the *canaille* [rabble], who were so frightening and fascinating at the same time: the kind that always seemed to add debauchery to mischief; that could truly be called criminal and that knew the thousand-and-one shelters in the capital where accomplices, loot and adventurous plans could be hidden; the kind that the bourgeoisie squarely equated with 'the people' in general. Nighttime Paris was a kind of backstage that justified all forms of police actions, including the most sordid. Here was gathered a population for which criminal activity was, most of the time, a way of life, something that did not at all resemble the Paris of the mornings and afternoons, the traces of which were to be found at the commissionership.

The 3000 people arrested by Inspector Poussot's men in fact revealed a side of Paris that the ruling order wanted to get rid of. These arrests can be interpreted as a will for police presence in all of the secret places of the capital, as well as for royal interventions at all levels, from the streets to the households. At the same time one can anticipate the futility of such an enterprise, even more so when one gets a few inklings of the way in which petty criminality operated. It was furtive, dynamic, and already organised: built on a family model (delinquency often involved the entire family) or on a certain ritualisation of male and female relationships, delinquency always seemed to rise from its own ashes. The King's orders hit this elusive population, and death did not put an end to its activities.

Similarly, breaches of military and religious discipline allowed the rapid incarceration of restless soldiers or of clergymen who did not abide by the usual rules. The number of clergymen thus placed in solitary confinement is very impressive: a study by H. [Henri] Debord[6] estimates the number of *lettres de cachet* sent against clergymen all across France between 1741 and 1775 at 6000 (as opposed to 17,000 to 18,000 letters sent against the lay). Even if these are approximate figures, it is important to highlight their scale.

Furthermore, one should not forget that the power of these royal letters was not limited to that of incarceration. They could be grafted onto the actions of the courts to add to, confirm or aggravate sentences. It often happened that, on the King's order, the Lieutenant General attempted to retain in prison some suspects, who had not been convicted by the ordinary courts because of a lack of evidence. The system of royal order not only coexisted with the regular procedure but also crept in to amend it, thus in a way perverting it from within.

The requests from the families

The *lettre de cachet* involving families was not a royal order different from the others: like any other social group, the family owed the King transparency. In private and public life alike, order was necessary: the family was the privileged site in which tranquillity in private life would in turn establish a certain kind of public order. Thus the King had the right to follow the family's operations and its ups and downs.

The *lettre de cachet* authorised a system of familial repression, which opened a particular site of social organisation where a curious battle – the balance of powers that were often unequal – took place between the representatives of a familial authority and one of its members. The two sides were not alone in the confrontation: they drew with them their own networks of social relations that testified for them. The letter ordering incarceration imposed its punishment on a familial fabric that itself was stitched together by relationships with other people. And this is certainly one of the first aspects to highlight: the *lettre de cachet* involving families, despite the insistence put on privacy, was never just about the family. That shows that the family is necessarily imbricated with the surrounding world and its impossible isolation even when this was desired.

In Paris, the family's requests for incarceration followed a procedure unique to the capital: the noble families sent their petition (placet) to the King himself, or to the minister of the *Maison du Roi*. It was in the royal council, in the actual presence of the King, that the placet was carefully reviewed.

The common people proceeded in quite a different fashion; they submitted their petition to the Lieutenant General of Police who reviewed it in his bureau, led the investigation, and pronounced the sentence. The inquiry inevitably kept the District Commissioner well informed of the case; he delegated his power of information to the Police Inspector. The popular family was considerably involved in its neighbourhood and integrated into an intense urban life, and could not exclude itself from this social capillarity. The urban fabric – neighbours, commissioners, parish priests, merchants, tenants – was a breeding ground without which the popular family could not exist. The Police Lieutenant then informed, wrote a detailed report to the minister and waited for the Secretary of State to send in further instructions. This was at least the most common procedure used under Louis XIV; and it was soon to transform and go at an ever quicker pace under the reign of Louis XV. One would often see Lieutenant Generals writing but very brief notes and not even waiting for the royal response, taking it upon themselves to execute the order of the King.

This intervention of the Lieutenant General of Police was a unique Parisian feature. It also explains the constant slippage between ordinary trials and royal order as the two were practically ruled by the same person. Other kinds of procedure existed in the provinces: in Languedoc, for example, it was the 'military authorities [...] that ensure[d] familial order and, as protector of the rights of the nobility, received complaints and recriminations coming from that class'.[7] The military authorities accepted placets from other social backgrounds: the confinement of family members was not the preserve of the aristocracy.

The *lettre de cachet* involving families made private repression legal: the royal power granted the legal authority to imprison somebody at the request of the family, but did not bear in any way the cost of detaining the prisoner. To punish one's relative without going through the ordinary and public system of justice, on the one hand, one had to beg the King and convince him of one's misery so that he deigned to send the official order. On the other hand, one had to help the King financially, as the royal administration did not have to bear the cost of the incarceration. The signature of the order had a price: the money added weight to the tales of woe.

That was a traditional practice at the time. It was one of the functions that the government was expected and requested to fulfil. This explains the enormous size of the files for each case, as well as the energetic drive with which the placets were written. Writing to the Lieutenant General of Police to make him aware of the unbearable conditions that prevailed in one's family was an adventure in the real sense of the term, especially if one was a member of the lower classes. First, one had to go and find a public scribe who, with the usual forms of respect due to His Majesty, would convey every detail of a tumultuous daily life. Upon reading the dossiers, one is astonished by the mass of domestic details and by the enormous amount of paperwork generated by private miseries that in fact concerned the intimacy and the dark shadow of family relationships. With the letter also came neighbours' testimonies: sometimes they signed at the bottom and added their occupation, sometimes they wrote separately and recounted in their way what they saw, heard and knew. Distant relatives of the family, the local café-owner, the grocer at the bottom of the staircase, and tenants on the same floor were the main signatories. To ensure that the petition had a greater force of conviction, it was useful to convince the parish priest – an influential person in the neighbourhood – as well as the principal tenant – that feared, hated and respected guarantor of Parisian buildings – to act as signatories.

If what was requested was the incarceration of one's child, and if the father was dead or absent, then the mother could apply for the request. She then surrounded herself with her relatives, and it was the *avis de parents* [relatives' opinion] that could add more weight to her request. The placet was received by a secretary of the Lieutenant General of Police who sent it to a Commissioner and to the Police Inspector of the area to *verify the facts and account for them*. Normally, they had to carry out their investigations separately, but in reality one took charge of the investigation and produced a report on the petition while the other annotated this report. Witnesses, neighbours and signatories were heard by the Inspector, and then the Commissioner reported to the Lieutenant General of Police. Whether the report was detailed or not depended on the case and the Commissioners. The Lieutenant then drew up his own report and sent it to the King's secretary. That step was often a pure formality: sometimes he did not expect any response to enforce the order of confinement.

1728–1758: A survey

Careful examination of this type of documents at the Archives de la Bastille shows that they are incomplete. On the one hand, there are only few requests for confinement for family reasons before the 1720s. On the other hand, documents related to this are very rare in the Archives de la Bastille for the years after 1760.

In fact these two findings do not have the same explanation. Among the King's orders that have been preserved, from the end of the seventeenth to the start of eighteen century, political and religious affairs constitute the largest proportion: affairs of the Convulsionnaires of Saint-Médard and of the Jansenists, affairs related to spies and foreign agents, and then all the small fry of astrologers, diviners, plotters and restless souls. The fact that the *lettres de cachet* mainly had this public usage and that their private use for family matters was quite rare seems to be confirmed by [Jean-Charles-Pierre] Lenoir, Lieutenant General of Police, if one were to believe the testimony that he left in the papers he wrote after he departed from his post, which were preserved at the Municipal Library in Orléans:

> The origin of the King's order that we call the *lettres de cachet* involving families dates back to the administration of M. d'Argenson [Marc-René de Voyer de Paulmy, marquis d'Argenson (1652–1721)]. Their use was best known during the administration of Berryer [Nicolas Berryer, seigneur de Ravenoville (1703–62)], and even more so during that of M. de Sartine [Antoine-Raimond-Jean-Gualbert-Gabriel, chevalier de Sartine (1729–1801)] than during my administration. At the time we held the principle that the dishonour of an individual affected his family, thus government and politics came to the rescue of the parents who had a legitimate fear of being disgraced. This measure is necessary in a large city like Paris where the youth is exposed to all sorts of dangers and corruption.[9]

We can therefore safely assume that the 1750s marked a real increase in requests for confinement for family reasons.

However the virtual disappearance of these requests from the Archives de la Bastille after 1760 is perplexing. We know that Sartine, at the end of Louis XV's reign, or even Lenoir – however 'restricted' he stated his practice to be – were reputed to have used this kind of procedure on a wide scale. Lenoir himself declared: 'In the last ten to twelve years, there were few Parisian families in which not a single person had to resort to the administrative magistrate of the general police in the city, for issues regarding their honour.' And when, in 1784, Breteuil [Louis Auguste le Tonnelier de Breteuil (1730–1807)] sent his famous circular to limit this practice, it is obvious that it had not fallen into disuse by that time. Thus family petitions had not ceased to be sent after 1760; yet the traces disappeared from the Archives de la Bastille. It must be assumed that such requests and the reports that accompanied them were archived in a different way during the period in question; they were then destroyed over time or dispersed to other places.

We thus had access to a rich documentation for the period 1720–1760 (this, of course, does not mean that we have all the petitions addressed by Parisian families for those forty years). We have chosen 1728 to be the starting point and 1758 to be the end point, two dates separated by the thirty years of one generation. No doubt the year 1758 coincides with Bertin de Bellisle's [Henri-Léonard-Jean-Baptiste, comte de Bourdeilles (1720–92)] brief office as Lieutenant General of Police, but verifications of the neighbouring years (1756 and 1760) show that, on this particular matter, his administration had not behaved in a peculiar manner. There are quite a number of documents attached to the years 1728 and 1758, their similarities are quite clear and indeed they are repetitive enough that we can assume that we have a representative sample (even if they do not allow any quantitative evaluation).

Close scrutiny of the years 1728 and 1758 shows that there were respectively 168 and 74 requests from families for incarceration; in the years 1756 and 1760 there were 67 and 76 dossiers on the same type of affairs: roughly one-fifth of the requests for incarceration. However precarious, unsound, and doubtlessly far removed from the quantitative reality these records are, we can dig into them and, case after case, find the tenuous threads in the history of families who had decided to expose their tears to the King, at the same time revealing their intimate lives, always mixing the tragic and the pathetic.

Notes

1. The definition for the *lettre de cachet* is very general: 'a letter written at the command of the King, countersigned by a Secretary of the State, and stamped by the seal of the King' (Guyot, *Répertoire de jurisprudence*, 1785 t. X). [Joseph Nicolas Guyot, *Répertoire universel et raisonné de jurisprudence*

civile, criminelle, canonique et beneficiale: ouvrage de plusieurs jurisconsultes, 1785, Tome Dixième.]

2. This contradicts the thesis of F.-X. [François-Xavier] Emmanuelli, 'Ordres du Roi et lettres de cachet en Provence à la fin de l'Ancien Régime: Contribution à l'histoire du climat social et politique', *Revue Historique*, 512 (1974), 3. Indeed, the request for confinement is not a process that only the upper classes would use. A rough social and occupational analysis attempted on the sources reveals that the process was used by a proportion ranging from half to two-thirds of people of the lower classes.

3. Germain Martin, *Lois, édits, arrêts et règlements sur les associations ouvrières au XVIIIe siècle, 1700–1792*. Doctoral thesis. Paris, 1900. [Paris: A. Rousseau, Faculté de droit et des sciences économiques, Université de Grenoble.]

4. Frantz Funck-Brentano, *La Bastille des comédiens, le For-l'Évêque* (Paris: Albert Fontemoing, 1903).

5. Bibliothèque de l'Arsenal, Archives de la Bastille, ms. 10141. An unpublished work devoted to the interpretation of Inspector Poussot's register.

6. Henri Debord, *Contribution à l'histoire des orders du Roi au XVIIIe siècle d'après les registres du secretariat d'État à la Maison du Roi, 1741–1775* (Paris: Domat-Montchrestien, 1938).

7. Nicole Castan, *Justice et repression en Languedoc à l'époque des Lumières* (Paris: Flammarion, 1980), 201. See also the pages devoted to *lettres de cachet* by Jean-Claude Perrot, *Genèse d'une ville moderne: Caen au XVIIIe siècle* (Paris: Mouton, 1975). And Claude Quétel, *'De par le Roy': Essai sur les lettres de cachet* (Toulouse: Éditions Privat, 1981).

8. Cf. Henri Debord, *Contibution à l'histoire des ordres du Roi au XVIIIe siècle, op. cit.*

9. Bibliothèque municipal d'Orléans, Fonds Lenoir, ms. 1423, fol. 21: Sûreté. Recall that Marc-René d'Argenson was Lieutenant General of Police from 1697 to 1718; Berryer from 1747 to 1757; Sartine from 1759 to 1774.

Translators' notes

The translators are extremely grateful to Robbie Duschinsky and Chloë Taylor for their encouragement, and to Arlette Farge and Jean Khalfa for their guidance. In order to avoid confusion, the notes from the original *présentation* are placed at the end of this translation. Note that endnote 8 does not actually appear anywhere in the original text.

[1] Editors' note: A *cas royal* was a crime that affected the person or the preroga-tives of the king, including lese-majesty (an offence against the dignity of the reigning sovereign or against the state), sedition, treason, rebellion, counter-feiting (of coins, for instance), forgery of the royal seal. A *cas royal* had to be dealt with exclusively by the royal court.

9

'That Dazzling, Momentary Wake' of the *lettre de cachet*:

The Problem of Experience in Foucault's Practice of History

Leon Antonio Rocha

Le Désordre des familles: Lettres de cachet des Archives de la Bastille au XVIIIe siècle is a volume edited by Arlette Farge and Michel Foucault, published in October 1982 by Gallimard. The book collects together 'poison-pen letters' from eighteen-century France, written to state institutions by ordinary men and women who wanted their 'deviant' or disgraced family members to be confined in a hospital, an asylum or a prison – the famous Bicêtre and Salpêtrière among others. Some of the responses given by the official institutions and the police dossiers are also included in Farge and Foucault's collection. There are commentaries throughout by the two scholars, along with a postscript entitled 'Quand on s'addresse au roi' ('When One Writes to the King').

At the time of writing this chapter (February 2012), *Le Désordre des familles* has still not found an English translator and publisher, and has sadly gone out of print in France. Arlette Farge explains that the lack of critical attention in France (and indeed elsewhere) is because *Le Désordre des familles* appears to readers and publishers to contain 'too many texts and not enough Foucault'.[1] Yet I argue in this chapter, which accompanies the English translation of Farge and Foucault's introduction to their book, that *Le Désordre des familles* is absolutely crucial to analysing Foucault's theorising in the late 1970s concerning experience and power. Indeed, I suggest that Farge and Foucault's collaborative project is integral to grasping Foucault's more general intellectual trajectory, including the shift from *History of Sexuality, Volume 1* to considerations of practices of the self in *History of Sexuality, Volume 2* and *Volume 3*. Moreover, *Le Désordre des familles* is important in understanding Foucault's relationship with the practice of history and his reception among contemporaneous historians.

The context of production

In the mid 1950s, Foucault uncovered the documents that eventually evolved into the *Le Désordre des familles* project.[2] At that time Foucault was working on his doctoral thesis, which would become *History of Madness* (first published in French as *Folie et déraison: Histoire de la folie à l'âge classique* in 1961). Between 1955 and 1960, Foucault worked as a cultural attaché in Sweden, but drove from Uppsala back to Paris to spend the summer months working on materials in the Parisian libraries and archives, including the *lettres de cachet* and their associated dossiers deposited at the Archives de la Bastille at the Bibliothèque de l'Arsenal. Very early on, Foucault already had in mind a book project on these documents, and in 1964 he signed a contract for a volume on the Bastille that was supposed to appear in the *Archives* series of books, founded and edited by Pierre Nora. The provisional title was *Les Fous: Michel Foucault raconte, du XVIIe au XIXe siècles, de la Bastille à Sainte-Anne, le voyage au bout de la nuit* – in English, *The Mad: Michel Foucault recounts the journey into the night, from the Bastille to the Sainte-Anne asylum, from the seventeenth to nineteenth century*.[3] An alternative title for the book was simply *Les Embastillés* – *The Imprisoned* (or specifically those imprisoned in the Bastille).[4] This book project was abandoned and Foucault concentrated instead on the manuscript for *The Order of Things*, the bulk of which was written in the middle of 1964.

What is the *Archives* series? Some remarks are warranted here, since Foucault's book on Pierre Rivière (1973) and *Le Désordre des familles* (1982) were also part of this enterprise; the two books were respectively numbers 49 and 91 in the series. *Collection Archives* was established by Pierre Nora in 1964, with Nora and Jacques Revel acting as general editors of this paperback imprint. It was first based at the Parisian publishing house Julliard, later on acquired by Gallimard. The entire collection ran for 105 volumes and was discontinued in 1998.[5] Many books in the series have unfortunately gone out of print, but some are still available as inexpensive paperbacks, sold for five to ten euros. Historians Pierre Nora and Jacques Revel are the third and fourth generation of the *Annales* School, with whom Foucault enjoyed a close relationship.[6] *Collection Archives* set out to publish archival materials – manuscripts, correspondences, notebooks, dossiers – on both well-known and more obscure episodes from predominantly European and American history, and addressing both heatedly debated and unusual historiographical problems. Many volumes were explicitly intended to be political interventions that spoke directly to contemporary affairs, for instance

Jacques de Launay's volume on Vichy documents (1967) or Yohanan Manor's contribution on Zionism (1981), while other publications in the series were more concerned with capturing and conveying the thick texture of quotidian lives, whether those of eighteenth-century French villagers and townspeople or early twentieth-century supporters of Olympique de Marseille football club.[7] Among the most well-known of the series in Anglophone academia includes Foucault and his collaborators' contribution on *'I, Pierre Rivière'* and Michel de Certeau's *La Possession de Loudun* (1970).[8] It is probably fair to say that there is no direct equivalent of the *Archives* series – or at least nothing on that scale and depth – in the English-language publishing market.

Most importantly, *Collection Archives* was not simply a reprint or collection of primary source materials; the books in the series were said to be 'presented' (presentée) – and not merely 'edited' (editée) – by scholars, who penned commentaries on the documents, explained some of their selection criteria and editorial decisions, described various historical connections and dissected previous interpretations, and occasionally revealed, in a self-reflexive manner, their relationship and attachment to the materials. The books tell us something about the 'backstage': those everyday practices of professional historians, their craftsmanship and self-fashioning, the emotional dynamics that could emerge as they confronted documents from the distant or recent past – whether it was joy, bafflement or anger. The commentaries were printed in italics in the series in order to distinguish the scholar's voice from the excerpts of primary sources. The books do show to some extent the 'historian in action', and are invaluable to those wishing to engage with a particular historical episode or the corpus of a particular historian, or to those who wish to think more deeply in general about the historian's identity, craft and archival practices.

The *Archives* series was most active during the 'archival boom' and 'memory boom' from the 1970s and early 1980s in French academia. Rather schematically, this involved academic trends such as: the recovery of popular memories for the construction of a French 'national identity' and 'national culture' in the Mitterrandian era (for instance, Nora's *Les Lieux de mémoire*);[9] multi-volume work on the mentalities and sensibilities of the people in eighteenth- and nineteenth-century France (for instance, Philippe Ariès and Georges Duby's *Histoire de la vie privée* project, and the followers of Ariès);[10] the rescue of obscure and deviant lives and the championing of marginalised voices 'from below' (certainly Arlette Farge's agenda);[11] the rise of 'micro-history' that sought to use local studies to illuminate the impact of large-scale and long-term social changes on a modest person or some peripheral community (for instance, the work of Emmanuel Le Roy Ladurie, Carlo Ginzburg and Canadian-American scholar Natalie Zemon Davis).[12]

The *lettres de cachet*, and the other documents at the Archives de la Bastille, evidently had a great effect on Michel Foucault. In 'The Lives of Infamous Men' (1977), he spoke of his mixture of emotions from that encounter: 'my taste, my pleasure, an emotion, laughter, surprise, a certain dread, or some other feeling [the] intensity [of which] I might have trouble justifying'.[13] Foucault said that he felt at the time a 'resonance' with those archival materials, which contained a 'kind of beauty' emanating from 'hastily drawn images', from 'lowly lives reduced to ashes in the few sentences that struck them down'.[14] And it was a resonance, a 'taste [that had] not diminished', an intense emotion that Foucault said he continued to experience, to haunt him perhaps, for almost twenty years – between his first encounter with the *lettres de cachet* in the 1950s and penning 'The Lives of Infamous Men'.[15] Given that Foucault discovered these documents while working on *History of Madness*, and was so clearly moved and impressed by them, it may come as a surprise that they rarely featured in that book. As Michael Sheringham observes,

> for long stretches of [*History of Madness*], Foucault's argument is based entirely on published works, or on source material already compiled by others [...] When Foucault does cite archival material in [*History of Madness*], it is often second-hand, deriving from the work of earlier scholars.[16]

These works included Frantz Funck-Brentano's classic study *Les Lettres de cachet à Paris: étude suivie d'une liste des prisonniers de la Bastille (1659–1789)* (1903) and Aristide Joly's much older *Les Lettres de cachet dans la généralité de Caen au XVIIIe siècle* (1864).

One possible, mundane explanation for the omission of archival citations is that Foucault already had the *Les Embastillés* project in mind, and thus reserved the materials for that book. Another reason is that, as Foucault himself admitted, the reliance on secondary sources in history was fairly typical in philosophy – one could, for that matter, argue that it is still somewhat typical for philosophers simply to help themselves to historical work done by others.[17] But it can be argued that there is a much deeper intellectual reason at work, and one supported by Foucault's own account of this period. Again, as Michael Sheringham points out, Foucault said in a 1977 interview that 'his object in writing

[*History of Mandess*] had been to locate a dimension of lived experience ignored by doctors and psychiatrists'.[18] To that end, Foucault said that he 'plunged body and soul into the dust of the archives'.[19] Throughout *History of Madness*, a recurrent phrase is the 'experience of madness'; indeed, Jean Khalfa points out that the word 'experience' is 'perhaps the most common in the book'.[20] But whenever Foucault discussed an 'experience' in *History of Madness*, he 'never [did] anything other than to point to a difference in historical configurations of practices, beliefs, and institutions'.[21] Put another way, Foucault elected to concentrate on medical, scientific, juridical, literary, philosophical and theological discourses that constructed this thing called 'madness', and there were few testimonies of the experiences of obscure men and women to be found. In 'The Lives of Infamous Men', Foucault explained that at the time of writing *History of Madness*, he 'lack[ed] the necessary talent' to 'restore [the intensity of the archival documents] in an analysis'.[22] What was that 'necessary talent' that Foucault presumably felt that he had developed in the intermittent period, between *History of Madness* and the late 1970s? This 'necessary talent' was precisely, I shall argue in the next section (following the work of philosopher Timothy O'Leary), a way of dissecting experiences 'along three fundamental axes: knowledge, normativity, and modes of subjectivity'.[23]

The *lettres de cachet* did not make appearances in Foucault's next major publications: *Birth of the Clinic* (1963), *The Order of Things* (1966), and *Archaeology of Knowledge* (1969). For that matter these works contain very few citations of archival materials. Yet the excavation of documents from the archives at the Bastille, the Hôpital Général, the Sainte-Anne asylum, the Bibliothèque Nationale and so forth was a constant preoccupation for Foucault. He never effectively left the archive behind. In the 1970s, the materials began to be mentioned in his works again. In *Psychiatric Power*, his Collège de France lectures for the 1973–74 academic year, Foucault gestured towards the *lettres de cachet* in a couple of lectures.[24] It was also in the early 1970s that Foucault and his collaborators discovered the Rivière case from a 1836 issue of *Annales d'hygiène publique et de medicine légale* and then the associated dossiers preserved at the Archives du Calvados in Caen. The resultant publication, '*I, Pierre Rivière, Having Slaughtered My Mother, My Sister, and My Brother*': *A Case of Parricide in the Nineteenth Century* (1973), contained fragments of the memoir penned by Rivière himself – a young farmer from Normandy who murdered three members of his family – as well as the legal documents, police files, medical reports and psychiatric evaluations, with short essays penned by Foucault and his collaborators. This book, as previously mentioned, belongs to Pierre Nora's *Archives* series. One *lettre de cachet* was directly quoted and analysed in the *Abnormal* lectures (1974–75); it involved a mother's request that her son, a delinquent who regularly lied and stole, be sent to the Bicêtre.[25] The question of these letters was raised once again in passing, in *Discipline and Punish* (1975), in relation to police power in eighteenth-century France. There, Foucault basically summarised his interest in the *lettres de cachet*:

> [Police supervision] did not function in a single direction. It was in fact a double-entry system: it had to correspond, by manipulating the machinery of justice, to the immediate wishes of the king, but it was also capable of responding to solicitations from below; the celebrated *lettres de cachet*, or orders under the king's private seal, which were long the symbol of arbitrary royal rules and which brought detention into disrepute on political grounds, were in fact demanded by families, masters, local notables, neighbours, parish priests; and their function was to punish by confinement a whole infra-penality, that of order, agitation, disobedience, bad conduct [...] In short, the eighteenth-century police added a disciplinary function to its role as the auxiliary of justice in the pursuit of criminals and as an instrument for the political supervision of plots, opposition movements or revolts. It was a complex function since it linked the absolute power of the monarch to the lowest levels of power disseminated in society; since, between these different, enclosed institutions of discipline (workshops, armies, schools), it extended an intermediary network, acting where they could not intervene, disciplining the non-disciplinary spaces; but it filled in the gaps, linked them together, guaranteed with its armed force an interstitial discipline and a meta-discipline. 'By means of a wise police, the sovereign accustoms the people to order and obedience.'[26]

When Foucault finished the first volume of *History of Sexuality* (1976), he began to focus again on the *lettres de cachet* and other archival documents, and initiated a project to produce 'an anthology of existences': 'Lives of a few lines or a few pages, nameless misfortunes and adventures gathered into a handful of words. Brief lives, encountered by chance in books and documents.'[27] This culminated in the launch of the *Les Vies parallèles* (Parallel Lives) series with Gallimard, for which Foucault published *Herculine Barbin dite Alexina B.* (1978). The series was probably meant to include *Le Désordre des familles* as well, and the well-known essay 'The Lives of Infamous Men' was originally intended to serve as the overall introduction to the series. On the back cover of *Herculine Barbin*, Foucault described the Parallel Lives series:

The Ancients like to display lives of famous men in parallel fashion. One could hear these exemplary shades converse across centuries.

Parallel lines, I know, meet at infinity. Let us imagine others, which would always diverge. No meeting point nor any place for them to be collected. Often their only echo is that of their condemnation. We would have to grasp them in the force of the movement that separates them; we would have to rediscover the dazzling, momentary wake left behind as they rushed into an obscurity from which 'nothing is heard', and where all 'fame' is lost. This would be the opposite side of the coin from Plutarch: lives so parallel that no one could join them.[28]

The Parallel Lives project was another aborted endeavour; the only other publication for that series was *Le Cercle amoureux d'Henry Legrand* (1979) by Jean-Paul Dumont and Paul-Ursin Dumont.[29] But Foucault carried on thinking about archival documents and the traces and testimonies, the 'dazzling, momentary wake' of obscure individuals from eighteenth-century France. In 1980, Arlette Farge – French historian and disciple of *Annales* scholar Robert Mandrou (1921–84) – received a small parcel from Foucault. The parcel contained photocopies of handwritten transcripts of materials from the Archives de la Bastille, including the *lettres de cachet*.

Arlette Farge and Michel Foucault had previously met. On 20 May 1978, Michelle Perrot and François Ewald led a roundtable on *Discipline and Punish*, involving Foucault and a group of historians: Maurice Agulhon, Nicole Castan, Catherine Duprat, Arlette Farge, Allésandro Fontana, Carlo Ginzburg, Rémi Gossez, Jacques Léonard, Pasquale Pasquino and Jacques Revel. These participants included: historians who were close to Foucault (Perrot and Revel), scholars associated with 'La Sociète de 1848' (Gossez and Agulhon), and regular members of Foucault's seminar group at the Collège de France (Ginzburg and Ewald). A volume edited by Michelle Perrot resulted from this roundtable – *L'Impossible Prison* (1980).[30] Foucault had read Arlette Farge's *Délinquance et criminalité: Le vol d'aliments à Paris au XVIIIe siècle* (1974) and *Vivre dans la rue à Paris au XVIIIe siècle* (1979).[31] The former was on the problem of food theft in eighteenth-century Paris, while the latter used archival materials to provide a detailed and vivid account of Parisian street-life. Foucault cited *Délinquance et criminalité* in *Discipline and Punish*, in his discussion on 'the double movement by which [...] crimes seemed to lose their violence, while punishments, reciprocally, lost some of their intensity, but at the cost of greater intervention'.[32] Farge was an admirer of *Discipline and Punish* and said that it inspired her to continue to 'study the phenomena of deviation and marginality'.[33] Although Farge and Foucault operated in the same intellectual circle, the two scholars were not particularly close. As Farge recalled, 'My meeting with Foucault was improbable because we were not at all working along the same lines.'[34]

Foucault's parcel of photocopies was accompanied by a letter. He asked what Farge thought of the documents. Farge was flattered and puzzled, but after much hesitation she replied to Foucault, informing him that she also thought that these archival materials were fascinating and would help to recover popular memories, but they would definitely require some sort of introduction and commentaries to aid readers. Foucault phoned back to say that he agreed with Farge, and Farge recalled that 'he [then] asked me to work with him on these texts'.[35] Thus marked the beginning of the two scholars' collaborative endeavour. Foucault had laboriously copied out the *lettres de cachet* in longhand, because of the fragility of the material – the letters were written on either parchment or rag paper, and were not in the best condition.[36] In any case, Foucault wanted to write out the materials by hand to have a greater intimacy with the texts; to him, photocopying is:

> so tempting [...] so easy [...] but it takes away the need to really read [...] And above all, it destroys the charm of the text, which becomes almost lifeless when you no longer have the printed page before your eyes and in your hands.[37]

Foucault's transcripts were then typed up by a secretary.[38] Not all of the documents transcribed by Foucault ended up in *Le Désordre des familles*; some of them found their way into Arlette Farge's contribution to the third volume (1986) of Philippe Ariès and Georges Duby's *Histoire de la vie privée* project.[39]

As Farge recalled, there was no rigid division of labour. The section on marital strife entitled 'La discorde des ménages' was largely Farge's work, while the longer section on parents who requested the confinement of their children was largely Foucault's effort. Apparently, Foucault was 'reluctant to be too closely involved in any discussion of relations between husbands and wives, and was apprehensive about the feminist wrath that might descend upon him if he pronounced too emphatically on that aspect of sexual politics'.[40] According to Farge, there were no major disagreements from beginning to completion, and Farge was full of praise of Foucault – she said that Foucault's 'intelligence – moving, malicious and sometimes hilarious – made me loquacious'.[41] On other occasions, she said that her collaboration with Foucault was the one that 'influenced me the most, but also the simplest and the easiest, the most humorous and joyful [...] an essential stage in my intellectual development'.[42] She added:

> Michel Foucault was my *great* encounter, completely improbable, I still do not know what else to say other than it moved me, enlivened me, impacted me, beyond what I could imagine. A meeting which was not at all obvious given our difference of age, of reputation, of intelligence, or quite simply because I was never a participant in his seminars [...] And if I had to 'situate' myself with one word, I would say that I am Foucauldean.[43]

The problem of experience

It may be inaccurate to characterise *Le Désordre des familles*, and indeed '*I, Pierre Rivière*' and *Herculine Barbin*, as some kind of 'archival turn' in Foucault's career, given that he was always interested in archival materials since the days of *History of Madness*. It is not quite right to describe it as a *return* to the archive either, given that he never really left it – rather, this is a new focus on showcasing these archival documents via his publications. The question remains: why did Foucault do this in the late 1970s and early 1980s? Why did Foucault at that particular moment act on his interest in the 'dazzling, momentary wake' left behind by men and women in the past?[44] I argue that the crucial way to understand Foucault's move is to read his body of work in relation to the question of 'experience'.[45]

Our starting point is the first few brilliant pages of Foucault's 1982–83 lectures at the Collège de France, *The Government of Self and Others*, as well as the unused 'Preface' to the *History of Sexuality, Volume 2*.[46] In the first lecture of *The Government of Self and Others*, Foucault provided his audience with an outline of 'some of the themes I have cut across or touched on over the last years, even over the ten or maybe twelve years [...] reference points that I have fixed for myself in my work'.[47] He explained that he wanted to differentiate his own intellectual project from two other entirely legitimate methods. The first of these two is the *history of mentalities* (of the *Annales* historians) – 'a history situated on an axis going from the analysis of actual forms of behaviour to the possible accompanying expressions which may precede them, follow them, translate them, prescribe them, disguise them, or justify them and so forth'.[48] The second method from which Foucault wanted to distance himself was the *history of representations*. This in turn involved two aspects: 'the analysis of the possible role played by representations either in relation to the object represented, or in relation to the subject who represents them to him or herself', and 'the analysis of the rep-resentational values of a system of representations, that is to say, the analysis of representations in terms of a knowledge (*connaissance*) [...] which is taken to be a criterion of truth'.[49]

Instead, what Foucault said that he wanted to do was the *history of thought*. By 'thought' Foucault meant 'an analysis of what could be called focal points of experience in which forms of a possible knowledge (*savoir*), normative frameworks of behaviour for individuals, and poten-tial modes of existence for possible subjects are linked together'.[50] And Foucault reiterates this in the next sentence: 'These three elements – forms of a possible knowledge, normative frameworks of behaviour, and potential modes of existence for possible subjects – these three things, or rather their joint articulation, can be called, I think "focal point of expe-rience"'.[51] With these three dimensions, Foucault then offers a brilliant retrospective of his major works up to the *History of Sexuality* project. Foucault said that in *History of Madness*, he tried to analyse 'madness', which he did not take to be an unchanging object throughout history. He did not want his analysis to be a study of the attitudes towards mad-ness over the centuries either. Instead, he tried to 'study madness as an experience within our culture'.[52] For Foucault, that involved first of all understanding madness as a point from which a whole variety of knowl-edges and 'expertise' were formed, and then the investigation of the changes of these knowledges over time – be they medical, psychiatric, psychological, sociological. Second, madness also involved a normative system that had to be unpacked, thus this required studying all of the technical, administrative, juridical apparatuses that served the purpose to isolate the insane from the normal, to pick it out 'as a phenomenon of deviance within society', and then taking custody of those classi-fied as mad. It also involved a set of norms of behaviour 'for normal individuals', professional rules and codes of conduct 'for doctors, psy-chiatric personnel, and so on'.[53] Third, Foucault said that he wanted to understand how the 'experience of madness defined the constitution of a certain mode of being of the normal subject, as opposed to and in relation to the mad subject'.[54]

In *The Government of Self and Others*, Foucault said that in *History of Madness* he 'more or less successfully and effectively tried to link together' these three axes – forms of a possible knowledge (savoir), normativity and constitution of the subject's mode of being.[55] But in the unused 'Preface to *History of Sexuality, Volume 2*', Foucault was more critical of himself. As a good number of scholars have noted – Colin Gordon, Gary Gutting, Jean Khalfa, Allan Megill, to mention but a few – *History of Madness* belonged to a transitional stage in Foucault's intellectual development, namely, his rejection of phenomenology.[56] In the 1950s, Foucault was very much preoccupied with the phenomenology. The influence was clearly on display in two pieces of work from 1954: *Mental Illness and Psychology* (which Foucault tried to suppress in the 1960s) and his introduction to the French edition of Swiss psychiatrist Ludwig Binswanger's 1930 text *Dream and Existence* (in which Foucault argued that phenomenology could offer a better account of the meaning of dreams than could psychoanalysis).[57]

But Foucault became hostile towards phenomenology. For him, phenomenology was wholly inadequate for explaining or even describing an experience. Phenomenology afforded primacy to the inner workings of our psyche; the privilege accorded to the category of the subject and the way that phenomenology placed subjective experience at the centre of intellectual inquiry was, for Foucault, problematic. This was because phenomenology seemed to fail to consider the extent that this subjective experience was dependent on social conditions and enabled by larger epistemic and political structures. Experience is not simply a confrontation between a subject and a world of objects, instead Foucault essentially argues that there is not even a subject existing independently of epistemic and political structures and preceding the experience itself. So this amounts to a *reversal* of phenomenology: the subject is not the foundation of the experience, rather, forms of subjectivity emerge in response to a range of experiences enabled by larger structures. The lack of space here will not allow me to launch a discussion on whether Foucault's characterisation of phenomenology was at all justified – Gary Gutting, for instance, argued that Foucault 'arbitrarily restrict[ed] phenomenology to the (Husserlian) claim that everything needs to be reduced to transcendental subjectivity', and that Foucault was unjust in his assessment of Jean-Paul Sartre and Maurice Merleau-Ponty.[58] Suffice it to say here that *History of Madness* left Foucault 'unsatisfied' with its 'theoretical weakness in elaborating the notion of experience'.[59] Foucault further criticised his usage of the word 'experience' in the book, which for him was 'very floating' – one might as well say 'undercooked'.[60]

'Experience' as a concept was practically evacuated from his subsequent works, until its return in the late 1970s. Yet a concern with the dimension of experience can be regarded as animating his work of the 1960s and early 1970s, despite its formal absence as a concept. Foucault stated that the work that he tried to do after the *History of Madness* consisted in analysing each of the three axes in turn – knowledge, normativity, subjectivity – to 'see what further work needed to be done on the methods and concepts for analysing them, first as dimensions of an experience, and then insofar as they were to be linked together'.[61] In his major works from the 1960s, Foucault concentrated on the first axis – the formation of forms of knowledge.[62] In *Birth of the Clinic* (1963), he took medicine and disease in eighteenth-century France, and demonstrated how the organisation for training, research and therapy were tied to a clinical medicine articulated on the development of pathological anatomy. The purpose of this was to illustrate the complex factors and reciprocal relationships that affect, on the one hand, the development of a particular kind of medical knowledge, and on the other hand, the 'transformations of an institutional field linked directly to social and political changes'.[63]

Then he moved on to the history of the human sciences in *The Order of Things* (1966). By that time, the so-called 'archaeological method' – which he would fully articulate in *Archaeology of Knowledge* (1969) – had been developed. The premise of Foucault's method was the existence of different 'epistemes', and by that Foucault meant that there were orderly rules and deep structures – beyond logic and grammar – underlying the production, regulation, circulation and operation of knowledge. Epistemes determine the possibilities of concepts and define the boundaries of thought in different historical periods, and they can be excavated and articulated. Foucault illustrated his method by showing the epistemes that governed the bodies of knowledge that, from around the seventeenth to early nineteenth centuries, 'had been charged with explaining certain aspects of human activity or existence: the wealth men produce, exchange and circulate; the linguistic signs they use to communicate; and the collectivity of living things to which they belong'.[64] Foucault showed that natural history, general grammar and theories of wealth all ordered their objects in terms of relations of representation or exchange, and the new sciences that emerged from these – biology, linguistics and economics – resulted from the transformation of the objects into historical ones. In sum, in the first phase of Foucault's career, which dissected the first axis of experience – forms of possible knowledge – he was not so much interested in analysing 'the development or progress of particular bodies of knowledge', or the history of the contents of the knowledge.[65] Rather, he wanted to identify the 'discursive practices which were able to constitute the matrices of possible bodies of knowledge'.[66]

In the early to late 1970s, Foucault moved on to the second of his three axes – the normative matrices of power. The works devoted to this included *Discipline and Punish* (1975), *History of Sexuality, Volume 1* (1976), and the bulk of his Collège de France lectures, for instance *Psychiatric Power* (1973–74), *Abnormal* (1974–75), *Society Must Be Defended* (1975–76) and *Security, Territory, Population* (1977–78). Foucault said of this shift:

> [It] did not consist in analysing Power with a capital 'P', or even institutions of power, or the general or institutional forms of domination. Rather, it meant studying the techniques and procedures by which one sets about conducting the conduct of others. That is to say, I tried to pose the question of norms of behaviour first of all in terms of power, and of power that one exercises, and to analyse this power as a field of procedures of government. Here again the shift consisted in passing from analysis of the norm to analysis of the exercise of power, and passing from analysis of the exercise of power to the procedures of, let's say, governmentality.[67]

The final phase of his career tackled the last axis – the constitution of the subject's mode of being. Here Foucault replaced the theory of the subject or the history of subjectivity with a historical analysis of the forms of subjectivation and the pragmatics of the self, in *History of Sexuality, Volume 2* and *Volume 3* (1984), and the final quartet of Collège de France lectures. With this tripartite schema of experience, we can also understand the radical shift in chronology from *History of Sexuality, Volume 1* (eighteenth to nineteenth century) to *History of Sexuality, Volume 2* (ancient Greece), and the abandonment of his initial plan for the *History of Sexuality* series (which was going to study children, mothers, 'perverts' and other sexual subjects) towards the techniques/technologies of the relation to self. As Foucault himself clarifies:

> In order better to analyse the forms of relation to the self, in and of themselves, I found myself spanning eras in a way that took me farther and farther from the chronological outline I had first decided on, both in order to address myself to periods when the effect of scientific knowledge and the complexity of normative systems [i.e. the first two axes of experience] were less, and in order eventually

to make out forms of relation to the self different from those characterising the experience of sexuality [...] rather than placing myself at the threshold of the formation of the experience of sexuality [i.e. the eighteenth century onwards], I tried to analyse the formation of a certain mode of relation to the self in the experience of the flesh. This called for a marked chronological displacement because it became obvious that I should study the period in late antiquity when the principal elements of the Christian ethic of the flesh were being formulated.[68]

Foucault did not mention how his three collaborative, archival books – *'I, Pierre Rivière'*, *Herculine Barbin* and *Le Désordre des familles* – should be situated in the first lecture of *The Government of Self and Others*. But in the unused 'Preface to *History of Sexuality, Volume 2*', he makes it absolutely clear how these works fit into his intellectual trajectory:

It is also these three axes and the play between types of understanding [*savoir*], forms of normality, and modes of relation to oneself and others which seemed to me to give individual cases the status of significant experiences – cases such as those of Pierre Rivière or Alexina B. [i.e. Herculine Barbin] – and to assign a like importance to that permanent dramatisation of family affairs which one finds in the *lettre de cachet* (whereby people committed their relatives to asylums) in the eighteenth century.[69]

Foucault himself acknowledged that things did not necessarily unfold so neatly, that 'there were many obscurities and hesitations along the way'.[70] However, the advantage of this tripartite formulation of experience as a reconstruction of Foucault's pathway is that we are now in a good position to understand why Foucault made *two* moves around the mid 1970s. He returned to the archival materials that bothered him from the 1950s and he reopened the discussion on 'experience'. Timothy O'Leary argues that Foucault's work 'in the decade 1966–76' should be regarded 'as in fact laying the groundwork for a much more sophisticated account of something that we could call "live experience" (or "everyday experience") – more sophisticated than he had achieved in the *History of Madness*, and also more sophisticated than he could have achieved using the tools of phenomenology'.[71] Foucault's major works dissected what he called 'important focal points of experiences in our culture' – madness, disease, criminality and sexuality.[72] Through doing this, and through the establishment of the archaeology and genealogy methods, Foucault finally felt that he had acquired 'that necessary talent' around 1977 – when he wrote 'The Lives of Infamous Men' – to process, as if in a *Nachträglichkeit*, that almost traumatic encounter with the documents at the Archives de la Bastille. He felt that he was finally able to restore, in his own words, 'their intensity in an analysis'.[73] Therefore, *Le Désordre des familles*, a seemingly unusual and obscure text in the Foucauldean canon, can be seen as an integral step in Foucault's late career, a culmination of his long engagement with the problem of experience.

History and the archive

Arlette Farge suggests that Foucault's return to the archive and the *lettres de cachet* project were also a response to his critics, particularly Foucault's contemporaneous historians in France. According to Farge, Foucault seemed quite touchy about the historians' assessment of his work; he was in fact 'more than sensitive, quite torn'.[74] What was the origin of this torn feeling, this 'malentendu persistant' between French historians and Foucault as Farge describes it?[75] One will have to return yet again to *History of Madness*, specifically its reception among historians. When the book was published in 1961, it was very enthusiastically received by historians. The *Annales* School applauded Foucault, with Robert Mandrou and Fernand Braudel heralding 'the birth of a great historian'.[76] Mandrou said that *History of Madness* was 'a decisive thesis [...] Seven hundred pages of rare beauty that will be crucial to our understanding of the classical period.'[77] Braudel suggested that to write a work like Foucault's would require 'a mind capable of being, alternately and not solely, a philosopher, psychologist, historian'.[78] Intellectual historian Gérard Noiriel suggests that, by drawing attention to the interdisciplinary qualities of *History of Madness*, Braudel was probably the first to 'accredit the idea that Foucault and the historians were addressing the same subject'.[79]

Arlette Farge and Jacques Revel, two historians sympathetic to Foucault's work, both point out that there was already a misunderstanding here. *History of Madness* was treated as 'a work of social psychology that magnificently illustrated the concept of the history of mentalities'.[80] As Arlette Farge argues, *History of Madness* was not merely a history of the confinement of the insane. *History of Madness* was also much more than a history of the way that objects, people, events regarding madness were felt, thought about or talked about in a particular age – that is to say, it was more than just a history of the general sensibility, mentality or perception about madness. Foucault set out to interrogate the categories that historians themselves often took to be unproblematic or even universal.[81] To elaborate, again in the first lecture of *The Government of Self and Others*, Foucault pointed to the three 'negativist aspects' of his intellectual project that put him at odds with his contemporaneous colleagues in history (particularly the *Annales* school):

> A historicising negativism, since it involves replacing a theory of knowledge, power, or the subject with the analysis of historically determinate practices. A nominalist negativism, since it involves replacing universals like madness, crime, and sexuality with the analysis of experiences which constitute singular historical forms. A negativism with a nihilistic tendency, if by this we understand a form of reflection which, instead of indexing practices to systems of values which allow them to be assessed, inserts these systems of values in the interplay of arbitrary but intelligible practices.[82]

When *Discipline and Punish* appeared in 1975, Farge described its 'rather simplistic reception'.[83] The book was taken to be a denunciation of the disciplinary society, whereas Foucault actually 'questioned how the objects of punishment were historically constituted, and at the same time showing how men, through these practices, became constituted as an object of knowledge in a field of power'.[84] The historians' debate on *Discipline and Punish*, particularly its historical accuracy, its methodology and its politics, reached a climax in the aforementioned May 1978 roundtable organised by Michelle Perrot and François Ewald, which resulted in *L'Impossible Prison* (1980). While Michelle Perrot was sympathetic to Foucault's work, other participants were critical. Historian of medicine Jacques Léonard, for instance, was very hostile. He complained that Foucault had a very superficial understanding of the sources that he used and that he did not 'perceive [those historical sources] from within' (whatever that means!).[85] Foucault's frequent use of pronominal verbs and the ambiguous personal pronoun *on* ('one does such and such') was, for Léonard, the telltale sign that Foucault did not really know or care who exactly was doing what to whom.[86] For Léonard, Foucault created a Kafkaesque universe: 'The vocabulary of geometry turns human society into a desert; [Foucault] speaks about spaces, lines, frameworks, segments, and dispositions', leaving the 'business of tidying up to the jobbers'.[87]

Another panellist, Maurice Agulhon, attacked Foucault for refusing to acknowledge that, thanks to the progress in the 'rights of man', prisoners in modern times are indeed treated much more 'humanely' than under the ancien régime.[88] Michelle Perrot recalled that Foucault 'tried to answer' these critics, but there appeared to be 'two parallel discourses' and Foucault and the historians talked past each other.[89] Overall, Foucault's ideas were taken to be mere 'theories', an impressive but ultimately vacuous edifice built upon superficial documentation, sloppy and selective use of data, over-reliance on outdated secondary sources and idiosyncratic interpretation of evidence. This was all wrapped up with Foucault's worldview that seemed at once cynical, romantic, nihilistic. Some historians went even further. Gérard Noiriel reported that, for instance, historian Charles O. Carbonnel accused Foucault and other 'metaphysicians, logicians, and epistemologists' of an 'outrageous imperialism'.[90] With regard to this 'barrier of incomprehension' that seemed to have arisen between Foucault and the historians, Michelle Perrot said that Foucault was 'sometimes bitter about this. He felt it was rejection.'[91]

In a January 1983 interview given to *Libération*, Foucault reflected on the disciplinary boundaries between history and philosophy. He said that '"theoretical" or "speculative" reflection has long had a rather distant and perhaps somewhat disdainful relationship with history'. There was an intellectual division of labour, whereby the philosophers 'did the thinking' and the historians 'went to the archives'. The modus operandi of philosophers – including to an extent Foucault's predecessors Gaston Bachelard and Georges Canguilhem – was to read historical works, 'in search of raw material that was considered "accurate"', and then 'all that was required was to reflect upon it, to provide it with a meaning and truth that it did not have on its own'. Foucault added: 'Free use of others' work was permitted – to the extent that no one even thought of hiding the fact that one was elaborating on work already done; that work was cited shamelessly.' To disrupt this state of affairs and to question the underlying assumptions and blindspots of *both* history and philosophy, Foucault volunteered to go 'to the bottom of the mine'.[92]

This is the context in which we can understand the first, somewhat mystifying sentence of the introduction in *Le Désordre des familles*: 'The idea that history is vowed to the "accuracy of the archive", and philosophy to the "architecture of ideas", seems nonsensical to us. That is not the way that we operate.'[93] How then are Foucault and Farge supposed to operate? In an interview, Foucault explains:

> What interests us is the history of thought. We don't believe that there is, on the one hand, the analysis of behaviours, and on the

other hand, the history of ideas. For us, there's thinking everywhere. In an eighteenth-century household, where the husband beats his wife, where the children look for freedom as they can, there's a system of representations, there's a play of passions with culture and social order. The history of ideas that I want to do has different requirements, different methods, because of the different objects compared to the history of societies.[94]

By 'history of thought', Foucault did not just mean some sort of scientific expertise, rather it is an analysis of precisely those 'focal points of experience' along three axes – forms of knowledge, normative frameworks, modes of subjectivity. Foucault said that he was interested in the 'play of true and false [...] ['thought'] is the basis for accepting or refusing rules, and constitutes human beings as social juridical subjects; it is what establishes the relation with oneself and with others, and constitutes the human being as ethical subject'.[95] The Foucauldean history of thought would analyse the:

speaking, doing, or behaving in which the individual appears and acts as knowing subject, as ethical or juridical subject, as subject conscious of himself and others. In this sense, thought is understood as the very form of action – as action insofar as it implies the play of true and false, the acceptance or refusal of rules, the relation to oneself and others. The study of forms of experience can thus proceed from an analysis of 'practices' – discursive or not – as long as one qualifies that word to mean the different system of action *insofar as* they are inhabited by thought as I have characterised it here.[96]

The result of Foucault's endeavour of doing this history of thought and bringing history and philosophy together, however, was that historians thought that Foucault was encroaching on, even invading, their territory. To his frustration and dismay, Foucault was accused of violating the standards of the historians' profession. But it would again be a mischaracterisation to suggest that Foucault was trying to placate his fellow historians, with '*I, Pierre Rivière*', *Herculine Barbin*, and *Le Désordre des familles*. In 'The Lives of Infamous Men', Foucault wrote:

I will be told: 'That's so like you, always with the same inability to cross the line, to pass to the other side, to listen and convey the language that comes from elsewhere or from below; always the same choice, on the side of power, of what it says or causes to be said. Why not go listen to these lives where they speak in their own voice?'[97]

This imaginary critic is presumably the professional historian, attacking Foucault for not being able to 'listen to these lives where they speak in their own voice'. This of course is a criticism that one still frequently encounters in debates on the 'uses' of Foucault. The kind of criticism roughly goes along these lines: Foucault does not do justice to historical events and actors because he reduces complex phenomenon to mechanical systems or flat descriptions, and in the process evacuates the 'agency' and 'voices' of historical actors, and so he is not a 'proper historian' and so forth. Foucault's response to this was defiant:

> [F]irst of all, would anything at all remain of what they were in their violence or in their singular misfortune had they not, at a given moment, met up with power and provoked its forces? Is it not one of the fundamental traits of our society, after all, that destiny takes the form of a relation with power, of a struggle with or against it? Indeed, the most intense point of life, the point where its energy is concentrated, is where it comes up against power, struggles with it, attempts to use its forces and to evade its traps. The brief and strident words that went back and forth between power and the most inessential existences doubtless constitute, for the latter, the only monument they have ever been granted. It is what gives them, for the passage through time, the bit of brilliance, the brief flash that carries them to us.[98]

Foucault's wish was to present the 'discourses that, in sorrow or in rage, [obscure men and women] exchanged with power'.[99] This was not the same as simply returning to the archives and recovering voices from the past, *as if* it was really possible to recover voices of ordinary folk who have 'played no appreciable roles in events or among important people', who have 'left no identifiable trace around them', and who have and never will have 'any existence outside the precarious domicile of these words'.[100] Foucault reiterates that these are lives 'destined to [...] disappear without ever having been told were able to leave traces – brief, incisive, often enigmatic – only at the point of their instantaneous contact with power'.[101] With *Le Désordre des familles*, Foucault went back to the *lettres de cachet* to refine his thinking about power, about ordinary people's encounters, collisions, intersections with institution and state authorities specifically with regard to their *family* affairs. Crucially, and

Foucault is absolutely right here, 'billions of existences [were] destined to pass away without a trace' had it not been for the production and preservation of precisely those 'traces' by apparatuses of power.[102]

Here Foucault makes a very important point, one that is sometimes elided and forgotten by historians as they proclaim that they aim to uncover, discover, recover all of those voices from the past, or attack others for failing to do so. These were people in eighteenth-century France who were not 'endowed with any of the established and recognised nobilities – those of birth, fortune, saintliness, heroism, or genius', and they certainly did not leave behind voluminous writings, correspondence, monuments erected in their memory or in their honour.[103] How exactly, then, would historians be able to consider these distant 'marginalised voices', murmurs that were barely audible? They have to rely on, presumably, the fragments of records that survived in the archives. But under what circumstances exactly and through which power mechanisms were these records actually generated in the first place, and then retained and preserved for the historians' investigation? These *lettres de cachet*, police dossiers, psychiatric records, patient case-files were the result of:

> the encounter with power; without that collision, it is very unlikely that any word would be there to recall their fleeting trajectory. The power that watched these lives, that pursued them, that lent its attention, if only for a moment, to their complaints and their little racket, and marked them with its claw was what gave rise to the few words about them that remain for us – either because someone decided to appeal to it in order to denounce, complain, solicit, entreat, or because he chose to intervene and in a few words to judge and decide [...] We may amuse ourselves, if we wish, by seeing a revenge in this: the chance that enabled these absolutely undistinguished people to emerge from their place amid the dead multitudes, to gesticulate again, to manifest their rage, their affliction, or their invincible determination to err – perhaps it makes up for the bad luck that brought power's lightning bolt down upon them, in spite of their modesty and anonymity. Lives that are as though they hadn't been, that survive only from the clash with a power that wished only to annihilate them or at least to obliterate them, lives that come back to us only through the effect of multiple accidents.[104]

Thus Foucault resisted the idea that historians could straightforwardly recover voices and subjectivities from people from the past, arguing that the very traces and fragments that historians worked with – and the very existence of the vast archive of documents itself – were the result of the product of power mechanisms and disciplinary apparatuses put in place in precisely the eighteenth and nineteenth century. With the *lettres de cachet*, Foucault said that he came back to them in the late 1970s because he 'suspected that they manifest[ed] a new beginning, or at any rate an important event, in which political mechanisms and discursive effects intersected'.[105] Around the beginning of the eighteenth century, Catholic confession – a pardoning mechanism – mutated into a recording mechanism that brought the quotidian into discourse, that surveyed the minute and seemingly unimportant details of everyday life, especially family life. The denunciation, the complaint, the police inquiry, the police report, spying, interrogation practices, all crystallised in the system of the *lettre de cachet* in eighteenth-century France. Tales on the miseries experienced and responded to through the family, including troubles and conflicts between generations, the abandonment and abuse of spouses and children, profligacy and squandered fortunes, debauchery and reckless violence brought on by drunkenness, rowdiness and disobedience of the youth, knavery and swindling, neighbourhood dispute and public altercations between family members – all of these small dramas were solicited by the state. Dossiers about all of these 'little orders of conduct' were meticulously compiled, mobilised to decide on the fates of individuals and their families and then archived away. For Foucault, the *lettres de cachet* system, even though it lasted only for a little over a century and was limited to France, brought about a number of consequences. He argued that political sovereignty 'penetrated into the most elementary dimension of the social body' and 'a whole political network became interwoven with the fabric of everyday life'.[106] Power was brought into play between the most humble of people, between members of the family, in matters of work, life, love and hate. Foucault continued:

> There was a kind of immense and omnipresent call for the processing of these disturbances and these petty sufferings into discourse. An unending hum began to be heard, the sound of the discourse that delivered individual variations of behaviour, shames, and secrets into the grip of power. The commonplace ceased to belong to silence, to the passing rumour of the fleeting confession. All those ingredients of the ordinary, the unimportant detail, obscurity, unexceptional days, community life, could and must be told – better still, written down. They became describable and transcribable, precisely insofar

as they were traversed by the mechanisms of a political power [...]
The birth, consequently, of an immense possibility for discourse.
A certain knowledge of the quotidian had a part at least in its origin,
together with a grid of intelligibility that the West undertook to
extend over our actions, our ways of being and of behaving.[107]

The *lettre de cachet* was therefore an important moment when a
society:

lends words, turns of phrases, and sentences, language rituals to
the anonymous mass of people so that they might speak of themselves – speak publicly of and on the triple condition that their
discourse be uttered and put in circulation within a well-defined
apparatus of power; that it revealed the hitherto barely perceptible
lower depths of social existence, and through the access provided
by that diminutive war of passions and interests, it offers power the
possibility of a sovereign intervention [...] How light power would
be, and easy to dismantle no doubt, if all it did was to observe, spy,
detect, prohibit, and punish; but it incites, provokes, produces. *It is
not simply eye and ear: it makes people act and speak.* This machinery
was doubtless important for the constitution of new knowledges.[108]

These new knowledges included psychiatry, medicine, forensics, criminology and so forth, couched in the categories of science and administration, which claim towards neutrality and objectivity. The historians
demanded that Foucault somehow 'cross that line', and listen to the
muffled voices from the 'other side' of power. But for Foucault, there
was no real line to cross, no other side of power, no elsewhere or below
that was somehow beyond power or outside it. The historians' claim to
be able to represent 'other voices', to search for some kind of 'authen-
ticity' that has been silenced and excluded, is thus really a conceptual
error. People *did* speak, but it seemed that they spoke precisely because
they were solicited, incited, invited, provoked in some way. They left
behind traces of their utterances because they were given the opportunity and enabled to speak by power, *not* in spite of it. Without the
apparatus of the *lettre de cachet*, we might have few clues about the lives
of these cobblers, army deserters, garment-sellers, scriveners, vagabond
monks, young libertines – those obscure and infamous lives of men and
women from the ancien régime. Without all sorts of power apparatuses,
we might have no information at all. The production and preservation
of the poison-pen letters, in other words, must be regarded as soaked

with power, drenched in it through and through. Experience can be addressed by the historian who attends to such documents, but never mediated by power/knowledge.

So in Foucault's reconsideration of the *lettres de cachet,* there was at once a reflection on historical method, namely the status of the archive and the documents. What 'voices', whose 'voices' are we trying to hear? How exactly are we supposed to do this, where are the resources that enable us to do this? And how, for what reason, under what circumstances, to what ends are these materials from the past generated? When we say that we want to listen and recapture marginalised voices, are we implicitly assuming to be able to hear these voices without the filter of power? Are we suspending our disbelief and thinking that there can be utterances that are not always already solicited by power in some way? Are we pinning our false hopes on some kind of 'reality' to be recovered that is untouched and uncontaminated by power? I argue that, as *Le Désordre des familles* shows, Foucault, *contra* the historians who criticised his lack of engagement with the questions of 'experience' and 'voices', took these two things absolutely seriously – with his dissection of 'experiences' *and* critical attention to the very history of the sources from which such 'experiences' are to be drawn. What we end up with, despite Foucault's ironic characterisation of his own programme as 'negative', is I argue a positive possibility – an analysis of experiences of historical actors in terms of knowledge, of normativity and of subjectivation *plus* a self-reflexive consideration of that very process of analysis. To paraphrase Gilles Deleuze, what we gain from following the Foucauldean method is not simply a history of 'mentalities' but of the conditions governing everything that has a mental existence; not simply a history of 'behaviours' but of the conditions governing everything that has a visible existence; not simply a history of 'institutions' but of the conditions governing their integration of different social relations and forces; not simply a history of 'private lives' but of the conditions governing the way in which the relation to oneself can constitute a private life; and not simply a history of 'subjects' but of the processes of subjectivation, the possible forms of subjects at a particular time.[109]

Conclusion

Thibaud Harrois and I translated the brief *présentation* at the suggestion of Robbie Duschinsky and Chloë Taylor, and were guided by Arlette Farge and Jean Khalfa. It is hoped that the translation of the introduction to *Le Désordre des familles*, along with this chapter on the background of the book, will renew attention to this publication both for its fascinating contents and for the insights that it offers into Foucault's thinking and career. I can only apologise here to the readers for the fact that, after reading the translated introduction and this chapter, they are not able to go on to read any of the *lettres de cachet*. A complete English translation of *Le Désordre des familles* is surely overdue. To sum up briefly, in this chapter I explored some of the dynamics of the French intellectual field and the context in which Foucault came to collaborate with Arlette Farge on the *lettres de cachet* in the late 1970s and early 1980s. Using Foucault's own experience of his oeuvre, codified in *The Government of Self and Others* and the unused preface of *History of Sexuality, Volume 2*, I situated *Le Désordre des familles* in Foucault's longer intellectual trajectory, specifically his thinking about the problem of experience and its interactions with power. I discussed the reception of Foucault's work among French historians and showed that *Le Désordre des familles* was connected to Foucault's reflections on the theory of power and the archive. Given the limit of space, a number of threads have to be left behind for another paper – for instance, the 'Collectif Maurice Florence' (Maurice Florence being one of Foucault's pseudonyms) that continued the political work of using archival materials to show people's collisions with power, or Arlette Farge's theorising on the aesthetics and ethics of the archive in her *Le Goût d'archive* (1989).[110] But certainly I hope to have shown that *Le Désordre des familles* cannot be accused of containing 'not enough Foucault'.

Notes

I would like to thank my co-editor Robbie Duschinsky, Arlette Farge, John Forrester, Jean Khalfa, Nicholas White and Chloë Taylor for all their advice on Foucault, and I am especially grateful to Simon Schaffer for extensive discussions on French intellectual history and historical practices. I also thank Michael Sheringham for his generous help and Thibaud Harrois for his help with some French documents. All mistakes remain my own.

1. David Macey's interview with Arlette Farge, quoted in David Macey, *The Lives of Michel Foucault* (London: Vintage, 1993), 456.
2. The basic account of Foucault's encounter with the *lettres de cachet* and the other documents deposited at the Archives de la Bastille, as well as his subsequent collaboration with Arlette Farge, can be found in a number of sources, chiefly: 'The lives of infamous men' (1977), Foucault, EW3, 157–75 and DE2, 237–53; an interview in *L'Express* with Farge and Foucault entitled 'L'âge d'or de la lettre de cachet' (1983), Foucault, DE2, 1170–1; biographies on Foucault, including Didier Eribon, *Michel Foucault*, Betsy Wing (trans.) (Cambridge, MA: Harvard University Press, 1991), 277; Macey, *The Lives*

of Michel Foucault, 75, 251, 360–1, 452–6; David Macey, *Foucault* (London: Reaktion Books, 2004), 135–7; as well as French intellectual history such as François Dosse, *History of Structuralism, Volume 2: The Sign Sets, 1967–Present,* Deborah Glassman (trans.) (Minneapolis, MN: University of Minnesota Press, 1997), 247–59; as well as Arlette Farge's interviews, including: Camille Deslypper and Guy Dreux, 'La parole comme événement – Entretien avec Arlette Farge', *Nouveaux regards,* 30 (2005), available at: http://www.parutions.com/index.php?pid=1&rid=4&srid=100&ida=6299 (last accessed 1 March 2012); Sylvain Parent, 'Entretien avec Arlette Farge', *Tracés: Revue de Sciences humaines,* 5 (2004), 143–8, available at: http://traces.revues.org/3383?lang=en (last accessed 1 March 2012); Jacques Lecomte, 'Foucault et les historiens: un malentendu persistant (entretien avec Arlette Farge)', *Sciences Humaines,* 44 (1994), 21; Arlette Farge, 'Travailler avec Michel Foucault', *Le Débat,* 41 (1986), 164–7; Arlette Farge, 'Michel Foucault et les archives de l'exclusion', in Elisabeth Roudinesco (ed.), *Penser la folie: Essais sur Michel Foucault* (Paris: Galilée, 1992), 63–78. I was also able to verify some of the details directly with Farge, currently director at the Centre National de la Recherche Scientifique (CNRS) in Paris.

3. Macey, *The Lives of Michel Foucault,* 453. The title appeared as forthcoming ('ouvrage à paraître') in some of the other books in the *Archives* series published in the 1960s, for instance in the back pages of Eugen Weber, *Satan franc-maçon: La mystification de Léo Taxil,* Archives No. 6 (Paris: Julliard, 1964).

4. Macey, *The Lives of Michel Foucault,* 135.

5. The first book of the *Archives* series was Michel Denis and Pierre Goubert's *1789: Les Français ont la parole – Cahiers de doléances des États-Généraux,* Archives No. 1 (Paris: Julliard, 1964), which was concerned with the list of grievances drawn up by each of the three Estates in France (clergymen, nobility, workers and peasants). This is cited in *Discipline and Punish,* see Foucault, D&P, 120 and 313 n. 7, in the discussion on the evolution of detention as one of the most general forms of legal punishment in France. The final volume of the *Archives* series was Pascal Ory, *Les Discours gastronomique français: Des origines à nos jours,* Archives No. 105 (Paris: Gallimard, 1998).

6. Pierre Nora is of course famous for directing the *Les Lieux de mémoire* project (Pierre Nora (ed.), *Les Lieux de mémoire,* 3 vols (Paris: Gallimard, 1984–1992; translated into English as *Rethinking France: Les Lieux de mémoire,* 4 vols (Chicago, IL: University of Chicago Press, 1999–2010); abridged translation Pierre Nora (ed.), *Realms of Memory: Rethinking the French Past,* 3 vols, Lawrence D. Kritzman (ed.) and Arthur Goldhammer (trans.) (New York: Columbia University Press, 1996)). Jacques Revel is well known for his impeccable scholarship on the social and cultural history of early modern Europe. Both scholars have been directors at the École des Hautes Études en Sciences Sociales (EHESS). On Foucault and the *Annales* historians, see for instance Peter Burke, *The French Historical Revolution: The* Annales *School, 1929–89* (Stanford, CA: Stanford University Press, 1990), 120; Dosse, *History of Structuralism, Volume 2,* 234–66, especially 260–6; Gérard Noiriel, 'Foucault and history: the lessons of a disillusion', *Journal of Modern History,* 66 (1994), 547–68; James A. Winders, 'Michel Foucault (1926–1984)', in Philip Daileader and Philip Whalen (eds), *French Historians 1900–2000: New Historical Writing*

in *Twentieth-Century France* (Oxford: Wiley-Blackwell, 2010), 252–70. On the *Annales* in general, see Burke, *The French Historical Revolution*; François Dosse, *L'histoire en miettes: des* Annales *à la 'nouvelle histoire'* (Paris: La Découverte, 1987), translated as *New History in France: The Triumph of the* Annales, Peter V. Conroy, Jr (trans.) (Urbana, IL: University of Illinois Press, 1994); André Burguière, *The* Annales *School: An Intellectual History*, Jane Marie Todd (trans.) (Ithaca, NY: Cornell University Press, 2009).

7. Jacques de Launay, *Le Dossier de Vichy*, Archives No. 32 (Paris: Julliard, 1967); Yohanan Manor, *Naissance du sionisme politique*, Archives No. 88 (Paris: Gallimard, 1981); Yves-Marie Bercé, *Croquants et nu-pieds: Les soulèvements paysans en France du XVIIe au XIXe siècle*, Archives No. 55 (Paris: Gallimard, 1974); Alfred Wahl, *Les Archives du football: Sport et société en France, 1880– 1980*, Archives No. 102 (Paris: Gallimard, 1989).

8. Michel de Certeau, *La Possession de Loudun* (Paris: Julliard, 1970), translated as *The Possession at Loudun*, Michael B. Smith (trans.), with a foreword by Stephen Greenblatt (Chicago, IL: University of Chicago Press, 2000).

9. Nora, *Les Lieux de mémoire*. See also Pierre Nora, 'Between memory and history: *Les Lieux de mémoire*', *Representations*, 26 (1989), 7–24; François Dosse, *Pierre Nora: Homo historicus* (Paris: Perrin, 2011).

10. Philippe Ariès and Georges Duby (eds), *Histoire de la vie privée*, 5 vols (Paris: Seuil, 1985–87), translated as *A History of Private Life*, 5 vols, Paul Veyne (ed.) and Arthur Goldhammer (trans.) (Cambridge, MA: Harvard University Press, 1992–98). On Ariès, see Patrick H. Hutton, *Philippe Ariès and the Politics of French Cultural History* (Amherst, MA: University of Massachusetts Press, 2004). On Ariès, Foucault and Farge, see 'Le style de l'histoire (entretien avec Arlete Farge et les journalistes du *Matin*, F. Dumont et J.-P. Iommi-Amunategui)', *Le Matin*, 2168 (21 February 1984), 20–1, reprinted in DE2, 1468–74.

11. See especially Arlette Farge's later work. Arlette Farge and Jacques Revel, *The Vanishing Children of Paris: Rumour and Politics before the French Revolution*, Claudia Miéville (trans.) (Cambridge, MA: Harvard University Press, 1991); Arlette Farge, *Fragile Lives: Violence, Power and Solidarity in Eighteenth-Century Paris*, Carol Shelton (ed.) (Cambridge, MA: Harvard University Press, 1993); Arlette Farge, *Subversive Words: Public Opinion in Eighteenth-Century France*, Rosemary Morris (trans.) (University Park, PA: Penn State University Press, 1995).

12. Emmanuel Le Roy Ladurie, *Montaillou: village Occitan de 1294 à 1324* (Paris: Gallimard, 1978), translated into English as *Montaillou: Cathars and Catholics in a French Village 1294–1324*, Barbara Bray (trans.) (New York: Vintage, 1979); Emmanuel Le Roy Ladurie, *Les Paysans de Languedoc* (Paris: Flammarion, 1969), translated into English as *The Peasants of Languedoc*, John Day (trans.) (Urbana, IL: University of Illinois Press, 1974); Carlo Ginzburg, *The Cheese and the Worms: The Cosmos of a Sixteenth-Century Miller*, John Tedeschi and Anne Tedeschi (trans.) (Baltimore, MD: Johns Hopkins University Press, 1980); Natalie Zemon Davis, *The Return of Martin Guerre* (Cambridge, MA: Harvard University Press, 1983).

13. Foucault, 'The lives of infamous men', EW3, 157.

14. Ibid., 158 and 167.

15. Ibid., 158 and 164.

16. Michael Sheringham, 'Michel Foucault, Pierre Rivière and the archival imaginary', *Comparative Critical Studies*, 8 (2011), 235–57 at 238.

17. Foucault's interview with *Libération* (21 January 1983), cited in Eribon, *Michel Foucault*, 274.

18. Sheringham, 'Michel Foucault, Pierre Rivière', 237.

19. Foucault, 'Le pouvoir, une bête magnifique: entretien avec M. Osorio', DE2, 368–82 at 372, quoted in Sheringham, 'Michel Foucault, Pierre Rivière', 237.

20. Jean Khalfa, 'Introduction', HOM, xiii–xxv at xx.

21. Ibid., xx.

22. Foucault, 'The lives of infamous men', EW3, 158.

23. Timothy O'Leary, 'Rethinking experience with Foucault', in Timothy O'Leary and Christopher Falzon (eds), *Foucault and Philosophy* (Oxford: Wiley-Blackwell, 2010), 162–84 at 172.

24. See Foucault, PSP, 7 and 125.

25. Foucault, ABN, 37–8.

26. Foucault, D&P, 214–15. The last sentence is a quotation from Swiss philosopher and legal thinker Emerich de Vattel, *The Law of Nations* (1758).

27. Foucault, 'The lives of infamous men', EW3, 157.

28. Foucault, quoted in Michael Lucey, *The Misfits of the Family: Balzac and the Social Forms of Sexuality* (Durham, NC: Duke University Press, 2003), 129; translation is Lucey's.

29. The book was based on the cryptic manuscripts of Henry-Alexandre-Alphonse Legrand (1814–76), preserved at the Bibliothèque Nationale, transcribed and presented by the anthropologist Jean-Paul Dumont and his father Paul-Ursin Dumont. Henry Legrand was apparently the only male member of an erotic and mystical secret society, who recorded his activities over three decades in 45 bulky manuscript volumes, writing in a code inspired by Sanskrit and Arabic. The manuscripts were discovered and deciphered in 1907 by French writer Pierre Louÿs (1870–1925).

30. Michelle Perrot (ed.), *L'Impossible Prison: Recherches sur le système pénitentiaire au XIXe siècle réunies par Michelle Perrot: Débat avec Michel Foucault* (Paris: Seuil, 1980). This book, *L'Impossible Prison*, is yet to be translated into English. See Macey, *The Lives of Michel Foucault*, 403. The French version of the roundtable session, heavily edited by Foucault, can be found in 'Table ronde du 20 mai 1978', DE2, 839–53. The English translation of this can be found in Michel Foucault, 'Questions of method: an interview with Michel Foucault', in Graham Burchell, Colin Gordon and Peter Miller (eds), *The Foucault Effect: Studies in Governmentality* (Chicago, IL: University of Chicago Press, 1991), 73–86; and Michel Foucault, 'The impossible prison', in Sylvère Lotringer (ed.), *Foucault Live: Collected Interviews, 1961–1984*, Lysa Hochroth and John Johnston (trans.) (New York: Semiotext(e), 1989), 275–86.

31. Arlette Farge, *Délinquance et criminalité: Le vol d'aliments à Paris au XVIIIe siècle* (Paris: Plon, 1974); and Arlette Farge, *Vivre dans la rue à Paris au XVIIIe siècle*, Archives No. 76 (Paris: Gallimard, 1979), which was also part of Pierre Nora and Jacques Revel's *Archives* series (No. 76).

32. Foucault, D&P, 75; citation of Farge in ibid., 77.

33. François Dosse's interview with Arlette Farge, quoted in Dosse, *History of Structuralism, Volume 2*, 258.

34. Ibid., 257.
35. Ibid., 258.
36. Macey, *The Lives of Michel Foucault*, 454; and personal correspondence with Arlette Farge, 10 November 2011.
37. Claude Mauriac, *Le Temps immobile 3, Et comme l'espérance est violente* (Paris: Livre de poche, 1986), 595, quoted in Macey, *The Lives of Michel Foucault*, 455.
38. Macey, *The Lives of Michel Foucault*, 454. In Foucault, ABN, 53 n. 6, Foucault mentioned that the quoted *lettre de cachet* came from the inventory 'produced by Christiane Martin on Michel Foucault's request. [She] died before completing the work.'
39. Macey, *The Lives of Michel Foucault*, 456. See Arlette Farge, 'Familles: L'honneur et le secret', in Philippe Ariès and Georges Duby (eds), *Histoire de la vie privée, Tome 3: De la Renaissance aux Lumières* (Paris: Seuil, 1986), 581–617, especially from 600 onwards. Th English translation of this can be found in Arlette Farge, 'The honour and secrecy of families', in Roger Chartier (ed.), *A History of Private Life, Volume 3: Passions of the Renaissance*, Philippe Ariès and Georges Duby (general eds) and Arthur Goldhammer (trans.) (Cambridge, MA: Harvard University Press, 1989), 571–609.
40. David Macey's interview with Arlette Farge, quoted in Macey, *The Lives of Michel Foucault*, 455.
41. Ibid.
42. Camille Deslypper and Guy Dreux, 'La parole comme événement – Entretien avec Arlette Farge', *Nouveaux regards*, 30 (2005), available at: http://www.parutions.com/index.php?pid=1&rid=4&srid=100&ida=6299 (last accessed 1 March 2012); my translation.
43. Ibid.; my translation.
44. Foucault, quoted in Lucey, *The Misfits of the Family*, 129; translation is Lucey's.
45. My analysis here is informed by the work of philosophers Thomas Flynn, Béatrice Han and especially Timothy O'Leary. See Thomas R. Flynn, *Sartre, Foucault, and Historical Reason, Volume 2: A Poststructuralist Mapping of History* (Chicago, IL: University of Chicago Press, 2005), 208–29; Béatrice Han, *Foucault's Critical Project: Between the Transcendental and the Historical*, Edward Pile (trans.) (Stanford, CA: Stanford University Press, 2002); Timothy O'Leary, 'Foucault, experience, literature', *Foucault Studies*, 5 (2008), 5–25; Timothy O'Leary, *Foucault and Fiction: The Experience Book* (London: Continuum, 2009); O'Leary, 'Rethinking experience with Foucault'.
46. Foucault, GSO, 1–23, especially 1–6. The 'Preface to the *History of Sexuality, Volume 2*' was not used in the final publication, and was collected in Foucault, DE2, 1397–1403 and Foucault, EW3, 199–205 (translated into English by William Smock). It initially appeared in *The Foucault Reader*, Paul Rabinow (ed.) (New York: Pantheon Books, 1984), 333–9. The pages in GSO and the unused 'Preface' share many similarities.
47. Foucault, GSO, 1.
48. Ibid., 2.
49. Ibid.
50. Ibid., 3.

51. Ibid.
52. Ibid.
53. Ibid.
54. Ibid.
55. Ibid.
56. See Colin Gordon, '*Histoire de la folie*: An unknown book by Michel Foucault', in Arthur Still and Irving Velody (eds), *Rewriting the History of Madness: Studies in Foucault's* Histoire de la folie (London: Routledge, 1992), 19–43; Gary Gutting, 'Foucault's philosophy of experience', *Boundary 2*, 29 (2002), 69–85; Gary Gutting, 'Foucault and the history of madness', in Gary Gutting (ed.), *The Cambridge Companion to Foucault*, 2nd edn (Cambridge: Cambridge University Press, 2005), 49–73; Jean Khalfa, 'Introduction', in Foucault's *History of Madness* (HOM); Allan Megill, 'Foucault, ambiguity and the rhetoric of historiography', in Still and Velody (eds), *Rewriting the History of Madness*, 86–104.
57. Michel Foucault, *Maladie mentale et personnalité* (Paris: Presses universitaires de France, 1954), translated into English as *Mental Illness and Psychology*, A. M. Sheridan-Smith (trans.) (New York: Harper and Row, 1976); Michel Foucault, 'Dream, imagination, and existence', in Keith Hoeller (ed.) and Forest Williams (trans.), *Dream, Imagination, Existence: An Introduction to Ludwig Binswanger's*, Dream and Existence (Atlantic Highlands, NJ: Humanities Press, 1993 [1954]), 31–105, cited in text as DIE. On Foucault's attempt to suppress *Mental Illness and Psychology*, see Eribon, *Michel Foucault*, 70.
58. Gutting, 'Foucault's philosophy of experience', 83. On Foucault and phenomenology, see also Todd May, 'Foucault's relation to phenomenology', in Gary Gutting (ed.), *The Cambridge Companion to Foucault*, 2nd edn (Cambridge: Cambridge University Press, 2005), 284–311.
59. Foucault, 'Preface', EW1, 201.
60. Ibid., 202.
61. Foucault, GSO, 4.
62. Foucault, 'Preface', EW1, 202–3.
63. Ibid., 203.
64. Ibid.
65. Foucault, GSO, 4.
66. Ibid.
67. Ibid.
68. Foucault, 'Preface', EW1, 204–5.
69. Ibid., 202.
70. Ibid.
71. O'Leary, 'Rethinking experience with Foucault', 169.
72. Foucault, GSO, 5.
73. Foucault, 'The lives of infamous men', EW3, 158.
74. François Dosse's interview with Arlette Farge, quoted in Dosse, *History of Structuralism, Volume 2*, 259.
75. Lecomte, 'Foucault et les historiens', 21.
76. Dosse, *History of Structuralism, Volume 2*, 254.
77. Robert Mandrou, 'Trois cles pour comprendre la folie à l'époque classique', *Annales: économies, sociétiés, civilisations*, 17 (1962), 771–2.

78. Fernand Braudel's addendum to Mandrou, 'Trois cles', 772. It is worth mentioning that by about the mid 1970s, Braudel's opinion of Foucault has shifted. For Braudel, Foucault was now a 'non-historian', a philosopher who 'spoke out on history with the greatest vehemence' and who in the process '[declaimed] loudly, perhaps even too loudly'. See Fernand Braudel, 'Foreword', in Traian Stoianovich, *French Historical Method: The* Annales *Paradigm*. (Ithaca, NY: Cornell University Press, 1976), 9–18 at 16–17.
79. Noiriel, 'Foucault and history', 551.
80. Dosse, *History of Structuralism, Volume 2*, 254.
81. Lecomte, 'Foucault et les historiens', 21.
82. Foucault, GSO, 5–6.
83. Lecomte, 'Foucault et les historiens', 21.
84. Ibid.; my translation.
85. Jacques Léonard, 'L'historien et le philosophe: A propos de *Surveiller et punir: Naissance de la prison*', in Michelle Perrot (ed.), *L'Impossible Prison: Recherches sur le système pénitentiaire au XIXe siècle réunies par Michelle Perrot: Débat avec Michel Foucault* (Paris: Seuil, 1980), 9–28 at 10.
86. Ibid., 14.
87. Ibid., 15 and 27. See also Patricia O'Brien, 'Michel Foucault's history of culture', in Lynn Hunt (ed.), *The New Cultural History* (Berkeley, CA: University of California Press, 1989), 25–46 at 29–31; Matthew Ramsey, 'Review essay: history of a profession, *Annales* style: the work of Jacques Léonard', *Journal of Social History*, 17 (1983), 319–38.
88. See Maurice Agulhon, 'Postface', in Perrot (ed.), *L'Impossible Prison*, 313–16 at 315–16.
89. François Dosse's interview with Michelle Perrot, quoted in Dosse, *History of Structuralism, Volume 2*, 255.
90. Charles O. Carbonnel, *Histoire et historiens: Une mutation idéologique des historiens français, 1865–1885* (Toulouse: Privat 1976), 7 and 575, quoted in Noiriel, 'Foucault and history', 553. For Michelle Perrot and others' reflections on the roundtable, see Rémi Lenoir and Jean-Jacques Yvorel (eds), *Michel Foucault,* Surveiller et punir: *la prison vingt ans après* (*Sociétés et Représentations*) (Paris: CREDHESS, 1996).
91. François Dosse's interview with Michelle Perrot, quoted in Dosse, *History of Structuralism, Volume 2*, 255.
92. All quotations from this paragraph from Michel Foucault, interview with *Libération*, 21 January 1983, cited in Eribon, *Michel Foucault*, 274.
93. Farge and Foucault, DEF, 9; translation by Rocha and Harrois.
94. Farge and Foucault, 'L'âge d'or de la lettre de cachet', Foucault, DE2, 1170; my translation.
95. Foucault, 'Preface', EW1, 200.
96. Ibid., 201.
97. Foucault, 'The lives of infamous men', EW3, 161.
98. Ibid., 161–2.
99. Ibid., 162.
100. Ibid., 161.
101. Ibid.
102. Ibid.
103. Ibid., 160.

104. Ibid., 161 and 163.
105. Ibid., 167.
106. Ibid., 167–8.
107. Ibid., 169.
108. Ibid., 172; my emphasis.
109. Gilles Deleuze, *Foucault*, Seán Hand (trans.) (Minneapolis, MN: University of Minnesota Press, 1988 [1986]), 116.
110. See Arlette Farge, *Le Goût d'archive* (Paris: Seuil, 1989). On Farge and Foucault on the 'aesthetics' of the archive, see also Lynne Huffer, 'Foucault's ethical ars erotica', *SubStance*, 38 (2009), 125–47; and Lynne Huffer, *Mad for Foucault: Rethinking the Foundations of Queer Theory* (New York: Columbia University Press, 2010), 249–53.

On the 'Collectif Maurice Florence': this collective includes Philippe Artières, Jean-François Bert, Pascal Michon, Mathieu Potte-Bonneville and Judith Revel. These historians, philosophers and sociologists are associated with the Centre Michel Foucault and are in charge of the Foucault archives deposited at the Institut Mémoires de l'Édition Contemporaine (IMEC). They are also editors of the 'Portail Michel Foucault' online. Artières in particular collaborated with Laurent Quéro and Michelle Zancarini-Fournel for a 2003 book on the archival documents from the Groupe d'Information sur les Prisons (GIP) founded by Foucault in 1970. The Collectif Maurice Florence stated that they wished to continue Foucault's work on experience and power in a contemporary perspective. To that end, they organised an exhibition at the Bibliothèque Municipale in Lyon and published *Archives de l'infamie* (Paris: Prairies ordinaires, 2009). The book included anthropometric notebooks, lists of deportees, judicial reviews of cases involving vagrant children, papers left behind by parents who abandoned their families, extracts from diaries of labourers, letters sent by political exiles and photographs from a report by Joséphine Guattari on psychiatric wards in Greece. 'Maurice Florence' was of course the pseudonym that Foucault used for his own entry in the 1981 *Dictionnaire des philosophes*. See Michel Foucault (as Maurice Florence), 'Foucault' in Denis Huisman (ed.), *Dictionnaire des philosophes, 1* (Paris: Presses universitaires de France, 1981), 942–4.

Afterword:

Foucault's Family Resemblances

Terrell Carver

No one since Marx has made a more profound change to the way that we think about society, power and politics than Foucault. In his thinking Marx had few, if any, disciplinary or sub-disciplinary boundaries to contend with; they didn't very much exist in the 1830s and 1840s, and in any case, his rather brief academic ambitions were thwarted. Very wisely he moved swiftly on, and fortunately for us, into journalism and freelance political/theoretical writing. Subject to varying forms of censorship and various considerations of medium and audience, he could cross any intellectual boundaries that he pleased, albeit mostly in geographical exile from his audience.

Foucault was not in the same position, but to say that he rethought sociology would be to underestimate and delimit his influence very considerably. Of course he was not a professional philosopher – thank goodness – but the depth of his thought has led, quite rightly, to a reading of him as a profound philosopher of society, and in that way, a contributor to any and all disciplines and sub-disciplines that centre humanity.

Indeed it is quite productive to engage in a Foucauldean reading of Marx's work, for instance; this may be an anachronistic projection, but it shows the power of Foucault's vision, rather than some genealogy of intellectual debt. The two do not have to be squared off in some kind of contest; the Library of Congress has awarded them happy family status by cataloguing most of their works as sociology, anyway. Readings like this can be productive (or not), and Foucault is nearer our times than Marx.

Indeed Foucault's recasting of sociology represents a supplement, in a sense, to Marx's vision and work. Marx was famously interested in human productive activities, and in particular in the historical changes associated with modern industry. Rather than working as an economist (the career did not of course exist at the time), he pushed his insights forward into the realm of political structure and ongoing events, touching on family structures and relationships, on cultural and imperial formations and on similar considerations as he went along.

Foucault famously focused on otherwise neglected institutions and issues – neglected even by sociologists, who are sometimes said to have got the leftovers after economics and political science organised themselves around fairly strictly defined concepts such as market and government. Family was one of those leftovers.

Foucault's accreditation as a sociological innovator is generally ascribed to his work on prisons – seemingly unpromising territory for sociological study, except in terms of more or less necessary pathologisations of behaviour. How much 'society' can there be in a prison that it is really interesting for, and exemplary of, the larger society that professional sociologists were aiming to improve? There might be some negative lessons there for criminologists to draw, but on the whole we know those already via rather uncontentious moral presumptions. Similarly Foucault's focus on the body was novel; of course people have bodies, but don't they belong to medicine? or sports science? or the performing arts? Individual consciousness was fine, albeit in its social context, as a functioning concept in sociological thinking. But the individual body? What was there to say? Birth, marriage and death emerge in conventional sociology as meaningful, symbolic, systemic activities – but in a rather disembodied and over-generalised way.

Then there is sexuality. Sociologists tended to follow the familiar bifurcations of the cultures that they lived in: heteronormative naturalisation (via Darwin or the Bible, or both, if necessary), and perverse pathologisations otherwise, possibly interesting in studies of deviant subgroups (where not a few participant-observers went native). However, the stars of the live-sex show were elsewhere – in anthropology and psychoanalysis. The former were far afield (often in the South Seas) looking at societies that were designated 'other' in exoticised ways (and often labelled primitive). The latter was darker territory – focusing on relationships very close to home, and indeed very literally so – but psychoanalytic practice (rather than the intellectual discipline) was fortunately rather less than scientific, so much so that even medicine didn't want it, and it was rather too commercial for academic psychology. As trained minds, sociologists could distance themselves from social subjects and follow standardised disclosure and debriefing procedures to ensure their objectivity; making sexuality a sociological subject might expose one to all kinds of unwelcome attention and comment, not least highly personal ones, as the Kinseys found out.

Foucault's historicism was itself quite novel. Sociology tended to have an oddly synchronic character, nested within rather vague assumptions that social science would lead to progress. While historical context was significant – whether for social concepts and structures or for individual opinions and values – it could usually be cribbed from historians, whose job it was to set these things up in the first place. Foucault's method was strikingly diachronic – history is all and you have to do it. His gift was to take unfashionable, dangerous and marginalised phenomena and give them very detailed histories. They were thus yanked into time, and in that way denaturalised. No one, of course, thought that prisons were natural objects but certainly everyone thought that human evil was a natural phenomenon, and a fairly obvious one at that. The body was a biological given, and couldn't have a history (other than in primatology, which is by definition about the not-yet-human). Sexuality might have different cultural expressions, and therefore histories, but it was biologically basic, surely, and the variants and pathologies of limited social significance.

Or rather, 'the family' stood in for a sociological consideration of sexuality. 'The family' in modern, Western terms – I shall persist with the scare-quotes as a gesture of constant de-naturalisation – has an ambiguous relationship with sexuality as such, but not one that sociologists cared to explore very much. The incest taboo was fine with them, and any variants in it could safely be left to anthropologists (or rather unsafely left to eugenicists). Infidelity and divorce were clearly pathologies, but then again they were rather too close to home; arguing for their significance might give people the wrong impression and expose oneself to scrutiny. Moral systems can be assumed, of course, but – short of suttee, stoning of adulterers and polygamy – the details could be left to local option and an objective distance thus reasonably maintained. The extent to which the family encouraged sex – rather than just permitted it – was hardly a polite subject for sociologists to study. This surely was private, and – as mentioned above – sexologists had a hard time and weren't acceptably mainstream. 'Romance', where all of this is in fact encapsulated and metonymised, is obviously entertainment, not sociology. It has been safely marginalised in cultural studies and feminist film criticism.

When Foucault made prisons the exemplar for social institutions generally – including all the 'good' ones such as education, healthcare, psychological therapies, social work and the like – he caused outrage.

When he focused on the body, he was thought weird. When he devoted himself to a massive history of sexuality, he caused a scandal: history wasn't sociology, and sexuality was not a project. What got Foucault to this point?

My contention is that it was the now rather banal power/knowledge conjunction. Seeing these as two sides of the same coin misses the profound philosophical interest of the insight that Foucault offers. My reading of his work – which of course could well be disputed, and productively so – is that they are *the same thing*. That is, one does not have knowledge *of power*, or *use power* to put knowledge into practice. Knowledge is already power by definition – whether used or not – and power isn't anything very significant without a knowledge-project, however bizarre and unscientific. Indeed knowledges and knowers don't have to be scientific or accredited in any sense at all. The very criteria that are offered to demarcate knowledge from nonsense or falsehood are themselves a knowledge-project and as such, power cranked up a notch. All this proceeds through discursive activity and generates power structures.

Foucault's 'regimes of truth' is an extraordinarily fecund move. While it may seem to relativise knowledge-projects as simply power structures, it more importantly exposes the apparatus of truth-production – via epistemologies and ontologies, via reason and revelation – as power-ridden, and far from benign or objective. Our problems are not therefore amenable to rationalities outside ourselves – whether of a material, transcendental or supernatural sort – but are rather power struggles all the way down. This cuts off all the easy routes to objectivity and any authorial or scientific claims to be the voice of truth.

This is a famously dark vision, and Foucault went for strikingly inverted studies that would show this up. Early modernity was a wonderful sourcebook for historical accounts of power/knowledge transformation, undermining what had previously appeared to be spaces and places of safety. This went straight to the normal/pathological boundary line, showing not that it was wrong, but that it was constructed, and that it was constructed in bizarrely different ways. In showing this, a number of other familiar binaries tumbled down: barbarism/civilisation, primitivism/modernity, kindness/cruelty, domination/liberation, public/private, even mind/body. Foucault has hardly destroyed all of these, which was not his point, anyway. Rather he exposed them as power projects, not effects of nature, universal moralities or Western progress.

What can we say about 'the family' now in that light? We have to be careful here not to go backwards. Merely mentioning the 'f'-word is likely to lock us into all of the casual, naturalised and unhistorical assumptions that Foucauldean scrutiny exposes as problematical. My suggestion is that we take our cues from him and begin with sexuality as – however inexplicably – a knowledge-project.

This is a profoundly inverted presumption. After all, sexuality is supposed to be bodily in an instinctive way, highly individualised as such, yet curiously uniform and universal. While most often practised in privacy (or such privacy as can be obtained), often this is constructed by looking away or not hearing. We constantly act it all out metaphorically in ways that are tautologically defined as public; as Butler noted, we perform repetitiously the meaningful activities through which we make ourselves intelligible. But over and above that, whenever we want to make sexuality intelligible, we resort to an unbounded reservoir of vocabularies: we experience sexuality in ways that preoccupy us and generate disclosure and confession, fantasy and dreaming. Foucault got a critical grip on all of this, and pursued his argument historically – nothing here is timeless or natural (and what is natural was – until Foucault – supposedly timeless).

Through the magic of abstraction Foucault departed from the traditional, and supposedly inescapable, man–woman–child scenario as biologically systemic and personally teleological. Moreover power-structures precede affect here, another unusual move. People are sexual, not because of their feelings, but because they are taught and disciplined – it's a knowledge-project with powerful institutions on board, and it's child-centred, or rather focused on the child as teleologically an adult. Indeed it is concepts of sexual maturity that create the child/adult distinction in the first place. Those who see humans as males and females, men and women (by and large), even those who are focused on these categories as knowledge-projects, can pause here, please. Famously Foucault says little about gender, and little to please feminists. Put simply, he lacked a 'woman-centred' perspective, and moreover tended to cast oppression in general 'human' terms. It's not that he's right (or indeed wrong), but rather that there may be a point to this apparent indifference to gender.

From the Foucauldean perspective nothing exists until power/ knowledge comes on the scene, even if we don't know when this took place, or notice it when it does. While this may appear to cut us loose from familiar foundations of certainty about the species, it usefully tips all the responsibility for what goes on back onto us collectively. We are what we make ourselves into; we are causes, not effects. Claims that humans have to have families, or always have families, are thus rightly exposed as knowledge-projects and power-trips. It also exposes state regulation of (and ethno-nationalistic investments in) kinship as not merely variable amongst societies but as dominatory practices to begin with. On this view any given 'family' structure is really the condensation of power/knowledge practices such that a normalisation/pathologisation boundary line is constructed – somewhere. It's a small step from this to seeing gender as an effect of kinship and 'family'.

As almost any feminist can tell you, centring 'woman' and gender risks reinscribing the categories of oppression in the very process of trying politically to dismantle them. *Finding* gender in Foucault, rather than noting its apparent omission or lack of centrality, starts to loosen the naturalising link between individuals with bodily sex and the usual process of gendering this into binary and hierarchical categories that disadvantage women. Kinship and 'family' are obviously structures through which individuals become known as who they are and what they are. They are categories and practices, not reflections of a supposed biology made manifest in the visible properties of individual humans. Foucault helps feminists to make this point about women and gender, although some had got there first or at least independently. However, Foucault didn't look to feminists for help, which is possibly one of his tragedies.

The next move I want to make is simply to note the ways that we operate the kinship and 'family' system metaphorically in order to preserve the categories that we are used to – while already knowing that they don't work. We now have a mishmash of kinship and 'family' categories, including egg mothers (two kinds), sperm fathers, surrogate mothers, adoptive parents and children, tolerated forms of plural marriage, divorce (that is to say 'ex-') relationships, trans-sex and transgender procedures and practices (including rules for entry into marriage and civil partnership), and of course gay marriage and adoption (including single parents, gay or otherwise). I'm sure this list isn't complete. My point is that these categories cover a variety of more or less consistent and inconsistent mapping exercises back to a supposed biological naturalism that is ever increasingly metaphorical. Adam and Eve really can be Adam and Steve. All of this Genesis-style two-by-two presumption merely raises the queries rehearsed above about what each person might be doing before, during and after this supposedly intimate association that we would choose to count as sexual. And we learn to count things as sexual by learning and recognising, one way or another, the very public terms of sex education, tabloid argot and popular idioms.

Foucault has thus not merely historicised and de-naturalised kinship and the 'family', he has done the same for sex and gender. Given his interest in power, discipline and suffering, however, it seems perverse to suggest that he excludes or 'doesn't get' gender and sex. He simply set up sexuality and oppression, and we can take it from there. It was feminists, rather than 'we', who did the work, as they were the ones with the political interest in gender, sex and 'the family', of course in highly varied ways. And there were certainly those among them who looked for certainty and promoted various kinds of naturalisation independent of history and society. However, Foucault's approach to power/ knowledge appealed to many in the feminist community, and they ran with it – irrespective of where it took them, in some cases.

Feminists indebted to Foucault have argued that sex itself as a biological construct is the work of knowledge communities with power agendas, indeed ones that propounded medico-scientific truth regimes (and rather prison-like therapies). Feminist work has self-consciously reproduced and extended Foucault's famous studies, for example of the hermaphrodite Herculine Barbin. Unlike Foucault, some of these writers were trained as cell biologists and medical researchers, which helped considerably.

Gender was in a sense somewhat less naturalised to begin with, but then as a focus of feminist investigation, it certainly benefited from a Foucauldean emphasis on bodily *surface* and public spectacle. Rather similarly bodily deportment – following Foucault's interest in etiquette and apparently minor kinds of social discipline – is but a very small step from a theory of gender as a similar sort of knowledge-project, rather than some mysteriously social emanation of one's 'inner' biology. However, it is a very large and difficult step convincing many people that this is so, given the vast political investments of various kinds in categorising and reproducing easily recognised and readily interpreted cookie-cutter 'identities', whether as 'woman' or anything else.

In his lectures on psychiatric power Foucault integrates 'the family' not into his 'theory' but into his theorisation of the relation between madness, asylums and the power-projects through which normality *for* individuals (not the normality *of* individuals) emerges. Historically, he says, individuals were extracted from 'the family' for treatment, and then the presumptions of the therapeutic regime were exported back into 'the family' via such strange new categories as 'student parents'. His focus, however, is the child, not 'woman'. With the child he is concerned to delineate the power/knowledge-project of creating some kinds of human subjectivities as normal, and struggling against the resistance and subversion manifested in recalcitrance. From some perspectives, this is woefully innocent of gender, whether construed as a biological determinant of behaviour or as a political project of liberation. My point here is not to defend this account in any sense, but to draw out its potential, positive implications.

Oppression is a key Foucauldean category, and feminists interested in 'the family' found plenty of it there, even if relatively few have seen the implications of full de-naturalisation. This would mean the abolition of the kinship structures through which personal identity – at the moment – is crucially construed. It's an open and interesting philosophical question whether one has to be 'son-of' or 'daughter-of' in order to exist as a person, even informally (most states insist on rather variable formalities and proofs in this regard). Indeed these days one can be first one and then the other anyway, given that sex assignment and gender-recognition have been cut loose (or rather loosened up) from the conventionally harsh disciplinary practices that Foucault and others have documented. Tabloid cases of misplaced babies and confusion over 'real' parents simply exposes the tenacity with which human life is made intelligible only in 'family' terms. According to Foucault's terms we are not looking at instincts or tradition; we are looking at power as an exercise of what we already think we know. His point is that we don't, but on the other hand, power/knowledge is what we do.

Historicisation of the family might have resulted in a typology of Wittgensteinian family resemblances, varying instances of a human universal, within which the differences are perhaps not as significant as we suppose – supposing that we were to drop some of our assumptions about civilisation and progress. De-naturalising 'the family' – as Foucault does by pulling us back to more general and even de-sexed concepts of the body and sexuality as such – is a more radical move. The Wittgensteinian family resemblances that he exposes are thus those between the knowledge-projects that constitute our worlds of power-relations, parallel practices of discipline, punishment and cruelty. These include nationhood, the state, education, the economy – and all else, including war, conflict and security. Foucauldean feminists have drawn this out in terms of gender, sex and – forming some interesting alliances – sexualities.

What, then, became of Marx? And of a Foucauldean reading of his work? From this perspective he emerges as profoundly concerned with oppression, albeit economic (rather than therapeutic). His analytical strategy is remarkably Foucauldean (rather than abstractly Hegelian or empirically positive), given his relentless historicisation of the variant ways that productive activities and social structures have emerged, faded out and looped back on each other. In particular he attacked any number of political economists for dehistoricising and thus naturalising the social structures and individualised subjectivities that they were – more or less – self-consciously promoting. Class structures, in Marx's account, tell you who you are and what you are in much the same way that kinship and 'family' structures do in Foucault. They are analysed as power/knowledge-projects, rather than presented as the 'givens' that normalising social sciences construct and thus insulate from critique in any depth.

However, Marx's project was of course a political one of liberation, rather than one of critical inversion and exposure, as was Foucault's. They started from different places, and headed in different directions, but not opposite ways by any means. Their paths crossed very significantly in intellectual terms, and they both changed the world by interpreting it. Feminists have benefited enormously from both, always with a critical edge, and somewhat against the grain. There has been highly significant work on 'the family' as and where feminists have found it, including an exposure of the linkages between kinship structures and individual identities. But I think there is still some way to go. When we have got there, I will drop the scare quotes.

Bibliography

Afary, Janet and Kevin B. Anderson, *Foucault and the Iranian Revolution: Gender and the Seductions of Islamism* (Chicago, IL: University of Chicago Press, 2005).

Agamben, Giorgio, *Homo Sacer: Sovereign Power and Bare Life*, Daniel Heller-Roazen (trans.) (Stanford, CA: Stanford University Press, 1998).

Agulhon, Maurice, 'Postface', in Michelle Perrot (ed.), *L'Impossible Prison: Recherches sur le système pénitentiaire au XIXe siècle réunies par Michelle Perrot: Débat avec Michel Foucault* (Paris: Seuil, 1980), 313–16.

Albistur, Maïté and Daniel Armogathe, *Histoire du féminisme français, du moyen âge à nos jours* (Paris: Éditions des femmes, 1978).

Alcoff, Linda, 'Dangerous pleasures: Foucault and the politics of paedophilia', in Susan J. Hekman (ed.), *Feminist Interpretations of Michel Foucault* (University Park, PA: Penn State University Press, 1996), 99–135.

Ariès, Philippe and Georges Duby (eds), *Histoire de la vie privée*, 5 vols (Paris: Seuil, 1985–87), translated as *A History of Private Life*, 5 vols, Paul Veyne (ed.) and Arthur Goldhammer (trans.) (Cambridge, MA: Harvard University Press, 1992–98).

Artières, Philippe, Laurent Quéro and Michelle Zancarini-Fournel (eds), *Le Groupe d'information sur les prisons: Archives d'une lutte, 1970–1972* (Paris: Éditions de l'IMEC, 2003).

Autès, Michel, *Les Paradoxes du travail social* (Paris: Dunod, 1999).

Bachmann, Christian, *Autour de Robert Castel* (Paris: Cedias-Musée Social, 1992).

Badinter, Elisabeth, *Mother Love: Myth and Reality* (New York: Macmillan, 1981).

Bartky, Sandra Lee, 'Foucault, femininity and the modernisation of psychiatric power', in Irene Diamond and Lee Quinby (eds), *Feminism and Foucault: Reflections on Resistance* (Boston, MA: Northeastern University Press, 1988), 61–86.

Baudrillard, Jean, *For a Critique of the Political Economy of the Sign*, Charles Levin (trans.) (St Louis, MO: Telos, 1981 [first published in French as *Pour une critique de l'économie politique du signe* (Paris: Gallimard, 1972)]).

Belkin, Lisa, 'The Opt-Out Revolution', *New York Times Magazine* (26 October 2003).

Bell, Vikki, *Interrogating Incest: Feminism, Foucault and the Law* (London: Routledge, 1993).

Bell, Vikki, 'Biopolitics and the spectre of incest: sexuality and/in the family', in Mike Featherstone and Scott Lash (eds), *Global Modernities* (London: Sage, 1995), 227–43.

Bercé, Yves-Marie, *Croquants et nu-pieds: Les soulèvements paysans en France du XVIIe au XIXe siècle*, Archives No. 55 (Paris: Gallimard, 1974).

Bericht des Bundesrates an die Bundesversammlung über das Volksbegehren, 'Für die Familie', *Bundesblatt*, 96 (10 October 1944), 868.

Berlant, Lauren, *The Queen of America Goes to Washington City: Essays on Sex and Citizenship* (Durham, NC: Duke University Press, 1997).

Bernauer, James, 'Beyond life and death', in Timothy Armstrong (ed.), *Michel Foucault, Philosopher: Essays* (Brighton: Harvester Wheatsheaf, 1992), 260–79.

Bessaguet, Anne, Michel Chauvière and Annick Ohayon, *Les socio-clercs: Bienfaisance ou travail social* (Paris: Maspero, 1976).

Bleuler, Eugen, *Lehrbuch der Psychiatrie* (Berlin: Julius Springer, 1916).

Bongie, Lawrence, *From Rogue to Everyman: A Foundling's Journey to the Bastille* (Montreal: McGill-Queen's University Press, 2004).

Bordo, Susan, 'Feminism, Foucault, and the politics of the body', in Caroline Ramazanoglu (ed.), *Up Against Foucault: Explorations of Some Tensions between Foucault and Feminism* (London: Routledge, 1993), 179–202.

Bourdieu, Pierre, 'Champ intellectuel et projet créateur', *Les Temps modernes*, 246 (1966), 865–906.

Bourdieu, Pierre, *Distinction: A Social Critique of the Judgement of Taste*, Richard Nice (trans.) (Cambridge, MA: Harvard University Press, 1984).

Bourdieu, Pierre, 'On the family as a realised category', *Theory, Culture and Society*, 13 (1996), 19–26.

Bourdieu, Pierre, *The Rules of Art: Genesis and Structure of the Literary Field*, Susan Emanuel (trans.) (Stanford, CA: Stanford University Press, 1996).

Bourdieu, Pierre, *Masculine Domination*, Richard Nice (trans.) (Stanford, CA: Stanford University Press, 2001), first published as *La Domination masculine* (Paris: Seuil, 1998).

Bourdieu, Pierre, *The Bachelors' Ball: The Crisis of Peasant Society in Béarn*, Richard Nice (trans.) (Cambridge: Polity, 2008).

Bourdieu, Pierre, Jean-Claude Chamboredon and Jean-Claude Passeron, *Le Métier de sociologue: préalables epistémologiques* (Paris-La Haye: Mouton-Bourdas, 1968).

Bourdieu, Pierre, et al., *La Misère du monde* (Paris: Éditions du Seuil, 1993); published in English as *The Weight of the World: Social Suffering in Contemporary Society*, Priscilla Parkhurst Ferguson (trans.) (Cambridge: Polity, 1999).

Braudel, Fernand, 'Foreword', in Traian Stoianovich, *French Historical Method: The* Annales *Paradigm* (Ithaca, NY: Cornell University Press, 1976), 9–18.

Broberg, Gunnar and Mattias Tydén, 'Eugenics in Sweden: efficient care', in Gunnar Broberg and Nils Roll-Hansen (eds), *Eugenics and the Welfare State: Sterilisation Policy in Denmark, Sweden, Norway, and Finland* (East Lansing, MI: Michigan State University Press, 2005), 77–149.

Brown, Wendy, *Politics out of History* (Princeton, NJ: Princeton University Press, 2001).

Brown, Wendy, *Walled States, Waning Sovereignty* (New York: Zone Books, 2010).

Burguière, André, *The* Annales *School: An Intellectual History*, Jane Marie Todd (trans.) (Ithaca, NY: Cornell University Press, 2009).

Burke, Peter, *The French Historical Revolution: The* Annales *School, 1929–89* (Stanford, CA: Stanford University Press, 1990).

Butler, Judith, 'Foucault and the paradox of bodily inscriptions', *Journal of Philosophy*, 86 (1989), 601–7.

Carbonnel, Charles O., *Histoire et historiens: Une mutation idéologique des historiens français, 1865–1885* (Toulouse: Privat, 1976).

Castel, Robert, '*Champ Social* a rencontré Robert Castel', *Champ Social*, 21 (1976), 4–5.

Castel, Robert, *Le Psychanalysme: L'ordre psychanalytique et le pouvoir* (Paris: Union Générale d'Éditions, 1976 [first published by François Maspero, 1973]).

Castel, Robert, 'De l'intégration sociale à l'éclatement du social: l'émergence, l'apogée et le départ à la retraite du contrôle social', *Revue internationale d'action communautaire*, 20 (1988), 67–78.

Castel, Robert, 'Du travail social à la gestion sociale du non-travail', *Esprit*, 3–4 (1988), 28–47.

Charlesworth, Simon, 'Bourdieu, social suffering and working-class life', in Bridget Fowler (ed.), *Reading Bourdieu on Society and Culture* (Oxford: Wiley-Blackwell, 2000), 49–64.

Christofferson, Michael Scott, *French Intellectuals Against the Left: The Anti-Totalitarian Moment of the 1970s* (Oxford: Berghahn Books, 2004).

Collectif Maurice Florence (Philippe Artières, Jean-François Bert, Pascal Michon, Mathieu Potte-Bonneville and Judith Revel (eds)), *Archives de l'infamie* (Paris: Prairies ordinaires, 2009).

Cusset, François, *French Theory: How Foucault, Derrida, Deleuze, & Co. Transformed the Intellectual Life of the United States*, Jeff Fort (trans.) (Minneapolis, MN: University of Minnesota Press, 2008).

d'Escrivan, Josette, 'Peut-on ne pas dénoncer l'inacceptable?' *Esprit*, 4–5 (1972), 33–7.

Davidson, Arnold I., *The Emergence of Sexuality: Historical Epistemology and the Formation of Concepts* (Cambridge, MA: Harvard University Press, 2001).

Davidson, Arnold I. (ed.), *Foucault and His Interlocutors.* (Chicago, IL: University of Chicago Press, 1997).

Davis, Natalie Zemon, *The Return of Martin Guerre* (Cambridge, MA: Harvard University Press, 1983).

de Certeau, Michel, *La Possession de Loudun* (Paris: Julliard, 1970), translated as *The Possession at Loudun*, Michael B. Smith (trans.), with a foreword by Stephen Greenblatt (Chicago, IL: University of Chicago Press, 2000).

de Launay, Jacques, *Le Dossier de Vichy*, Archives No. 32 (Paris: Julliard, 1967).

Defert, Daniel, 'L'émergence d'un nouveau front: les prisons', in Philippe Artières, Laurent Quéro and Michelle Zancarini-Fournel (eds), *Le Groupe d'information sur les prisons: Archives d'une lutte, 1970–1972* (Paris: Éditions de l'IMEC, 2003), 315–26.

Deleuze, Gilles, *Foucault*, Seán Hand (trans.) (Minneapolis, MN: University of Minnesota Press, 1988 [1986]).

Deleuze, Gilles and Félix Guattari, *Anti-Oedipus*, Robert Hurley, Mark Seem and Helen R. Lane (trans.) (London and New York: Continuum, 2004 [1972]).

Denis, Michel and Pierre Goubert, *1789: Les Français ont la parole – Cahiers de doléances des États-Généraux*, Archives No. 1 (Paris: Julliard, 1964).

Denizet-Lewis, Benoit, 'Boy crazy', *Boston Magazine* (May 2001), available at: http://www.bostonmagazine.com/articles/boy_crazy/ (last accessed 1 March 2012).

Deslypper, Camille and Guy Dreux, 'La parole comme événement – Entretien avec Arlette Farge', *Nouveaux regards*, 30 (2005), available at: http://www.parutions.com/index.php?pid=1&rid=4&srid=100&ida=6299 (last accessed 1 March 2012).

Dilts, Andrew, 'Michel Foucault meets Gary Becker: criminality beyond *Discipline and Punish*', in *The Carceral Notebooks*, 4 (2008), available at: http://www.thecarceral.org/journal-vol4.html (last accessed 1 March 2012).

Djaballah, Marc, *Kant, Foucault, and Forms of Experience* (London: Routledge, 2008).

Donzelot, Jacques, 'Une anti-sociologie', *Esprit*, 12 (1972), 835–55.

Donzelot, Jacques, 'Travail social et lutte politique', *Esprit*, 4–5 (1972), 654–73, reprinted in Philippe Meyer (ed.), *Normalisation et contrôle social (pourquoi le travail social?)* (Paris: Seuil, 1976), 99–120.

Donzelot, Jacques, 'Misère de la culture politique', *Critique*, 34 (1978), 572–86, available at: http://donzelot.org/articles/Misere%20de%20la%20culture%20 politique.pdf (last accessed 1 March 2012).

Donzelot, Jacques, *The Policing of Families*, Robert Hurley (trans.) (Baltimore, MD: Johns Hopkins University Press, 1979 [first published in French in 1977]).

Donzelot, Jacques, *L'Invention du social: Essai sur le déclin des passions politiques* (Paris: Seuil, 1984).

Donzelot, Jacques, 'À propos de la gouvernmentalité: Une discussion avec Colin Gordon' (2005), available at: http://donzelot.org/articles/ gouvernementalitecolingordon.pdf (last accessed 1 March 2012).

Donzelot, Jacques, 'Devenir sociologue en 1968: Petite topographie physique et morale de la sociologie en ce temps-là', *Esprit*, 344 (2008), 47–53.

Dosse, François, *L'histoire en miettes: des* Annales *à la 'nouvelle histoire'* (Paris: La Découverte, 1987), translated as *New History in France: The Triumph of the Annales*, Peter V. Conroy, Jr (trans.) (Urbana, IL: University of Illinois Press, 1994).

Dosse, François, *History of Structuralism, Volume 1: The Rising Sign, 1945–1966*, Deborah Glassman (trans.) (Minneapolis, MN: University of Minnesota Press, 1997).

Dosse, François, *History of Structuralism, Volume 2: The Sign Sets, 1967–Present*, Deborah Glassman (trans.) (Minneapolis, MN: University of Minnesota Press, 1997).

Dosse, François, *Gilles Deleuze and Félix Guattari: Intersecting Lives*, Deborah Glassman (trans.) (New York: Columbia University Press, 2011).

Dosse, François, *Pierre Nora: Homo historicus* (Paris: Perrin, 2011).

Dreyfus, Hubert L. and Paul Rabinow, *Michel Foucault: Beyond Structuralism and Hermeneutics*, 2nd edn, with an afterword by and an interview with Michel Foucault (Chicago, IL: University of Chicago Press, 1983).

Dubach, Roswitha, 'Zur "Sozialisierung einer medizinischen Massnahme": Sterilisationspraxis der Psychiatrischen Poliklinik Zürich in den 1930er-Jahen', in Marietta Meier, Brigitta Bernet, Roswitha Dubach and Urs Germann (eds), *Zwang zur Ordnung: Psychiatrie im Kanton Zürich, 1870–1970* (Zurich: Chronos, 2007), 155–92.

Duggan, Lisa, *The Twilight of Equality? Neo-Liberalism, Cultural Politics, and the Attack on Democracy* (Boston, MA: Beacon Press, 2003).

Dumont, Jean-Paul and Paul-Ursin Dumont (eds), *Le Cercle amoureux d'Henry Legrand. D'après ses mss. cryptographiques conservés à la Bibliothèque Nationale. Transcrit et présenté par Jean-Paul Dumont et Paul-Ursin Dumont* (Paris: Gallimard, 1979).

Eribon, Didier, *Michel Foucault*, Betsy Wing (trans.) (Cambridge, MA: Harvard University Press, 1991).

Euripides, *The Bacchae and Other Plays*, Philip Vellacott (trans.) (London: Penguin, 1973).

Farge, Arlette, *Délinquance et criminalité: Le vol d'aliments à Paris au XVIIIe siècle* (Paris: Plon, 1974).

Farge, Arlette, *Vivre dans la rue à Paris au XVIIIe siècle*, Archives No. 76 (Paris: Gallimard, 1979).

Farge, Arlette, 'Familles: L'honneur et le secret', in Philippe Ariès and Georges Duby (eds), *Histoire de la vie privée, Tome 3: De la Renaissance aux Lumières* (Paris: Seuil, 1986), 581–617.

Farge, Arlette, 'Travailler avec Michel Foucault', *Le Débat*, 41 (1986), 164–7.

Farge, Arlette, *Le Goût d'archive* (Paris: Seuil, 1989).

Farge, Arlette, 'The honour and secrecy of families', in Roger Chartier (ed.), *A History of Private Life, Volume 3: Passions of the Renaissance*, Philippe Ariès and Georges Duby (general eds) and Arthur Goldhammer (trans.) (Cambridge, MA: Harvard University Press, 1989), 571–609.

Farge, Arlette, 'Michel Foucault et les archives de l'exclusion', in Elisabeth Roudinesco (ed.), *Penser la folie: Essais sur Michel Foucault* (Paris: Galilée, 1992), 63–78.

Farge, Arlette, *Fragile Lives: Violence, Power and Solidarity in Eighteenth-Century Paris*, Carol Shelton (ed.) (Cambridge, MA: Harvard University Press, 1993).

Farge, Arlette, *Subversive Words: Public Opinion in Eighteenth-Century France*, Rosemary Morris (trans.) (University Park, PA: Penn State University Press, 1995).

Farge, Arlette and Michel Foucault, *Le Désordre des familles: Lettres de cachet des Archives de la Bastille au XVIIIe siècle* (Paris: Gallimard, 1982), cited in text as DEF.

Farge, Arlette and Jacques Revel, *The Vanishing Children of Paris: Rumour and Politics before the French Revolution*, Claudia Miéville (trans.) (Cambridge, MA: Harvard University Press, 1991).

Feder, Ellen K., *Family Bonds: Genealogies of Race and Gender* (Oxford: Oxford University Press, 2007).

Feder, Ellen K. 'The dangerous individual('s) mother: biopower, family, and the production of race', *Hypatia*, 22 (2007), 60–78.

Fisher, Jaimey, *Disciplining Germany: Youth, Re-education, and Reconstruction after the Second World War* (Detroit, MI: Wayne State University Press, 2007).

Flynn, Thomas R., *Sartre, Foucault, and Historical Reason, Volume 1: Toward an Existentialist Theory of History* (Chicago, IL: University of Chicago, 1997).

Flynn, Thomas R., *Sartre, Foucault, and Historical Reason, Volume 2: A Poststructuralist Mapping of History* (Chicago, IL: University of Chicago Press, 2005).

Forrester, John, 'Michel Foucault and the history of psychoanalysis', in *The Seductions of Psychoanalysis: Freud, Lacan and Derrida* (Cambridge: Cambridge University Press, 1991), 286–316.

Foucault, Michel, *Maladie mentale et personnalité* (Paris: Presses universitaires de France, 1954), translated into English as *Mental Illness and Psychology*, A. M. Sheridan-Smith (trans.) (New York: Harper and Row, 1976).

Foucault, Michel, *Folie et déraison: Histoire de la folie à l'âge classique* (Paris: Plon, 1961).

Foucault, Michel, *Histoire de la folie à l'âge classique* (Paris: Union générale d'éditions, 1964).

Foucault, Michel, *The Order of Things: An Archaeology of the Human Sciences*, Alan Sherdian (trans.) (New York: Pantheon Books, 1970 [first published in French in 1966]).

Foucault, Michel, *L'Ordre du discours* (Paris: Gallimard, 1971).

Foucault, Michel, 'Appendix: the discourse on language', in *The Archaeology of Knowledge and the Discourse on Language*, Rupert Swyer and Alan Mark

Sheridan-Smith (trans.) (New York: Pantheon Books, 1972 [first published in French in 1969]), 215–37, cited in text as DOL.

Foucault, Michel, *The Birth of the Clinic: An Archaeology of Medical Perception*, A. M. Sheridan Smith (trans.) (New York: Pantheon Books, 1973 [first published in French in 1963]).

Foucault, Michel (ed.), *'I, Pierre Rivière, Having Slaughtered My Mother, My Sister, and My Brother': A Case of Parricide in the Nineteenth Century*, Frank Jellinek (trans.) (Lincoln, NB: University of Nebraska Press, 1975 [first published in French in 1973]), cited in text as IPR.

Foucault, Michel, *The History of Sexuality, Volume 1: An Introduction*, Robert Hurley (trans.) (New York: Pantheon, 1978 [first published in French, Paris: Gallimard, 1976]), reprinted as *The Will to Knowledge* (London: Penguin, 1998), cited in text as HS1.

Foucault, Michel, *Discipline and Punish: The Birth of the Prison*, Alan Sheridan (trans.) (London: Penguin, 1979 [first published in French in 1975]), cited in text as D&P.

Foucault, Michel, *Herculine Barbin: Being the Recently Discovered Memoirs of a Nineteenth-Century French Hermaphrodite*, Richard McDougall (trans.) (New York: Pantheon, 1980), cited in text as HBA.

Foucault, Michel (as Maurice Florence), 'Foucault', in Denis Huisman (ed.), *Dictionnaire des philosophes, 1* (Paris: Presses universitaires de France, 1981), 942–4.

Foucault, Michel, 'L'âge d'or de la lettre de cachet', interview with Michel Foucault and Arlette Farge conducted by Yves Hersant, *L'Express*, 1638 (1982), 83–5, reprinted in Michel Foucault, *Dits et écrits, II, 1976–1988*, Daniel Defert and François Ewald (eds), with the collaboration of Jacques Lagrange (Paris: Quatro Gallimard, 2001), 1170–1.

Foucault, Michel, 'Discourse and truth: the problematisation of *Parrhesia*: six lectures given by Michel Foucault at the University of California, Berkeley, October–November 1983 – Lecture 2, *Parrhesia* in the Tragedies of Euripides', available at: http://foucault.info/documents/parrhesia/foucault. DT2.parrhesiaEuripides.en.html (last accessed 1 March 2012).

Foucault, Michel, *The History of Sexuality, Volume 2: The Use of Pleasure*, Robert Hurley (trans.) (New York: Pantheon, 1985 [first published in French, Paris: Gallimard, 1984]), cited in text as HS2.

Foucault, Michel, *The History of Sexuality, Volume 3: The Care of the Self*, Robert Hurley (trans.) (New York: Pantheon, 1986 [first published in French, Paris: Gallimard, 1984]), cited in text as HS3.

Foucault, Michel, *Politics, Philosophy, Culture: Interviews and Other Writings, 1977–1984*, Lawrence D. Kritzman (ed.) (London: Routledge, 1988), cited in text as PPC.

Foucault, Michel, 'The impossible prison', in Sylvère Lotringer (ed.), *Foucault Live: Collected Interviews, 1961–1984*, Lysa Hochroth and John Johnston (trans.) (New York: Semiotext(e), 1989), 275–86.

Foucault, Michel, 'Questions of method', in Graham Burchell, Colin Gordon and Peter Miller (eds), *The Foucault Effect: Studies in Governmentality* (Chicago, IL: University of Chicago Press, 1991), 73–86.

Foucault, Michel, 'Dream, imagination, and existence', in Keith Hoeller (ed.) and Forest Williams (trans.), *Dream, Imagination, Existence: An Introduction to Ludwig*

Binswanger's, Dream and Existence (Atlantic Highlands, NJ: Humanities Press, 1993 [1954]), 31–105, cited in text as DIE.

Foucault, Michel, *Ethics: Subjectivity and Truth: Essential Works of Foucault, 1954–1984, Volume 1*, Paul Rabinow (ed.) (New York: New Press, 1998), cited in text as EW1.

Foucault, Michel, *Aesthetics, Method, and Epistemology: Essential Works of Foucault, 1954–1984, Volume 2*, James D. Faubion (ed.) (New York: New Press, 1998), cited in text as EW2.

Foucault, Michel, *Power: Essential Works of Foucault, 1954–1984, Volume 3*, James D. Faubion (ed.) (New York: New Press, 2001), cited in text as EW3.

Foucault, Michel, *Dits et écrits, I, 1954–1975*, Daniel Defert and François Ewald (eds), with the collaboration of Jacques Lagrange (Paris: Quarto Gallimard, 2001), cited in text as DE1.

Foucault, Michel, *Dits et écrits, II, 1976–1988*, Daniel Defert and François Ewald (eds), with the collaboration of Jacques Lagrange (Paris: Quarto Gallimard, 2001), cited in text as DE2.

Foucault, Michel, *Madness and Civilisation: A History of Insanity in the Age of Reason*, Richard Howard (trans.) (London: Routledge, 2001 [1967]).

Foucault, Michel, *Abnormal: Lectures at the Collège de France, 1974–1975*, Arnold I. Davidson (ed.) and Graham Burchell (trans.) (London: Verso, 2003), cited in text as ABN.

Foucault, Michel, *Society Must Be Defended: Lectures at the Collège de France, 1975–1976*, Arnold I. Davidson (ed.) and Graham Burchell (trans.) (New York: Picador, 2003), cited in text as SMD.

Foucault, Michel, 'Preface', in Gilles Deleuze and Félix Guattari, *Anti-Oedipus: Capitalism and Schizophrenia*, Robert Hurley, Mark Seem and Helen R. Lane (trans.) (London and New York: Continuum, 2004), pp. xiii–xvi, cited in text as PAO.

Foucault, Michel, *The Hermeneutics of the Subject: Lectures at the Collège de France, 1981–1982*, Arnold I. Davidson (ed.) and Graham Burchell (trans.) (Basingstoke: Palgrave Macmillan, 2005), cited in text as HES.

Foucault, Michel, *History of Madness*, Jean Khalfa (ed.) and Jonathan Murphy and Jean Khalfa (trans.) (London: Routledge, 2006), cited in text as HOM.

Foucault, Michel, *Psychiatric Power: Lectures at the Collège de France, 1973–1974*, Arnold I. Davidson (ed.) and Graham Burchell (trans.) (Basingstoke: Palgrave Macmillan, 2006), cited in text as PSP.

Foucault, Michel, *Security, Territory, Population: Lectures at the Collège de France, 1977–1978*, Arnold I. Davidson (ed.) and Graham Burchell (trans.) (Basingstoke: Palgrave Macmillan, 2007), cited in text as STP.

Foucault, Michel, *The Birth of Biopolitics: Lectures at the Collège de France, 1978–1979*, Arnold I. Davidson (ed.) and Graham Burchell (trans.) (Basingstoke: Palgrave Macmillan, 2008), cited in text as BOB.

Foucault, Michel, *The Government of Self and Others: Lectures at the Collège de France, 1982–1983*, Arnold I. Davidson (ed.) and Graham Burchell (trans.) (Basingstoke: Palgrave Macmillan, 2010), cited in text as GSO.

Foucault, Michel and Michael Bess, 'Power, moral values, and the intellectual: an interview with Michel Foucault', *History of the Present*, 4 (1988), 1–2, 11–13, available at: http://www.vanderbilt.edu/historydept/michaelbess/Foucault%20Interview (last accessed 1 March 2012).

Frijhoff, Willem, 'Foucault reformed by Certeau', in John Neubauer (ed.), *Cultural History after Foucault* (New York: Walter de Gruyter, 1999), 83–91.

Funck-Brentano, Frantz, *Les Lettres de cachet à Paris: étude suivie d'une liste des prisonniers de la Bastille (1659–1789)* (Paris: Imprimerie Nationale, 1903).

Galton, Francis, *Inquiries into Human Faculty and its Development*, 1st edn (London: Macmillan, 1883).

Gendron, Bénédicte, 'Why emotional capital matters in education and in labour? Toward an optimal exploitation of human capital and knowledge management', *Les Cahiers de la Maison des Sciences Economoqies*, série rouge, 113 (Paris: Université Panthéon-Sorbonne, 2004), available at: http://econpapers.repec.org/paper/msewpsorb/r04113.htm (last accessed 1 March 2012).

Ginzburg, Carlo, *The Cheese and the Worms: The Cosmos of a Sixteenth-Century Miller*, John Tedeschi and Anne Tedeschi (trans.) (Baltimore, MD: Johns Hopkins University Press, 1980).

Goldberg Moses, Clara, *French Feminism in the Nineteenth Century* (Albany, NY: SUNY Press, 1984).

Goldstein, Jan, *Foucault and the Writing of History* (Oxford: Wiley-Blackwell, 1994).

Gordon, Colin, '*Histoire de la folie*: An unknown book by Michel Foucault', in Arthur Still and Irving Velody (eds), *Rewriting the History of Madness: Studies in Foucault's Histoire de la folie* (London: Routledge, 1992), 19–43.

Gordon, Colin, 'Foucault in Britain', in Andrew Barry, Thomas Osborne and Nikolas Rose (eds), *Foucault and Political Reason: Liberalism, Neo-Liberalism, and Rationalities of Government* (Chicago, IL: University of Chicago Press, 1996), 253–70.

Gordon, Robert, 'Review of Michel Foucault, *History of Madness*, Jean Khalfa (trans.) (London: Routledge, 2006)', *Notre Dame Philosophical Reviews*, 23 February 2007, available at: http://ndpr.nd.edu/news/25226-history-of-madness/ (last accessed 1 March 2012).

Grignon, Claude and Jean-Claude Passeron, *Le Savant et le populaire: Misérabilisme et populisme en sociologie et en littérature* (Paris: Gallimard, 1989).

Gutting, Gary, 'Foucault's philosophy of experience', *Boundary 2*, 29 (2002), 69–85.

Gutting, Gary, 'Foucault and the history of madness', in Gary Gutting (ed.), *The Cambridge Companion to Foucault*, 2nd edn (Cambridge: Cambridge University Press, 2005), 49–73.

Haag, Pamela, *Consent: Sexual Rights and the Transformation of American Liberalism* (Ithaca, NY: Cornell University Press, 1999).

Halperin, David, *Saint Foucault: Towards a Gay Hagiography* (Oxford: Oxford University Press, 1995).

Han, Béatrice, *Foucault's Critical Project: Between the Transcendental and the Historical*, Edward Pile (trans.) (Stanford, CA: Stanford University Press, 2002).

Harcourt, Bernard E., *The Illusion of Free Markets: Punishment and the Myth of Natural Order* (Cambridge, MA: Harvard University Press, 2011).

Harkins, Gillian, *Everybody's Family Romance: Reading Incest in Neoliberal America* (Minneapolis, MN: University of Minnesota Press, 2009).

Harvey, David, *A Brief History of Neoliberalism* (Oxford: Oxford University Press, 2005).

Hause, Steven C. and Annie Kenney, *Women's Suffrage and Politics in the French Third Republic* (Princeton, NJ: Princeton University Press, 1984).

Hauss, Gisela and Béatrice Ziegler, 'Norm und Ausschluss in Vormundschaft und Psychiatrie: Zum institutionnellen Umgang mit jungen Frauen', in Véronique Mottier and Laura von Mandach (eds), *Pflege, Stigmatisierung und Eugenik: Integration und Ausschluss in Medizin, Psychiatrie und Sozialhilfe* (Zurich: Seismo, 2007), 63–75.

Huffer, Lynne, 'Foucault's ethical ars erotica', *SubStance*, 38 (2009), 125–47.

Huffer, Lynne, *Mad for Foucault: Rethinking the Foundations of Queer Theory* (New York: Columbia University Press, 2010).

Hunt, Lynn, *The Family Romance of the French Revolution* (Berkeley, CA: University of California Press, 1993).

Hutton, Patrick H., *Philippe Ariès and the Politics of French Cultural History* (Amherst, MA: University of Massachusetts Press, 2004).

Jackson, Spencer, 'The subject of time in Foucault's tale of Jouy', *SubStance*, 39 (2010), 39–51.

Jenkins, Philip, *Moral Panic: Changing Concepts of the Child Molester in Modern America* (New Haven, CT: Yale University Press, 1998).

Joly, Aristide, *Les Lettres de cachet dans la généralité de Caen au XVIIIe siècle: d'après des documents inédits* (Paris: Imprimerie Impériale, 1864).

Khalfa, Jean, 'Introduction', in Michel Foucault, *History of Madness*, Jean Khalfa (ed.) and Jonathan Murphy and Jean Khalfa (trans.) (London: Routledge, 2006), xiii–xxv.

Kincaid, James, *Child-Loving: The Erotic Child and Victorian Culture* (London: Routledge, 1992).

Koopman, Colin, 'Two uses of genealogy: Michel Foucault and Bernard Williams', in C. G. Prado (ed.), *Foucault's Legacy* (New York: Continuum, 2009), 90–108.

La Revue français de service social, 107 (1973).

Lancaster, Roger N., *Sex Panic and the Punitive State* (Berkeley, CA: University of California Press, 2011).

Laqueur, Thomas W., *Solitary Sex: A Cultural History of Masturbation* (New York: Zone Books, 2003).

Le Roy Ladurie, Emmanuel, *Les Paysans de Languedoc* (Paris: Flammarion, 1969), translated into English as *The Peasants of Languedoc*, John Day (trans.) (Urbana, IL: University of Illinois Press, 1974).

Le Roy Ladurie, Emmanuel, *Montaillou: village Occitan de 1294 à 1324* (Paris: Gallimard, 1978), translated into English as *Montaillou: Cathars and Catholics in a French Village 1294–1324*, Barbara Bray (trans.) (New York: Vintage, 1979).

Lecomte, Jacques, 'Foucault et les historiens: un malentendu persistant (entretien avec Arlette Farge)', *Sciences Humaines*, 44 (1994), 21.

Lenoir, Rémi, *Généalogie de la morale familial* (Paris: Seuil, 2003).

Lenoir, Rémi and Jean-Jacques Yvorel (eds), *Michel Foucault, Surveiller et punir: la prison vingt ans après (Sociétés et Représentations)* (Paris: CREDHESS, 1996).

Léonard, Jacques, 'L'historien et le philosophe: A propos de *Surveiller et punir: Naissance de la prison*', in Michelle Perrot (ed.), *L'Impossible Prison: Recherches sur le système pénitentiaire au XIXe siècle réunies par Michelle Perrot: Débat avec Michel Foucault* (Paris: Seuil, 1980), 9–28.

Lévi-Strauss, Claude, *The Elementary Structures of Kinship*, Rodney Needham (ed. and trans.) (London: Eyre and Spottiswoode, 1969 [1949]).

Lovell, Terry, 'Thinking feminism with and against Bourdieu', in Bridget Fowler (ed.), *Reading Bourdieu on Society and Culture* (Oxford: Wiley-Blackwell, 2000), 27–48.

Lucey, Michael, *The Misfits of the Family: Balzac and the Social Forms of Sexuality* (Durham, NC: Duke University Press, 2003).

Macey, David, *The Lives of Michel Foucault* (New York: Vintage, 1993).

Macey, David, *Foucault* (London: Reaktion Books, 2004).

Mandrou, Robert, 'Trois cles pour comprendre la folie à l'époque classique', *Annales: économies, sociétiés, civilisations*, 17 (1962), 771–2.

Manor, Yohanan, *Naissance du sionisme politique*, Archives No. 88 (Paris: Gallimard, 1981).

Mauriac, Claude, *Le Temps immobile, 3, Et comme l'espérance est violente* (Paris: Livre de poche, 1986).

May, Todd, 'Foucault's relation to phenomenology', in Gary Gutting (ed.), *The Cambridge Companion to Foucault*, 2nd edn (Cambridge: Cambridge University Press, 2005), 284–311.

McNay, Lois, 'The Foucauldean body and the exclusion of experience', *Hypatia*, 6 (1991), 125–37.

McWhorter, Ladelle, *Racism and Sexual Oppression in Anglo-America: A Genealogy* (Bloomington, IN: Indiana University Press, 2009).

Megill, Allan, 'The reception of Foucault by historians', *Journal of the History of Ideas*, 48 (1987), 117–41.

Megill, Allan, 'Foucault, ambiguity and the rhetoric of historiography', in Arthur Still and Irving Velody (eds), *Rewriting the History of Madness: Studies in Foucault's* Histoire de la folie (London: Routledge, 1992), 86–104.

Monrose, Murielle, 'Une lecture statistique de l'histoire des travailleurs sociaux', in Jean-Noël Chopart (ed.), *Les Mutations du travail social: Dynamiques d'un champ professionnel* (Paris: Dunod, 2000), 13–21.

Moreno Pestaña, José Luis, *Foucault, la gauche et la politique* (Paris: Textuel, 2011).

Mottier, Véronique, 'Narratives of national identity: sexuality, race, and the Swiss "Dream of Order"', *Swiss Journal of Sociology*, 26 (2000), 533–58.

Mottier, Véronique, 'From welfare to social exclusion: eugenic social policies and the Swiss national order', in David Howarth and Jacob Torfing (eds), *Discourse Theory in European Politics: Identity, Policy, Governance* (London: Palgrave MacMillan, 2005), 255–74.

Mottier, Véronique, 'Eugenics and the Swiss gender regime: women's bodies and the struggle against "difference"', *Swiss Journal of Sociology*, 32 (2006), 253–67.

Mottier, Véronique, 'Eugenics, politics and the state: social-democracy and the Swiss gardening state', *Studies in History and Philosophy of Biological and Biomedical Sciences*, 39 (2008), 263–9.

Mottier, Véronique, 'Eugenics and the state: policy-making in comparative perspective', in Alison Bashford and Philippa Levine (eds), *The Oxford Handbook of the History of Eugenics* (Oxford: Oxford University Press, 2010), 134–53.

Mottier, Véronique and Natalia Gerodetti, 'Eugenics and social democracy: or, how the European left tried to eliminate the "weeds" from its national gardens', *New Formations*, 20 (2007), 35–49.

Mottier, Véronique and Laura von Mandach (eds), *Pflege, Stigmatisierung und Eugenik: Integration und Ausschluss in Medizin, Psychiatrie und Sozialhilfe* (Zurich: Seismo, 2007).

Moulin, Raymond and Paul Veyne, 'Entretien avec Jean-Claude Passeron: Un itinéraire de sociologue', *Revue européenne des sciences socials*, 34 (1996), 275–354.

Muel-Dreyfus, Francine, *Le Métier d'éducateur: Les instituteurs de 1900, les éducateurs spéclialisés de 1968* (Paris: Minut, 1983).

Nietzsche, Friedrich, *Thus Spoke Zarathustra*, R. J. Hollingdale (trans.) (London: Penguin, 1969).

Noiriel, Gérard, 'Foucault and history: the lessons of a disillusion', *Journal of Modern History*, 66 (1994), 547–68.

Nora, Pierre, 'Between memory and history: Les Lieux de mémoire', *Representations*, 26 (1989), 7–24.

Nora, Pierre (ed.), *Les Lieux de mémoire*, 3 vols (Paris: Gallimard, 1984–92), translated as *Rethinking France: Les Lieux de mémoire*, 4 vols (Chicago, IL: University of Chicago Press, 1999–2010), abridged translation Pierre Nora (ed.), *Realms of Memory: Rethinking the French Past*, 3 vols, Lawrence D. Kritzman (ed.) and Arthur Goldhammer (trans.) (New York: Columbia University Press, 1996).

Nowotny, Helga, 'Women in public life in Austria', in Cynthia Fuchs Epstein and Rose Laub Coser (eds), *Access to Power: Cross-National Studies of Women and Elites* (London: George Allen and Unwin, 1981), 145–58.

Nye, Robert, *Masculinity and Male Codes of Honour in Modern France* (Oxford: Oxford University Press, 1993).

O'Brien, Patricia, 'Michel Foucault's history of culture', in Lynn Hunt (ed.), *The New Cultural History* (Berkeley, CA: University of California Press, 1989), 25–46.

O'Leary, Timothy, 'Foucault, experience, literature', *Foucault Studies*, 5 (2008), 5–25.

O'Leary, Timothy, *Foucault and Fiction: The Experience Book* (London: Continuum, 2009).

O'Leary, Timothy 'Rethinking experience with Foucault', in Timothy O'Leary and Christopher Falzon (eds), *Foucault and Philosophy* (Oxford: Wiley-Blackwell, 2010), 162–84.

Ory, Pascal, *Les Discours gastronomique français: Des origins à nos jours*, Archives No. 105 (Paris: Gallimard, 1998).

Parent, Sylvain, 'Entretien avec Arlette Farge', *Tracés: Revue de Sciences humaines*, 5 (2004), 143–8, available at: http://traces.revues.org/3383?lang=en (last accessed 1 March 2012).

Passeron, Jean-Claude, 'Le sociologue en politique et *vice versa*: Enquêtes sociologiques et réformes pédagogiques dans les années 1960', in Jacques Bouveresse and Daniel Roche (eds), *La Liberté par la connaissance: Pierre Bourdieu (1930–2002)* (Paris: Odile Jacob, 2004), 15–104.

Passeron, Jean-Claude, *Le Raisonnement sociologique: Un espace non poppérien de l'argumentation* (Paris: Albin Michel, 2006).

Pearson, Karl, 'The scope and importance to the state of the science of national eugenics', in Lucy Bland and Laura Doan (eds), *Sexology Uncensored: The Documents of Sexual Science* (Cambridge: Polity Press, 1998 [1909]), 176–7.

Perrot, Michelle (ed.), *L'Impossible Prison: Recherches sur le système pénitentiaire au XIXe siècle réunies par Michelle Perrot: Débat avec Michel Foucault* (Paris: Seuil, 1980).

Pettit, Philip, *Republicanism: A Theory of Freedom and Government* (Oxford: Oxford University Press, 1997).

Philo, Chris, 'Foucault's children', in Louise Holt (ed.), *Geographies of Children, Youth and Families: An International Perspective* (London: Routledge, 2011), 27–54.

Poster, Mark, *Critical Theory of the Family* (New York: Pluto Press, 1978).

Ramsey, Matthew, 'Review essay: history of a profession, *Annales* style: the work of Jacques Léonard', *Journal of Social History*, 17 (1983), 319–38.

Reay, Diane, 'Gendering Bourdieu's concept of capitals? Emotional capital, women and social class', in Lisa Adkins and Beverley Skeggs (eds), *Feminism after Bourdieu* (Oxford: Wiley-Blackwell, 2004), 57–74.

Rose, Nikolas, *Powers of Freedom: Reframing Political Thought* (Cambridge: Cambridge University Press, 1999).

Rose, Nikolas, *Governing the Soul: The Shaping of the Private Self* (London: Free Associations Books, 1989; new edn 2001).

Rose, Nikolas, *The Politics of Life Itself: Biomedicine, Power, and Subjectivity in the Twenty-First Century* (Princeton, NJ: Princeton University Press, 2006).

Sawicki, Jana, *Disciplining Foucault: Feminism, Power and the Body* (London: Routledge, 1991).

Shapiro, Michael J., *For Moral Ambiguity: National Culture and the Politics of the Family* (Minneapolis, MN: University of Minnesota Press, 2001).

Sharpe, Andrew N., *Foucault's Monsters and the Challenge of Law* (London: Routledge, 2010).

Sheringham, Michael, 'Michel Foucault, Pierre Rivière and the archival imaginary', *Comparative Critical Studies*, 8 (2011), 235–57.

Simons, Jon, 'Foucault's mother', in Susan J. Hekman (ed.), *Feminist Interpretations of Michel Foucault* (University Park, PA: Penn State University Press, 1996), 179–209.

Skeggs, Beverley, 'Context and background: Pierre Bourdieu's analysis of class, gender and sexuality', *Sociological Review*, 52 (2004), 19–33.

Spivak, Gayatri Chakravorty, 'Can the subaltern speak?', in Cary Nelson and Lawrence Grossberg (eds), *Marxism and the Interpretation of Culture* (Urbana, IL: University of Illinois Press, 1988), 271–313.

Stedman Jones, Gareth, 'The determinist fix: some obstacles to the further development of the linguistic approach to history in the 1990s', *History Workshop Journal*, 42 (1996), 19–35.

Tarbouriech, Ernest, *La Cité future: Essai d'une utopie scientifique* (Paris: P. V. Steck, 1902).

Taylor, Charles, 'Foucault on freedom and truth', *Philosophy and the Human Sciences: Philosophical Papers 2* (Cambridge: Cambridge University Press, 1985), 152–84.

Taylor, Chloë, 'Foucault and familial power', *Hypatia*, 27 (2012), 201–18.

The Foucault Reader, Paul Rabinow (ed.) (New York: Pantheon Books, 1984).

The Scottish Report on the Sexualisation of Young People 4.2, *Identities and Consumption*, available at: http://www.scottish.parliament.uk/s3/committees/equal/reports-10/eor10-02.html (last accessed 1 March 2012).

Vachss, Andrew, 'How we can fight child abuse', *Parade* (20 August 1989).

Vachss, Andrew, 'Today's victim could be tomorrow's predator', *Parade* (3 June 2000).

Vachss, Andrew, 'The difference between "sick" and "evil"', *Parade* (14 July 2002).

Verdès-Leroux, Jeannine, *Le Travail social* (Paris: Minuit, 1978).

Veyne, Paul, *Foucault: His Thought, His Character*, Janet Lloyd (trans.) (Cambridge: Polity, 2010).

von Krafft-Ebing, Richard, *Psychopathia Sexualis: With Especial Reference to the Antipathic Sexual Instinct: A Medico-Forensic Study*, Franklin S. Klaf (trans. from 12th German edn, original 1st German edn published in 1886) (New York: Arcade Publishing, 1965).

Wahl, Alfred, *Les Archives du football: Sport et société en France, 1880–1980*, Archives No. 102 (Paris: Gallimard, 1989).

Weber, Eugen, *Satan franc-maçon: La mystification de Léo Taxil*, Archives No. 6 (Paris: Julliard, 1964).

Wecker, Regina, 'Vom Verbot, Kinder zu haben, und dem Recht, keine Kinder zu haben: Zu Geschichte und Gegenwart der Sterilisation in Schweden, Deutschland und der Schweiz', *Figurationen*, 02/03 (2003), 101–9.

Weeks, Jeffrey, 'Foucault for historians', *History Workshop Journal*, 14 (1982), 106–19.

Winders, James A., 'Michel Foucault (1926–1984)', in Philip Daileader and Philip Whalen (eds), *French Historians 1900–2000: New Historical Writing in Twentieth-Century France* (Oxford: Wiley-Blackwell, 2010), 252–70.

Young, Robert J. C., 'Foucault on race and colonialism', *New Formations*, 25 (1995), 57–65.

Yuval-Davis, Nira and Floya Anthias (eds), *Woman–Nation–State* (London: Macmillan, 1989).

Ziegler, Béatrice, 'Frauen zwischen sozialer und eugenischer Indikation: Abtreibung und Sterilisation in Bern', in Veronika Aegerter, Nicole Graf, Natalie Imboden, Thea Rytz and Rita Stöckli (eds), *Geschlecht hat Methode: Ansätze und Perspektiven in der Frauen- und Geschlechtergeschichte* (Zurich: Chronos, 1999), 293–301.

Index